COLONIAL AMERICA
AND THE
AMERICAN REVOLUTION
THE 25 BEST SITES

Colonial America and the American Revolution The 25 Best Sites is the fourth book in the Greenline Historic Travel Series (GHTS). The series, *extraordinary guides for extraordinary times*, was introduced on December 7, 2002 with *The 25 Best World War II Sites: Pacific Theater*. This was followed by *The 25 Best World War II Sites: European Theater* in 2004, and *The 25 Best Civil War Sites* in 2005. GHTS is published by Greenline Publications, which aims to provide readers with unique and significant travel experiences through a willingness to explore new approaches to guidebooks, combined with meticulous research.

Colonial America and the American Revolution The 25 Best Sites is an independent guide. We welcome your views on our selections. The information contained in this book was checked as rigorously as possible before going to press. The publisher accepts no responsibility for any changes that may have occurred since or for any other variance of fact from that recorded here in good faith.

ISBN-10: 0-9766013-2-X; ISBN-13: 978-0-9766013-2-6
Library of Congress Control Number: 2006925607
Distributed in the United States and Canada by National Book Network (NBN)
Printed in the United States on recycled paper containing 30% postconsumer waste.
Copyright © 2006 Greenline Publications
All rights reserved

Series Editor	Christina Henry de Tessan
Copy Editor	Marisa Solis, Elizabeth Stroud
Cover Designer	Samia Afra
Original Book Design	DeVa Communications
Production Editor	Jo Farrell
Cartographer	Chris Gillis
Photographer	Clint Johnson
Indexer	Karen Bleske

To reach us or for updated information on all Greenline books, visit the Greenline Publications website at **greenlinepub.com**.

GREENLINE PUBLICATIONS
P.O. Box 590780
San Francisco, CA 94159-0780

Greenline Publications is an imprint of ASDavis Media Group, Inc.

TO all the readers at Emmaus Public Library Hope you enjoy travelling

COLONIAL AMERICA
AND THE
AMERICAN REVOLUTION

THE 25 BEST SITES

Clint Johnson

CLINT JOHNSON

Book Expo 2006

GREENLINE PUBLICATIONS • SAN FRANCISCO, CALIFORNIA

OVERVIEW MAP

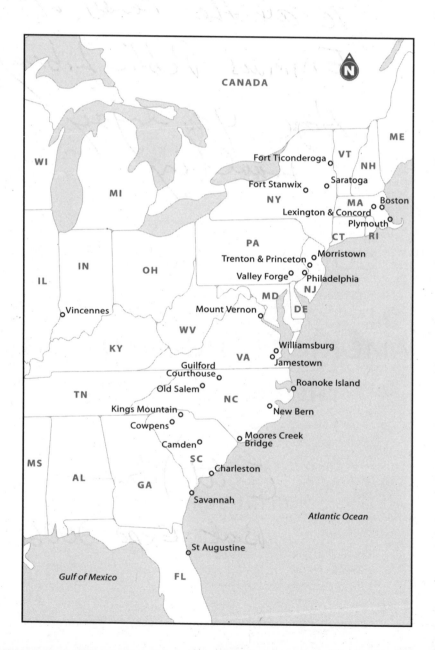

TABLE OF CONTENTS

CHRONOLOGY OF NEW WORLD COLONIZATION AND THE AMERICAN REVOLUTION

1513

March 23: Florida is claimed for Spain by Juan Ponce de Leon.

1565

France establishes a small colony at the mouth of the St. Johns River.

St. Augustine, Florida, is founded as a result of the discovery of the French colony, which is driven off by the occupying Spanish.

1584

July 13: The first English explorers land on the Outer Banks of North Carolina, and claim the land for Queen Elizabeth.

1585

July 27: The first settlers arrive on Roanoke Island and build a fort.

1587

July 22: A second, more substantial colonization effort begins at Roanoke. No sign is found of the 15 men who had been left at the colony two years earlier.

August 18: Virginia Dare, the first known child of colonists, is born in The New World. John White, founder of the colony, leaves for England to bring more supplies.

1589

August 17: White, delayed·by war with Spain, finally returns to Roanoke Island to find the colony abandoned. Only the word Croatoan, the name of a nearby Indian tribe, is found to give clues to what happened to the settlers. They are never found.

1607

May 14: First settlers from the Virginia Company arrive on Jamestown Island, Virginia.

1619

July 30: The first general assembly to establish some form of government in the New World is held at Jamestown.

1620

November 21: The Pilgrims arrive at Cape Cod, Massachusetts.

December 21: The Pilgrims land at Plymouth.

1624

The Crown revokes the Virginia Company's charter and makes Jamestown a Crown colony.

1626

Colony of New York is founded on Manhattan Island.

1653

The colony in North Carolina is refounded after the aborted Roanoke Island colony in 1585 disappeared. These successful colonists come from the already established colony of Virginia.

1663

Colony of South Carolina is founded as "Carolina." The colony would be split into North and South Carolina in 1729.

1664

Colony of New Jersey is founded.

1672

Construction on Castillo de San Marcos, a tabby fort, is begun in St. Augustine, Florida, to protect the Spanish colony.

1682

Colony of Pennsylvania is founded.

1698

The Crown moves the Virginia colonial capital to Williamsburg from Jamestown and the first English colony is abandoned to the elements.

1733

Georgia, the last of the English colonies, is founded more than 50 years later than most of the others and 120 years after Virginia. Georgia is the only colony to ban slavery and the importation of liquor.

1765

England, seeking a way to pay for governing the colonies, passes the Stamp Act, requiring that every paper document be taxed by a revenue agent with the tax money returning to England.

The Quartering Act is passed, requiring that the colonies provide barracks for British troops, an act the colonies correctly perceive as a thinly veiled effort by the Crown to make sure the other tax acts were followed.

The first grumbling voices began to be heard that the increasing numbers of taxes being imposed on the colonies were "taxation without representation" in the Parliament. The Parliament replies that it represents all English people, including those in the colonies.

1766

The Stamp Act is repealed as a means of trying to quiet the discontent of the colonies.

1770

March 5: Five Boston civilians are shot down by a British detachment after a mob's taunting of a British sentry outside the Customs House became unruly.

1771

May 16: North Carolina farmers called Regulators, angry at taxation without representation, finally fight with Crown militia at the Battle of Alamance, North Carolina. They were routed with deaths on both sides totaling at least 20. Another 10 Regulators are hanged as an example to other rebels. This is the first massed, armed resistance to the Crown.

1773

May: The Tea Act is passed in Parliament, but it is not a new tax. The Act allows Britain's tea importers to sell tea directly and cheaper to colonial merchants, which dissident colonials fear will soften the growing sense that the colonies should become more independent.

December 16: Bostonians throw loads of tea into Boston Harbor rather than unload it and sell it. The Boston Tea Party was not a protest of unfair taxation, but a provocation by independence-minded colonials to keep profit-minded colonial tea merchants in line.

1774

September 5–October 26: The First Continental Congress meets in Philadelphia's Carpenters Hall, not to talk about freedom from England, but how the colonies should be governed. Among the ideas is creation of an American Parliament that would have veto power over England's Parliament when dealing with American issues.

1775

April 18: Paul Revere and William Dawes leave Boston to warn the Patriots that the British are marching on Concord to capture the colonists' supply of gunpowder.

April 19: British and Patriots skirmish at Concord and Lexington, Massachusetts.

May 10: Fort Ticonderoga is captured by Patriots without firing a shot.

May 10: On the same day, the Second Continental Congress opens to discuss the fighting at Concord and Lexington. Noted by the Second Congress was that King George III had not responded to demands sent to him by the First Congress. The Second Congress would not officially dissolve until 1789.

May 20: In Mecklenburg County, North Carolina (present day Charlotte), a group of Scots-Irish issue the Mecklenburg Declaration declaring themselves free of the British Crown. It is the first written document demanding freedom from England.

June 15: George Washington, a hero of the British during the French and Indian War, is appointed general of the Continental Army by the Second Continental Congress.

June 17: Battle of Bunker Hill—really Breed's Hill—sees the first heavy combat of the war. The Americans occupy some heights north of Boston and the British dislodge them. The British win the battle, but suffer losses approaching 40 percent.

1776

February 27: Battle of Moores Creek Bridge, North Carolina, pits Loyalists against Patriots for the first time. The Tories suffer heavy casualties in this first Patriot victory in the South.

July 4: Second Continental Congress issues the Declaration of Independence.

December 25–26: George Washington's army crosses the cold Delaware River under cover of darkness and surprises the Hessian garrison at Trenton, New Jersey, capturing or killing most of them while losing few of their own.

1777

January 3: Washington follows up his Trenton victory with a second at Princeton.

September 9–11: Battle of Brandywine, Pennsylvania, is one of Washington's more humiliating defeats because he had been warned repeatedly about the approach of the British.

September 19: First Battle of Saratoga or Freeman's Farm, a British defeat.

October 7: Second Battle of Saratoga or Bemis Heights, is a second British defeat resulting in the complete surrender of the British army.

1778

June 27: Battle of Monmouth, New Jersey, is a confusing battle fought to a draw, though it proved that Washington was capable of rescuing an army that was close to panicking.

1779

February 25: George Rogers Clark and 200 Rangers capture Fort Sackville, driving the British out of their westernmost fortifications.

October 9: After Savannah, Georgia, had been captured with little resistance the previous year, the French join with Americans to try to force the English out. The British hold and the French retreat.

1780

May 12: Charleston, South Carolina, surrenders after a five-week siege. More than 5,000 Patriot soldiers are captured, the largest single surrender the Americans suffered during the war.

August 12: General Horatio Gates, a man who once believed he should be the Patriot commander over George Washington, loses almost his entire force at the Battle of Camden, South Carolina. It is one of the worst battlefield defeats of the Patriots.

October 7: Buoyed by their victory at Camden, the British send a force of Tories deep into the interior of South Carolina. They are met at Kings Mountain, South Carolina, by a force of backwoods Patriots. The British, despite having the high ground, lose to the Patriots, who are better shots in the woods. Many of the captured Tories are tortured and killed by Patriots angry at rumors of atrocities committed by the British. After Kings Mountain, the South turns solidly in favor of the Patriot cause.

1781

January 17: The Battle of Cowpens, South Carolina, is another crushing defeat of the British when wily General Daniel Morgan, a hero in the northern colonies, successfully fools the ruthless British commander, Banastre "Bloody" Tarleton. Morgan orders his militia to run after just two volleys, a feat Tarleton misinterprets as a panic. Morgan's regulars poured a devastating fire into Tarleton's troops.

March 15: The Battle of Guilford Courthouse, North Carolina, is a tactical victory for the British under Lord Cornwallis, but a strategic defeat because he had lost so many men that he had to march for the coast to refit and resupply. Cornwallis's goal is Portsmouth, Yorktown, Virginia, where he expects to meet the British fleet.

September 28–October 19: During the summer a still-confident Cornwallis marches unchecked through Virginia. During the fall, he finds himself facing fresh French troops, George Washington's army, which had secretly left New York, and a French fleet that had already defeated a resupplying British fleet.

Cornwallis is trapped in trenches at Yorktown, Virginia. He surrenders more than 8,000 troops.

1783

February 4: England officially declares that hostilities are over in America.
September 3: The Treaty of Paris is finally signed by both nations, officially ending the war.

INTRODUCTION

1776—it is the most famous year in the American Revolution. On July 4, the Second Continental Congress issued the Declaration of Independence. That document, beginning "When in the course of human events," bluntly informs King George III and the Parliament that the 13 colonies have decided to go their own way.

Sadly, that pretty much sums up all that some people know about the colonization of the New World and the early days of the United States' long and involved struggle for independence.

This book is written for people who not only want to know how the Declaration came to be, but who also want to know more about the places where this nation's fight for independence took place. The nation we know as the United States did not just pop up on July 4, 1776. Our colonial history dates back to 1513 when Ponce de Leon first sighted Florida and ends over two-and-a-half centuries later in 1783 when England finally pulled its last soldiers out of the colonies.

I hope that the readers of this book are those history travelers and armchair historians who want to experience the sites that were so important to the country's history. This book brings alive through photographs and current descriptions all those old history-book mentions of faraway places like St. Augustine, Lexington, and Plymouth. It also shows people how to find and appreciate historically important places that do not get as many tourists, such as Fort Ticonderoga, Morristown, Kings Mountain, and Cowpens.

By visiting these sites, readers might find their own answers to some interesting questions of the colonial period and the American Revolution:

What compelled England to build colonies in the New World? How did those first colonists, and the slaves who came shortly afterward, survive in a new and unfamiliar world that they they knew very little about? What skills did it take to survive and thrive?

How did those colonists learn what plants, vegetables, and fruits would grow in the New World? How did they know what wild foods were safe to eat? How did they know which plants would produce medicines?

What event launched the American Revolution? Once the Revolution was under way, how did armies find each other in vast wildernesses that lacked not only road maps, but roads? What were the obstacles that had to be overcome? How were military tactics different or the same as in later wars?

Why would men stand shoulder to shoulder and shoot at each other from distances of less than 100 yards? What must it have been like to watch a red-coated battle line marching forward with bayonets pointed at you?

What was really going through the heads of Patriots as they fought battles against Tories who spoke the same language and might even be relatives living just down the road?

Thanks to the historic sites covered in this book, the public can learn that the colonial period and the American Revolution are not just dusty, forgotten episodes in the nation's past. These sites live and breathe every day with the help of dedicated historians and interpreters who realized long ago that a nation cannot march forward into the future without honoring its past. They stretch from Florida to upstate New York and as far west as Indiana.

I used several overlapping methods to rate these sites. First, the sites have to be accessible to the public—as opposed to some important sites that are on private property. Second, something important to the overall history of the nation had to have taken place there. There are scores of Revolutionary War skirmishes and battles that occurred, but those engagements were not always as vital to the outcome of the war as the battles covered here. Third, the sites must have some type of educational value to them. For instance, Old Salem in Winston-Salem, North Carolina, did not see a Revolutionary War battle, but the historic preservation of this 18th-century settlement describes the Moravian religion, a religion that is not well known around the nation, but which was known during the American Revolution.

Regarding accommodations, I've chosen bed-and-breakfasts that try to reflect the colonial period. With the exception of one motel in Rome, New York, which is right across the street from Fort Stanwix and two in Vincennes, Indiana, you won't find economy motels in this book.

Although it was unlikely that anyone then could foresee that the United States would one day become the most powerful nation on earth, these early days reveal a great deal about how the nation developed. By exploring these sites—standing where soldiers fought, triumphed, and fell; witnessing the difficulties of life in a colonial village; standing in the buildings where unprecedented ideas were debated—visitors will have the opportunity to bring history to life and experience it in an accessible way. In addition to gaining a better understanding of our past, visiting these sites also affords people the opportunity to honor those who fought for what they believed in and in many cases died for a country that did not even formally exist yet.

Points of Interest Ratings

Individual points of interest are awarded scores of one to five stars based on the following rough description:

★★★★★	Major site, must visit
★★★★	Extraordinary site or development
★★★	Worth a side trip
★★	Interesting, not vital
★	Only if you have time or special interest

SITE
1

Boston

Massachusetts

The Old North Church bell tower

THE WAR YEARS

I f the American Revolution could be said to have an epicenter, it would have to be Boston. It was here that wealthy merchants tired of paying taxes, and would-be politicians determined that they wanted to be free of England. Boston's historic areas are well preserved, making the entire city a rewarding site for those interested in learning more about the nation's early years.

Dubbed "the city on the hill" by its early settlers in 1633, Boston was an immediate success as a colonial city, growing to be the colonies' third largest with around 16,000 inhabitants by the mid-1700s. (Only New York and Philadelphia were larger.) Boston had a good port, a clear route to England, and a number of smaller towns on three sides that could keep it supplied with crops and goods that could be exported to England.

Boston's success eventually attracted the attention of King George III and his advisors. At the completion of the French and Indian War in 1763 (which ended with the French being driven from the colonies into Canada), the Crown began to look for a way to pay off its war debts. In addition, England needed to find a way to pay for future expenses that would be incurred in managing the colonies. The king and his advisors reasoned that a prosperous city such as Boston, and its colony Massachusetts, could contribute to the ever-growing expenses of maintaining civilization more than 3,000 miles from Mother England. Starting in the 1760s, the Crown began suggesting—gently at first—that the colonies help in their own governance by paying increased taxes on imported and exported items. Their first suggestion was The Stamp Act of 1765, which intended to tax virtually every piece of paper that changed hands.

The merchants of Boston did not like the idea of increased taxes, and they particularly did not like the idea of such a ubiquitous tax as one on paper. They reasoned that they were doing fine with low or no taxes, and besides, the colonies did not have any representatives in England's Parliament who could speak for them. Those merchants contacted local leaders in the other colonies and learned that they were also unhappy with the tax proposal.

England heard the grumbling but dismissed it, unaware that the colonists were forming secret groups, such as the Sons of Liberty, to oppose taxes. On June 10, 1768, a merchant named John Hancock refused to allow his merchant ship, the *Liberty*, to be boarded by customs agents who suspected he was hiding cargo from them. The ship was seized by British warships, and a Boston mob retaliated by attacking the agents.

King George responded by sending troops to garrison Boston in October 1768. That only aggravated the citizens, who learned that the off-duty soldiers were seeking scarce jobs. On the night of March 5, 1770, a British sentry outside the Customs House struck a heckler in the head with his musket. A crowd formed and tried to accost the British soldier. Other British soldiers arrived to protect him. The civilian crowd grew more unruly and the British soldiers more nervous. When a club sailed through the crowd and struck a British soldier, he retaliated by firing. Soon other British soldiers—without orders—began firing. Shortly after, four civilians lay dead, one would die later, and several more were severely wounded. This came to be known as the Boston Massacre.

Though a subsequent trial would find most of the British soldiers innocent (with only two discharged for not following orders), firebrands in Boston made sure the story of how a British army had fired on unarmed civilians spread throughout the colonies. One rebel leader, Samuel Adams, commissioned a local artist, Paul Revere, to make an engraving showing the British, under orders, firing into the crowd. The engraving, which was reproduced and scattered throughout the colonies, was false, but Adams knew that it would stoke the fires of rebellion.

Stung by the violence in reaction to the suggested taxes, the Crown retreated from their earlier tax proposals. They repealed almost all of them with the exception of a tax on tea coming from India. Thanks to complicated merchandising maneuvers back in London, tea going to the colonies actually cost less than tea that the colonists had been smuggling in from Holland. King George III was doing the colonies a favor by shipping the lower-priced tea to them. At the same time, the king was saving face back home by being able to state that the colonies were paying at least one tax.

That made no difference to the Sons of Liberty. On December 16, 1773, the Sons of Liberty boarded three British merchant ships and threw their cargo of tea into Boston Harbor in protest of the tea tax. That was the last straw. The king ordered the port of Boston closed and more troops to be permanently quartered in the city. He revoked the right of citizens to meet in regular town hall meetings.

The king's every effort to reign in Boston had the opposite effect. Instead of cowing the residents, they showed increased sympathy to the rebels. On April 19, 1775, the British troops leaving Boston to capture military stores in Concord and Lexington limped back under fire to a sneering populace of Bostonians.

On June 17, 1775, the only fighting Boston would see occurred when the British attacked a Patriot position on Breed's Hill, near Bunker Hill, both of which were located in Charlestown, across the Charles River from Boston. The British saw the battle as a chance to crush the small untrained army of rebels, while the rebels wanted to draw the British into a battle that forced them to attack an elevated, fortified position.

One of the Patriots' commanders, Israel Putnam, issued one of the most famous orders of the war in order to conserve his limited reserve of gunpowder: "Don't fire until you see the whites of their eyes and then fire low." He did not want his men to waste a single shot. They did not. Nearly 100 British soldiers fell in the first charge. More fell in a second charge. A third charge succeeded, and the British were in the Americans' lines.

The British took Breed's Hill, but their casualties approached 50 percent, with more than 220 dead. The dug-in Americans suffered heavy losses themselves. In the first true stand-up battle of the rebellion, the British army had been bloodied much more than they ever expected to be.

On March 7, 1776, 11,000 British troops boarded ships and evacuated Boston after an eight-month siege.

SITE
1

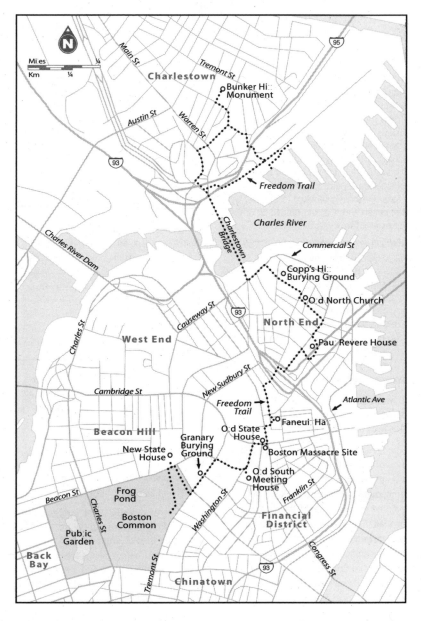

N

Miles ¼
Km ¼

Main St

Tremont St

Charlestown

○ Bunker Hill Monument

Austin St

Warren St

93

Charles River Dam

Charlestown Bridge

Freedom Trail

Charles River

Commercial St

○ Copp's Hill Burying Ground

○ Old North Church

Charles St

Causeway St

93

North End

West End

○ Paul Revere House

Cambridge St

New Sudbury St

Atlantic Ave

Freedom Trail

Beacon Hill

○ Faneuil Hall

New State House ○

Granary Burying Ground

Old State House ○

○ Boston Massacre Site

Beacon St

Charles St

Frog Pond

○ Old South Meeting House

Franklin St

Boston Common

Financial District

Public Garden

Washington St

Congress St

Back Bay

Tremont St

93

Chinatown

95

BOSTON TODAY

Though it long ago lost its colonial distinction as the nation's third-largest city, Boston remains an important metropolis. Today, Boston's population of 569,000 makes it the nation's 24th largest. Like many northeastern cities, Boston has been slowly losing population to Sun Belt cities. This is partly because Boston is not in a position to expand geographically: land mass is naturally blocked to the east by the ocean and it is surrounded by other cities and towns in other directions.

Tourists hoping to find a quaint, 18th-century setting where the spirit of the American Revolution was born over drinks and spirited conversations in local taverns are going to be disappointed. Though the important colonial and Revolutionary War sites are preserved, they are located right in the middle of a fast-paced metropolis. Tourists thinking about John Adams, Samuel Adams, and the Boston Tea Party are going to find that they are competing for sidewalk space with bankers and lawyers going about their day without any thoughts of the Revolution.

That said, tourists looking for more than just colonial history will find Boston very appealing. It has professional sports teams playing in every season, an entertaining and educational science museum, the John F. Kennedy Museum and Library, several arts museums, and even a museum dedicated to the display of medieval armor going back to the 13th century. A thorough visit to Boston requires a stay of several days.

POINTS OF INTEREST

Freedom Trail ★★★★★

Downtown Boston to Bunker Hill
Monument in Charlestown
2.5-mile (one way) walking trail

The Freedom Trail is a 2.5-mile walking tour of downtown Boston and Charlestown. It is marked either by two red bricks embedded in the concrete, or by a thick, painted red line when it travels over asphalt. The trail winds its way through downtown Boston, taking tourists to most of the significant colonial sites before crossing the Charles River to end (or begin) on Breed's Hill, the site of the Battle of Bunker Hill.

The entire trail is negotiable by wheelchair, but like any city sidewalk, there are potholes along the way. Tourists should probably avoid taking shortcuts off the red-bricked trail, as Boston's winding streets can be confusing enough—even with the Freedom Trail map in hand. Maps of the Freedom Trail are available at many hotels and all visitor centers.

One alternative visitors may want to consider if they want to avoid the hassle of parking in Boston is to park in Charlestown (there is parking available in several shopping malls) and then follow the trail in reverse from the Bunker Hill Monument into Boston.

The following are short descriptions of the more prominent colonial sites found along the trail, beginning in the Boston Common bordered by Tremont, Beacon, Arlington, and Boylston Streets near the center of the central business district.

Boston Common ★★ today is a relatively spacious 40-acre public park frequented by business people on their lunch breaks. In the 1600s, it was a popular colonial gathering spot, as well as a cow pasture and militia training ground. It was also the rallying point from which British troops left on their fateful march to Lexington and Concord in April 1775. There are some interesting statues of Patriots scattered around the Common.

New State House ★★★ was completed in 1798 on land once owned by John Hancock. Free tours are available Mon–Fri 10am–4pm that point out magnificent architecture, historical events that transpired here, and paintings depicting events that led to the American Revolution. It was designed by Charles Bullfinch (who later won a contract to design the United States Capitol).

Granary Burying Ground ★★★★★, adjacent to the Park Street Church, a block away from the start of the Freedom Trail, is where visitors will find the graves of some of the most important men in our history: John Hancock (president of the Second Continental Congress, first governor of Massachusetts, and first to sign the Declaration of Independence), Paul Revere (one of the riders who warned the residents of Lexington and Concord of the approaching British), Samuel Adams (one of the founders of the Sons of Liberty and an important force behind the Boston Tea Party), the victims of the Boston Massacre, and James Otis (who is credited with coining the phrase "no taxation without representation").

Old South Meeting House ★★★★★, at 310 Washington Street, was once one of the largest buildings in Boston, making it a natural choice when some 5,000 angry colonials wanted to meet to discuss grievances. Built in 1729 by the Puritans, the most famous colonial act of rebellion that occurred here was the planning of the Boston Tea Party in 1773.

Old South Meeting House is open daily 9:30am–5pm April through October and 10am–4pm November through March. Admission is $5. A group ticket to the Old South Meeting House, Old State House, and the Paul Revere House can be purchased here for $11. Today, through interactive exhibits and artifacts, visitors can learn about the many debates that have taken place here through the years and the nation's long legacy of protest.

Boston Massacre Site ★★, outside the Old State House may not be much to look at—just a circle of cobblestones in front of the building—but it is hugely significant historically. On March 5, 1770, a group of colonists were taunting a lone, nervous British sentry on this spot when he called for assistance. A small detachment rushed to his aid. They too were quickly surrounded by the growing crowd. Reports vary as to what occurred next, but rocks were thrown and shots were fired. When the smoke cleared, four colonists lay dead in the street and several more were wounded.

Colonists who were pressing for more freedom from England used the incident as an example of how England did not respect the Bostonians. A trial was held later that year with future president John Adams representing the British soldiers. All but two were acquitted of manslaughter. Boston would remain restless for another five years until the battles for Lexington and Concord brought war to a head.

Old State House ★★★, built in 1713, is the oldest official building in Boston. Located at the corner of State and Washington Streets, it is open daily 9:30am–5pm. Admission is $5. It is now operated as a museum and research library. It was from the balcony overlooking State Street (then King Street) that the Declaration of Independence was first read to eager Bostonians on July 18, 1776. The building housed the government for only another three years, until the New State House was finished. Among the permanent exhibits is a light and sound show explaining the Boston Massacre. Plan to spend at least an hour, maybe two, as the exhibits give a good description of how Massachusetts moved from a religious colony to one of the most rebellious of the colonies pushing for independence.

Faneuil Hall ★★★ was similar to the Old South Meeting House in that it was a place where members of the Sons of Liberty met to discuss freedom from England. Today it shares its name with nearby Quincy Market, which is a shopping center (not an inauthentic use for Faneuil Hall, however, as it was originally built to house shops). The third floor is a museum. National Park Service rangers hold lectures on the colonial history of Faneuil Hall every 30 minutes (free).

Paul Revere House ★, at 19 North Square, was built in 1680 and is the home from which Revere left to warn colonists of the British marching on Lexington and Concord. Historians believe Revere's role in warning citizens that "The British are coming!" was overly dramatized by Henry Wadsworth Longfellow in his famous poem, but Revere did make the ride, even though he was captured.

The house is open daily 9:30am–5:15pm except during the winter months when it closes at 4:15pm. It is closed on Mondays January through March. Admission is $3. Call 617-523-2338 for details. A visit takes at least a half hour. Watch carefully for the house when traveling along the north end on the trail; it is easy to walk by it without even noticing it since it is not very well marked.

Old North Church ★★★, at 193 Salem Street, was built in 1723. It got its reputation from the same Longfellow poem that made Revere famous when the sexton hung two lanterns in the steeple to alert Patriots across the river in Charlestown that the British were on their way. Longfellow's poem mentions that two lanterns would be hung if the British were invading "by sea." Revere's signal of two lanterns actually meant that the British would be rowing across the Charles River rather than leaving from another location on the land.

The church is still an active congregation but it also opens its doors to tourists. Call 617-523-6676 for visiting details.

Copp's Hill Burying Ground ★★★ is an interesting, accessible graveyard that is most valuable for its old tombstones. Many of them are each topped with skull and crossbones, a symbol of mortality dating back to the Middle Ages. It was about this time that pirates adapted the Christian symbol for their flags. In the 1800s, the emblem came to be used to symbolize poison, thus forever changing what was originally meant to be a Christian symbol. The most famous person buried here is Cotton Mather, a Puritan minister who greatly influenced the early colonial sense of morals thanks to his extensive writings. (While he did not preside at the Salem witch trials, Mather did talk to the judges and urged them to be wary of the witches. Most of the women accused of being witches were burned at the stake.)

After walking a half mile and crossing over the Charles River, visitors following the red-brick trail will reach the **Bunker Hill Monument ★★★★**. The tall obelisk resembling the Washington Monument is actually on Breed's Hill, the site of the battle. For reasons even park rangers cannot easily explain, the battle was always named after Bunker Hill (where no fighting took place) instead of Breed's Hill, where all of the fighting took place. There is a small museum and diorama of the battle in the nearby visitor center.

It is 294 steps to the top of the monument. (But if you don't feel like making the climb, photographs in the visitor center show the view from the top.) None of the original battlefield or the entrenchments remains. Actually, because of the surrounding houses, it is difficult to see what must have been Breed's Hill and Bunker Hill, as the slopes disappeared long ago under residential development.

The Battle of Bunker Hill is a good example of how untrained people getting into a war make mistakes. In late May 1775, the Americans decided to occupy Charlestown because it looked down on British-occupied Boston. Occupying high ground is always a good military decision, but the Americans did not occupy the highest ground, Bunker Hill. Instead, they moved 600 yards closer to the city to Breed's Hill, which was also that much closer to the British cannons on board ships in Boston. It also had a milder slope that would give any British troops coming up it an easier attack. Worst of all, Breed's Hill was farther into the peninsula pointing at Boston. If British ships sailed up the Charles River and disembarked troops behind their lines, the Americans would be trapped.

Instead of sailing up the river and attacking the American rear, the British, under Lord Howe, landed on the eastern side of the peninsula to begin a frontal assault. The overconfident British believed the Americans would run at the first sight of a strong line of red-coated regular soldiers, but that did not happen. The Americans waited in their trenches and obeyed one of the most famous orders in American military history—"Don't fire until you see the whites of their eyes."

When the British advanced to within 50 yards, the Americans opened up with three volleys. Nearly 100 British troops were killed in that first attack. Within a few minutes, it became clear that the Americans did not have the gunpowder to resist another attack. The British soon breached their trenches and the Americans began to fall back to Bunker Hill. Most of the 140 Americans killed in the battle died on this retreat as they were bayoneted by advancing British.

When the battle was over, the British were shocked by the tally of their victory. More than 1,000 of their force of 2,400 had been killed or wounded. Heavy casualties had not been expected, particularly not at the hands of a ragtag army made up of farmers armed with rifles normally used for squirrel hunting. One British general, Henry Clinton, wrote to a friend that Bunker Hill was "a dear-bought victory; another such would have ruined us."

The Patriots had suffered far fewer casualties even though they had lost the battle. In the space of just a month, they had humiliated the British by sniping at them from Concord through Lexington and nearly all the way back to Boston. Now they had decimated that same army in the type of stand-up combat that the British supposedly liked to fight. Even in defeat, the Patriots felt confident that they could win their independence.

GETTING TO AND AROUND BOSTON

Getting to Boston by air is easy, as it is served by Logan International Airport, which hosts 30 different airlines. Visitors hoping to tour Boston in their own car will be making a mistake. Even with near-completion of the "Big Dig," which put most of I-93 heading through downtown in an underground tunnel, the city is notoriously difficult to negotiate by car. There are no tourist-friendly signs on the underground interstate directing people to historical sites. Above ground the problem is just as bad. Construction of surface streets seems to be ongoing all over the city. Even with I-93 underground, there is still lots of traffic present. Boston's colonial-era streets were not laid out in a sensible grid, and the street names often change without warning. A detailed map of Boston is necessary to move anywhere downtown.

The best bet for tourists may be to leave the driving to a local tour company such as Old Town Trolley Tours, which offers a one-hour-and-45-minute tour of 100 sites, plus free on-and-off privileges, for $29 per person. The tour visits all of the colonial sites, including Bunker Hill across the river from Boston.

If visitors must arrive by car, they should take Exit 27 from I-93 in Charlestown, north of Boston. Park in a shopping center near Bunker Hill Community College, then hike the several blocks to Bunker Hill itself. This is normally the terminus of the Freedom Trail, the red-bricked sidewalk winding through Boston, but it can be walked in either direction. Follow the bricks back over the Charles River to see all of the Boston sites and then retrace your steps back to Charlestown. Note that this will be a walk of more than six miles, but the hassle of parking and driving can be avoided.

SOURCES & OTHER READING

A People's History of the American Revolution: How Common People Shaped the Fight for Independence, Ray Raphael, Perennial, 2002

Boston 1775: The Shot Heard Around the World (Campaign Series 37), Brendan Morrissey, Osprey Publishing, 1995

Boston and the American Revolution, Barbara C. Smith, National Park Service, 1998

The First American Revolution: Before Lexington and Concord, Ray Raphael, New Press, 2003

The Founding of a Nation: A History of the American Revolution 1763–1776, Merrill Jensen, Hackett Publishing Company, 2004

Rebels and Redcoats: The American Revolution through the Eyes of Those Who Fought and Lived It, George Scheer and Hugh Rankin, DeCapo Press, 1957

ACCOMMODATIONS

Beacon Hill Bed and Breakfast

27 Brimmer St., Boston
T: 617-523-7376
$200–$275

This six-story Victorian is located on the "flat" of Beacon Hill, a historic neighborhood of brick row houses, gas-lit tree-lined streets, and hidden gardens. It's a short walk to Boston Common, the subway, the Freedom Trail, and Quincy Market.

Bunker Hill Bed and Breakfast

80 Elm St., Boston
T: 617-241-8067
bunkerhillbedandbreakfast.com
$135–$145

Bunker Hill Bed and Breakfast is a Victorian home built in 1885, renovated with 21st-century conveniences, and furnished with antiques. It is 10 minutes from the airport and the following landmarks: the USS *Constitution,* the Bunker Hill Monument, and the Charlestown Navy Yard. It is pet friendly.

The Herbert Carruth House

30 Beaumont St., Boston
T: 888-838-8900 or 617-436-8260
carruthhouse.us
$85–$125

The Herbert Carruth House, built around 1877, is one of the landmark historic properties in the Ashmont section of Dorchester in Boston. The house is a convenient five-minute walk to the Red Line's Ashmont Station. Downtown Boston is a 15-to-20 minute direct train ride on the Red Line from Ashmont.

Herbst Haus

108 Appleton St., Boston
T: 617-266-5537
herbsthaus.com
$125–$180

This 1870s Victorian Townhouse is just minutes to Beacon Hill, the Public Garden, the Boston Common, the Theater District, Symphony Hall, the Museum of Fine Arts, the Freedom Trail, Fenway Park, the Charles River, and Boston Harbor.

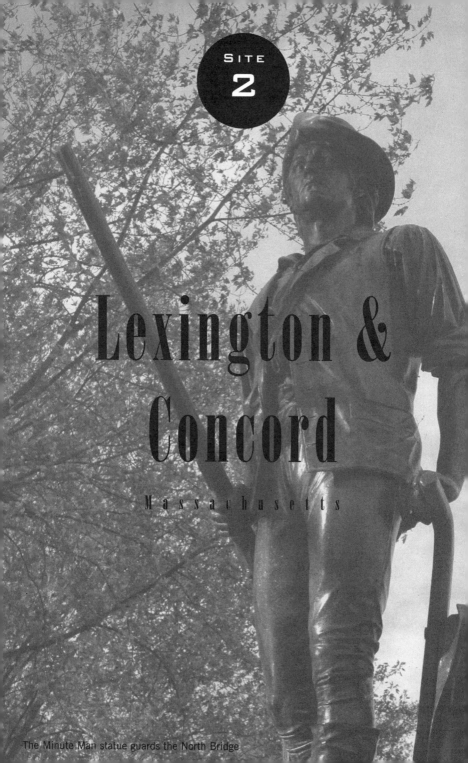

Lexington &
Concord

Massachusetts

The Minute Man statue guards the North Bridge

THE WAR YEARS

These two small towns have always symbolized the American Revolution, largely thanks to one iconic statue and the enduring line in a poem by Ralph Waldo Emerson about "the shot heard 'round the world."

The leaders of the growing rebellion in Boston knew they had to store their arms far enough away from Boston's occupying British forces that they could not be easily seized. They chose the quiet village of Concord, 20 miles west of the city.

On the evening of April 18, 1775, British General Thomas Gage woke his 700 soldiers and ordered them to go to Concord to seize whatever arms they could find. As dawn of April 19 lit the way to Concord, the British discovered that night riders such as Paul Revere and William Dawes had alerted the outlying villages west of Boston to their approach. As the red-coated soldiers marched smartly in step, cat calls could be heard from doorways, from behind trees and fences, and from bolder colonists standing out in the open by the side of the dirt road.

By midmorning, the British column had reached Lexington, a village about halfway to Concord. There on the Green in the center of the town, the startled British saw about 70 civilians armed with hunting rifles. As a precaution, the British commander of the expedition, Major John Pitcairn of the Royal Marines, put his troops into the standard battle formation of three ranks. Pitcairn was not concerned that any shots would be fired, as he had 700 men, at least 10 times the number he could see confronting him. He ordered the civilians to put down their arms and disperse.

Patriot militia Captain John Parker did not reply directly to Pitcairn. Instead, according to legend, he spoke the three sentences to his men that would launch a revolution. Parker moved among the ranks saying, "Stand your ground. Don't fire unless fired upon. If they want to have a war, let it begin here." (Apparently, in reality, he ordered his men to walk backward away from the British lines, but more significantly, he did not order his militia to put down their arms as Major Pitcairn had ordered.)

History is not clear on who fired the first shot, but it appears that at least one civilian was not willing to give way to the British army. A shot was fired, apparently from the militia ranks. More undisciplined shots followed, again apparently coming from the militia. There was no immediate reply from the British.

The British soldiers, who were in reality just as inexperienced in real combat as the Patriot civilians, retaliated with one and then a second undisciplined volley into the ranks of the militia without awaiting any orders from Pitcairn. Captain Parker, who stood his ground, was run through with a bayonet.

Eight civilians were killed on the Lexington Green and 10 more were wounded. Only one British soldier was slightly wounded. In the first clash of fire from British Brown Bess muskets versus civilian rifles, the British had won a decisive victory. Though he was livid that his men had fired without orders, Pitcairn was at least impressed with the evidence that the professional soldier proved to be superior to the undisciplined rebel farmer.

The British continued their march to Concord, confident that the bloodletting at Lexington would send the militia flying into the safety of their houses, but the redcoats were wrong. The fighting on Lexington Green had only riled the Concord militia further.

No accurate tally has ever been made of the number of militia who turned out, but they numbered in the hundreds, perhaps thousands at one point in the day somewhere along the return route to Boston. At Concord, another, larger force of militiamen fired a full volley from their rifles at the British. Three British soldiers fell dead and another nine were wounded. It was this military-style volley from the militia that Ralph Waldo Emerson described in his 1836 Hymn Sung at the Completion of the Concord Monument as "the shot heard 'round the world."

The British commander of this leading force in Concord, Colonel Francis Smith, having found no cache of arms, gathered his dead and began the 20-mile march back to Boston. It was like no other march the mighty British army had ever experienced from a supposedly civilized enemy. From behind trees and stone walls, snipers fired into the British ranks and ran. The British army was used to fighting other armies, not men who would not stand and fight.

At this same time, a column of reinforcements was marching from Boston toward Smith. They too found themselves under fire from behind walls. The reinforcements met up with the advance column at Lexington and then turned back toward Boston. All along the way they faced opposition. In an attempt to stop the sniping, the British set fire to houses alongside the road to destroy the cover the rebels were using. When they saw a man with a rifle, they tried to kill him.

By the end of the day, the British, who had been marching or fighting for more than 30 hours, finally arrived back in Boston. Their losses were appalling. Seventy-three soldiers were dead. Another 26 were missing and presumed dead. One hundred and seventy-four were wounded.

Details of losses on the rebel side were less clear. Tallies were 49 dead, five missing, and 41 wounded. Of those dead, eight had been killed in Lexington, when they were mostly unprepared for the volley that hit them. The rebels learned quickly after that volley how to avoid the British army's slow method of aiming muskets according to precise orders and shouted commands.

The violence at Lexington and Concord had been unexpected. The Second Continental Congress, then meeting in Philadelphia, had not ordered any resistance to the British. Neither had the British officers been given any orders to force a confrontation. The shots fired on Lexington Green by both sides had not necessarily been accidental, but were not planned by anyone in power. Regardless, the American Revolution was on. The British Crown could not allow any rebel force to fire on its army without retaliation.

On May 10, 1775, Fort Ticonderoga, New York, and its supply of cannons, was captured by the Patriots. With the expected use of artillery, it was clear that a real war was going to be fought.

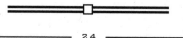

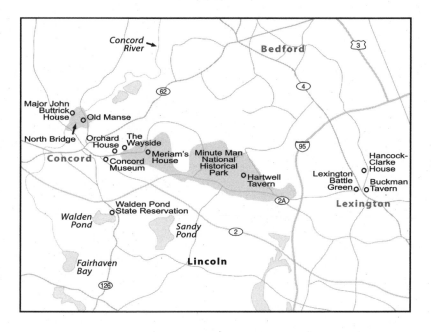

SOURCES & OTHER READING

The First American Revolution: Before Lexington and Concord, Ray Raphael, New Press, 2003

Iron Tears: America's Battle for Freedom, Britain's Quagmire: 1775–1783, Stanley Weintraub, Free Press, 2005

Lexington and Concord: The Beginning of the War of the American Revolution, Arthur Tourtellot, W.W. Norton, 2000

The Minute Men: The First Fight—Myths and Realities of the American Revolution, John Galvin, Potomac Books, 1996

Paul Revere's Ride, Paul Hackett Fisher, Oxford University Press, 1995

Websites:

americanrevolution.com/LexingtonandConcord.htm

americanrevwar.homestead.com/files/lexcon.htm

patriotresource.com/battles/lexington.html

Lexington and Concord retain the feel of colonial villages. Lexington has a population of 30,000. Concord is smaller with a population of 17,000.

Both are bedroom communities for Boston. The farmers and shopkeepers from these towns and surrounding villages who harassed the redcoats have long since been replaced by prosperous professionals.

Strict zoning laws mean that older homes are prevalent in both towns. While few true colonial-era homes are still standing, the flavor of the towns reminds visitors of that time period.

Both towns are welcoming to tourists, though visitors trying to drive slowly through Minute Man Park during morning and afternoon rush hour may experience some exasperation from more-hurried locals. Out-of-state drivers who have yet to experience "rotaries" (otherwise known as roundabouts or traffic circles) will find them in both towns. Remember that the vehicle already in the rotary always has the right of way.

POINTS OF INTEREST

Buckman Tavern ★★

1 Bedford St., Lexington
T: 781-862-1703
lexingtonhistory.org/buckman_2002.html
May–October daily 10am–4pm; tours every half hour
Admission: $5

Seventy-seven nervous militiamen gathered at Buckman Tavern before dawn on April 19, 1775, to wait on the British marching from Boston. This is the only colonial-era building still standing on the Lexington Green. A few musket ball holes can still be seen in the building's walls. On display is the original front door, which has a bullet hole in it. The Tavern is located beside the Lexington Visitor Center.

Hancock-Clarke House ★★★

36 Hancock St., Lexington
T: 781-862-1703
lexingtonhistory.org/hancockclarke_2002.html
June–October daily; tours at 11am, noon, 1pm and 2pm.
Admission: $5

Sons of Liberty members Samuel Adams and John Hancock were guests of the Rev. Jonas Clarke on the night of April 18, 1775, when two riders, William Dawes and Paul Revere, arrived separately to warn them that the British were on their way to arrest them. Hancock's grandfather had built the house in 1639. Today, the house has many period furnishings and British Major John Pitcairn's horse pistols. The pistols were captured when his horse threw him on his way back to Boston and the horse ran over to the American side.

Lexington Battle Green ★★★★★

Massachusetts and Bedford Streets, across the street from Buckman Tavern

It was here that colonial militia first stood up against the British troops who were advancing westward from Boston. A monument lists the names of the eight men who were killed here. A statue of a militia-man stands in front of the Green.

One irony of the action here in Lexington is that British law led to the confrontation. It had long been Crown law that every able-bodied man be ready to fall out with arms in the event of a military emergency. Every man in the colony was expected to own a rifle or a musket and have powder and shot for it. What King George III and the British army did not know was that many of these farmers had already agreed among themselves that their militia was ready to fight against the Crown rather than in defense of it.

Under stronger military commanders and with more experienced men holding their muskets, both sides might have evaded bloodshed at Lexington Green. Militia leader Captain John Parker later said that he had no intention of firing on the British. They were goaded into firing when a junior redcoat officer had ridden up to his men and demanded that they drop their weapons. Parker then claimed this same officer ordered his soldiers to fire on the farmers. Major John Pitcairn, the com-mander of the British soldiers, was furious that his men had fired without his person-al order. One of his lieutenants later reported that "the men were so wild that they could hear no orders."

Minute Man National Historical Park ★★★★★

Lexington Visitor Center, Rte. 2A east of Lexington
T: 978-369-6993
nps.gov/mima/
Visitor Center: Late-March–late-September daily 9am–5pm; October-November daily 9am–4pm; closed December–March; Grounds open dawn to dusk year-round. Suitable for biking, walking, and wheelchairs
Admission: Free

Minute Man National Historical Park is unique in that it encompasses an active Massachusetts highway, Rte. 2A. This road is on the historic roadbed of the Lexington Road, the same road on which the British marched while the Patriots sniped at them. Inside the visitor center, tourists should begin their tour by watching *The Road to Revolution*, a multimedia presen-tation that describes the action on April 19, 1775, as well as the incidents that led up to the events that day.

The Park Service suggests taking the five-mile park tour from west to east after leav-ing the visitor center, which is on the east side of the park. Visit Concord after taking this tour. The highlights of the trail are listed below:

Meriam's Corner ★★★★★, beside the Meriam House built in 1705, marks the spot where the militia began their all-day sniping at the British trudging back toward Boston after their final on-field clash at Concord. The house is being restored by members of the Meriam family. There are restrooms and a parking lot here, making this an ideal starting spot for those who want to walk the entire five-mile trail. Beside the parking lot are farming fields that have remained in cultivation for near-ly 300 years. Look for tiny Mill Brook passing under the road just west of the parking lot at Meriam's Corner. In 1775 there was a wooden bridge over the brook that formed a natural bottleneck for the British marching back toward Boston. The Patriots used this to their advantage and caught the British in a crossfire as they crossed the bridge.

Hartwell Tavern ★★★★

Mid-April–mid-May Sat-Sun 9am–5:30pm; daily late-May–late October 9:30am–5:30pm; closed in winter. Built in 1733 as an inn for travelers on their way west from Boston, Hartwell

Tavern was a landmark along the road used to rally militiamen. The Hartwells had three sons who were militiamen. After the running battle had passed by, the Hartwells moved into the road, retrieved the bodies of at least two British redcoats, and buried them nearby. Neighbors did not object as they knew the Hartwell sons were Patriots and that their parents were merely taking care of the dead. The Tavern was added to the park in the 1930s.

Just to the west of Hartwell Tavern is the mistakenly named **Bloody Angle** ★★, which actually should be named Bloody Curve since it marked a sharp turn in the original roadbed. The Patriot militia set up an ambush from behind a stone and log wall at this spot.

Just to the east of Hartwell Tavern is the site where **Paul Revere was captured** ★★★★, bringing to an end his famous "midnight ride." The night before the battles, Revere had been rowed across the Charles River. He had borrowed a horse so that he could ride to Lexington to warn Sons of Liberty leaders Samuel Adams and John Hancock that the British intended to arrest them. Revere arrived at the Hancock-Clarke house around midnight and was admonished by a uniformed sentry outside the house where Adams and Hancock were sleeping that he was making too much noise.

"Noise?!" Revere shouted to the sentry. "You'll have noise enough before long. The regulars are coming out!"

As Adams and Hancock were throwing on their clothes, Adams said, "What a glorious morning this is!" When Hancock looked at him with a shrug, Adams continued, "for America, I mean." Adams had been agitating for years for the British army to make a provocative move against the colonists. He sensed that it was about to come at Lexington (but he never ordered the militia to fire on the British).

After giving his warning, Revere continued his ride west, joined by William Dawes and Samuel Prescott. All three were determined to make it to Concord to warn the Patriots there, who were hiding weapons and powder. It was here that a British patrol stopped Revere, who had ridden ahead of the other two. Dawes and Prescott had hung back to rouse the militiamen living west of Lexington.

When Revere honestly told the British officer in charge of the patrol that he had already given the alarm to scores of houses, the officer released him. The British officer apparently believed the column had already lost the element of surprise and that holding the civilian would only slow them down. However, he did confiscate Revere's horse. Revere walked back to Lexington and was shocked to see Adams and Hancock still loitering around the Hancock-Clarke House. Revere packed them up and led them to a road that led to Philadelphia that was well out of the way of any British marching from Boston.

From here, visitors should drive three more miles into Concord. There are two sites on the way to Concord for those interested in 19th-century literature.

The Wayside ★

455 Lexington Rd., Concord
T: 978-369-6993
cr.nps.gov/nr/travel/pwwmh/ma47.htm
June–October; tours: Wed–Thu 2pm and 4pm, Fri–Sun 11am, 1:30pm, 3pm, and 4:30pm.
Admission: Free

The Wayside was one of the childhood homes of Louisa May Alcott, author of *Little Women*, and the only home owned by Nathaniel Hawthorne, author of *The House of Seven Gables* and *The Scarlet*

Letter. Children's book writer Margaret Lathrop, author of *The Five Little Peppers,* preserved the house.

Orchard House ★

399 Lexington Rd., Concord
T: 978-369-4118
louisamayalcott.org
April 1–October 31 Mon–Sat
10am–4:30pm, Sun 1–4:30pm;
November 1–March 31 Mon–Fri
11am–3pm, Sat 10am–4:30pm, and Sun
1–4:30pm
Admission: $8

This is the house where Louisa May Alcott grew up and where she wrote *Little Women.* In that book she also described the Wayside next door. Tours are offered every half hour. About 75 percent of the furnishings in the house were owned by the Alcott family. There have been no structural changes made to the house, so readers will recognize it from her book.

Old Manse ★★★

Monument St., Concord
T: 978-369-3909
concord.org/town/manse/old_manse.html
Mid-April–October 31 Mon–Sat
10am–5pm, Sun noon–5pm;
closed in the winter.
Admission: $5

The house itself was built in 1770, but the land under the Old Manse was used as a seasonal Indian camping ground for hundreds of years before Concord was settled by colonists. The first owner of the house was fiery preacher William Emerson, who may have been on the ridge with the militia when the British arrived at the North Bridge. The house was apparently unharmed even though the battle raged just 100 yards away to the north.

Emerson's grandson, Ralph Waldo Emerson, often visited the house and is reputed to have written his first published work, *Nature,* in its attic. Emerson wrote his poem *Concord Hymn* for the 1875 dedication of the Minute Man monument just north of the house. The poem begins, "By the rude bridge that arched the flood, Their flag to April's breeze unfurled; Here once the embattled farmers stood; And fired the shot heard 'round the world."

Nathaniel Hawthorne also lived in the house for three years. Henry David Thoreau was employed as a handyman and planted a vegetable garden for the Hawthornes. Thoreau at that time was living in a cabin set on the shores of nearby Walden Pond.

North Bridge ★★★★★

Monument St. 0.5 mile north of downtown, Concord

It was here at the North Bridge over the Concord River that the first true stand-up battle between Minute Men and British soldiers took place around 9am on April 19, 1775, about three hours after the British fired on the more passive militiamen at Lexington Green.

The Concord militia did not know that the British had already fired on their compatriots at Lexington, but they were prepared to fight anyway, as the British had already searched the nearby house of Colonel James Barrett looking for weapons and powder (from which the munitions had been removed earlier).

Three companies of British soldiers waiting on the south side of the bridge watched as hundreds of militiamen began to gather on a ridge northwest of the North Bridge over the river. Buoyed by their growing numbers, the Americans advanced on the British, who were outnumbered by at least five to one. The British, their blood up since firing on the militia at Lexington just hours earlier, fired first. The Americans returned fire and their superior numbers drove the British back over the bridge. In the brief exchange, three British soldiers were killed and eight were wounded. Two Americans were killed.

The first of many atrocities committed by both sides during the war took place here at this bridge. A wounded British soldier left behind was killed by a teenage Patriot who hit him in the head with an axe.

Just before the bridge, there is a monument over the graves of the British who were buried here. The original wooden bridge deteriorated long ago, but the reproduction is faithful to Emerson's description "the rude bridge that arched the flood."

On the north side is the famous statue of a Minute Man, sculpted by Daniel Chester French, who also carved the statue of Abraham Lincoln in the Lincoln Memorial in Washington, DC.

North Bridge Visitor Center

174 Liberty St., Concord
T: 978-369-6993
Late-March–late-October daily 9am–5pm; reduced hours in winter.
Admission: Free

The Concord River occasionally floods, closing the path leading to the visitor center on top of the hill behind the statue. If that is the case, the visitor center can be reached by driving to the north end of Monument Avenue and turning left. The visitor center features period drawings of the battles and a history of the famous bridge. It also offers ranger programs that start at 11am, 2pm, and 4pm daily.

Major John Buttrick House ★

Across the street from visitor center

Major John Buttrick was one of the commanders of the militia at Concord. He is most famous for giving the simple, direct order to his men, "Fire! For God's sake! Fire!" This order was the first military order given to the militia and may be considered the first true military response to the British march. After this order was given, the American Revolution was officially under way.

Concord Museum ★★★

200 Lexington Rd., Concord
T: 978-369-9763
concordmuseum.org/
January–March Mon–Sat 11am–4pm, Sun 1–4pm; April–December Mon–Sat 9am–5pm, Sunday noon–5pm.
Admission: $8

Among the Revolutionary artifacts here is one of the lanterns Revere had hung in the Old North Church. The museum is also noted for having most of the possessions of Henry David Thoreau, who lived at nearby Walden Pond.

Walden Pond State Reservation ★

915 Walden St., Concord
T: 978-369-3254
mass.gov/dcr/parks/northeast/wldn.htm
Admission: Free

For two years Henry David Thoreau, a native of Concord, lived in a cabin he built on land owned by Ralph Waldo Emerson on the shores of Walden Pond. During that time he wrote about the importance of living within the bounds of nature. He later became involved in movements to end slavery and social inequality. There is a trail leading around the entire pond that passes near Thoreau's home site.

Getting to and around Lexington & Concord

Concord and Lexington are about 20 miles west of Boston, making Logan International Airport the closest major airport. From the airport by rental car, take the Ted Williams Tunnel to the Massachusetts Turnpike to I-95 north. Leave I-95 at Exit 30B onto Rte. 2A, the road that passes between the two towns.

Public transit is available to and from Boston. Concord is on the Metropolitan Boston Transit Authority commuter train line, but Lexington is not. Visit the MBTA's website, mbta.com, for more details.

The towns are walker-friendly, but moving between them may be a challenge without a car. While the Concord Bridge can be reached by a not-too-lengthy hike from downtown Concord, Lexington Green is six miles to the east. Biking to Lexington from

Concord is possible along the Battle Road Trail within the confines of Minute Man Park, but that protected trail ends about a mile west of downtown Lexington. That leaves bikers to compete with traffic on Massachusetts Avenue if they want to continue into downtown Lexington.

Public buses do not run between Concord and Lexington, but a tour bus called Liberty Ride does from mid-June through mid-October. This tour of all the sites within Minute Man Park departs daily at 10am, 11:30am, 1pm, 2:30pm, and 4pm from the National Heritage Museum at 33 Marrett Road (Rte. 2A and Massachusetts Avenue), a mile southeast of downtown Lexington. The 90-minute tour costs $20 per person. The bus ticket can be shown at a number of private sites for discounts, including on food at historic restaurants.

Accommodations

Colonel Roger Brown House

1694 Main St., Concord
T: 800-292-1369 or 978-369-9119
colrogerbrown.com
$110–$180

Built in 1775, the house has fine architectural details like hand-hewn beams and wainscoting, while incorporating modern features such as DSL and cable TV. Each of its suites has a mix of period, reproduction, and modern furnishings.

Concord's Colonial Inn

48 Monument Sq., Concord
T: 800-370-9200 or 978-369-9200
concordscolonialinn.com
$245–$615 depending on season

This inn, which is listed on the National Register of Historic Places, was built in

1716 and has operated as a hotel since 1889. It has three original buildings and is noted for its meals and its nightly entertainment in the Village Forge Tavern. In 1775, one of the inn's original buildings was used as a storehouse for arms and provisions. Henry David Thoreau lived in what is now Colonial Inn from 1835 to 1837 while he attended Harvard.

Morgan's Rest Bed and Breakfast

205 Follen Rd., Lexington
T: 781-652-8018
morgansrestbandb.com
$95–$115

Morgan's Rest is located in East Lexington, convenient to Boston and the Lexington-Concord area.

Plymouth

Massachusetts

The docked *Mayflower II* in downtown Plymouth

THE EARLY YEARS

Plymouth, Massachusetts, may be the only place in the former colonies where a visitor can step back into 1627 and come away with a reasonable idea of what it must have been like to survive an ocean crossing, disease, and an unfamiliar land and climate. This town is host to a living-history village, where daily survival—not the politics of living under a distant king—was the primary concern.

Religion in England in the early 1600s was fairly simple—you were a member of the Church of England thanks to King Henry VIII's break from the Roman Catholic Church nearly 100 years earlier. It was not a good idea to openly practice anything other than what the church's leaders told you to believe. Practicing other beliefs often led to persecution, even torture.

By the early 1600s, some people were challenging the church. One group, the Scooby Separatists, named after the town where they were centered, did not care for the church rituals and wanted to break from it. Understandably, they were not a popular group to associate with as they attracted undue attention from authorities. They moved around frequently, so often that they picked up the unwanted nickname Pilgrims for their constant "pilgrimages" to various towns. The Pilgrims thought of themselves as equals among many and toyed with the idea of a government independent from the king—a radical idea for the 1600s. They even went so far as to encourage dissenting opinions among themselves.

Another group wanted to purify the existing church, leading them to be called Puritans. Instead of the finery they saw priests wear, the Puritans preferred to wear plain black clothes. Though they disliked control from the Church of England, they also disliked anyone opposing their own church leaders.

The Pilgrims were the first separatists to leave England successfully (the Puritans came later). In 1608, the Scooby Separatists moved from England to Holland in an attempt to practice their religion. In time, the Dutch grew tired of the Separatists and the former Englishmen realized that they were about to undergo another round of harassment. Their leaders started to look west to the New World in hopes that they could establish their own society without fear that they would be banished.

On September 16, 1620, a single ship called the *Mayflower* sailed with 106 people aboard. Their destination was vaguely described as "Virginia." There was to be a second ship, but it proved unseaworthy, and rather than wait for another ship to be found, the separatists set sail out of fear that the powers that be in England would have second thoughts about letting religious dissidents leave the country. They sailed from England after leaving Holland before that country could discriminate against them too.

No one on board the *Mayflower* had given much thought to the fact that they would soon be landing in unfamiliar territory right at the beginning of winter.

The ship landed on what would later become known as Cape Cod, Massachusetts, in November. Anxious to start their new lives, the colonists thought briefly about reneging on the contracts they had signed with the Virginia Company stating that they would indenture themselves to the company for seven years in exchange for passage to the new colony. Knowing that this could kill the colony before it got started, the church leaders convinced the colonists to keep their word and sealed the deal by writing the Mayflower Compact before they even set foot on shore. The Mayflower Compact was a simple document that bound the signers to a government that would govern for the common man and be chosen by common consent. It was a remarkable document that spoke of a people governing themselves democratically rather than waiting to see what a faraway king would rule.

For some reason, the colonists did not feel the urgent need to find a final site for their settlement. After sailing around and exploring for awhile, they finally landed on the mainland at Plymouth on December 21, more than a month after they had reached Cape Cod. This scouting would prove to be a mistake because by this time colder weather had arrived. The colonists barely had time to scout out the lay of the land and begin building cabins before winter hit.

At least half of the colonists died that winter from malnutrition and exposure to the cold. The following spring, a small crop of corn was raised from some seed corn that the colonists had discovered buried in the sand on Cape Cod. (The origin of that seed corn has always been a mystery. Was it seed corn the local Indians had buried for their own use that was intentionally or accidentally appropriated by the Pilgrims, or was the corn intended by the Indians to be a gift to these pale strangers who had landed from big canoes? The speculation continues.)

By October 1621, nearly a year after the Pilgrims had landed, their leader, William Bradford, declared that it was time for a harvest feast—not quite "Thanksgiving," but close enough for myth-making historians. And it lasted not for one afternoon, but for three days. The colonists served up ducks, geese, and wild turkeys. They invited their friendly Indian neighbors, the Wampanoag, who brought oysters and venison. Both the Pilgrims and the Indians shared the vegetables from their gardens. Curiously, this first celebration of their settlement in America was not repeated the following year.

The colony survived the first cruel year and began to flourish. A treaty with the Indians was signed and honored by both sides. The idea of indentured servants was eventually abandoned in favor of the principle of independent labor. To pay off the colony's London investors, who held the seven-years labor contracts, the colony developed a prosperous fur trade. The colonists never did develop a good cash crop that would thrive in the rocky coastal soil, which the Virginia Company had originally thought would be the source of the return on their investment, but the furs provided the same profit margin.

Over the next several years more colonists arrived. As the colony grew, people moved out to start their own towns. By 1638, the towns were operating under a kind of county government. In 1691 the colony was officially merged with the younger but rapidly growing colony of Massachusetts. Though Plymouth was nearly 100 years older, the city of Boston grew much more rapidly, probably because it had a larger port that could accommodate bigger ships. As Boston grew, the importance and memory of Plymouth as the pioneering colony in New England faded.

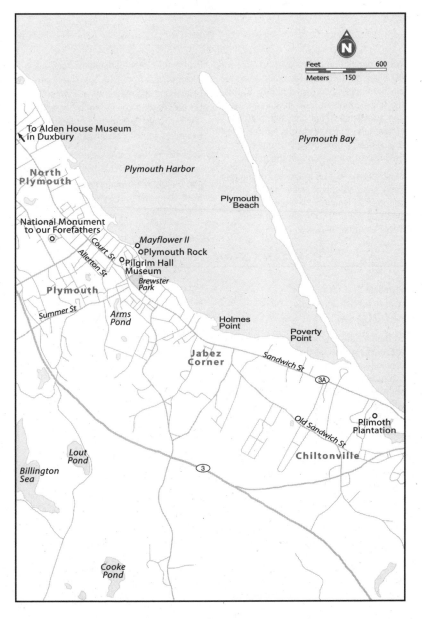

To Alden House Museum
in Duxbury

Plymouth Bay

North
Plymouth

Plymouth Harbor

Plymouth
Beach

National Monument
to our Forefathers

Mayflower II

Court St.

Plymouth Rock

Allerton St

Pilgrim Hall
Museum

Plymouth

Brewster
Park

Summer St

Arms
Pond

Holmes
Point

Poverty
Point

Jabez
Corner

Sandwich St

3A

Old Sandwich St

Plimoth
Plantation

Lout
Pond

Chiltonville

Billington
Sea

3

Cooke
Pond

Feet   600
Meters   150

N

PLYMOUTH TODAY

With a population of just over 50,000 only 40 miles from Boston, Plymouth is an ideally situated bedroom community. But as the first permanent town in Massachusetts and a settlement that has been featured in elementary school textbooks for decades, it also has its own identity as one of the best-known small towns in the nation.

Most tourists will be interested in the relatively short stretch of waterfront where the shops and Plymouth Rock are found. Don't be put off by the souvenir shops. There are other places to visit.

Plymouth is very tourist-conscious. Signs direct drivers from Rte. 3 to downtown via Exit 6, and the road ends at Plymouth Harbor. Beyond downtown, other signs direct visitors to Plimoth Plantation about two miles south of downtown.

Even during the cooler seasons, Plymouth can be quite busy. That may mean traffic, particularly when visitors are turning to leave the waterfront to make their way to Plimoth Plantation.

POINTS OF INTEREST

Plymouth Rock ★★★
Waterfront under pavilion
Admission: Free

To their credit, tourist officials in Plymouth make no claims that the *Mayflower* voyagers stepped onto the granite rock with the date 1620 carved into it. After all, it should be obvious that no trained seaman who had just crossed the Atlantic Ocean would intentionally steer his fragile wooden rowboat directly toward a rock that could sink him and his passengers. One hundred twenty years after the *Mayflower* arrived, a 95-year-old man living in Plymouth asked his neighbors if they would take him down to the waterfront so he could see the rock one more time before he died. He told the story that, as a child, he had listened to the original settlers describe how they had stepped on the rock when they first landed. Only two written accounts survive from the early days of Plymouth about the landing—on

Plymouth beach. Neither one mentions anything about the rock.

Still, the story of Plymouth Rock has persisted. Since 1741 the residents of Plymouth, with a wink and nod, have honored this rock. It has been moved numerous times and was dropped and broken in half at least once. It once was at least twice as large but water action and souvenir hunters have whittled it down to about the size of a loveseat. It is now protected by an iron fence. True or not, no study of the early colonial days of the nation would be complete without a trip to Plymouth Rock.

Mayflower II ★★★★★
Waterfront
T: 508-746-1622
plimoth.org/visit/what/mayflower2.asp
April–November daily 9am–5pm
Admission: $8 for visiting only the ship, $24 for a combination two-day pass including admission to Plimoth Plantation.

The ship is not wheelchair accessible.

Built in 1957 in England, the *Mayflower II* is 106 feet long and 25 feet wide. The dimensions of the original *Mayflower* are unknown, but surviving ship plans show this to be a typical cargo ship of its period. While it may look top heavy to the landlubber, the *Mayflower II* is an accurate reproduction of the ships of the day. It still sails on occasion and has proven seaworthy. The only concessions to modern amenities on board are the placement of electric lights below so visitors can see in the dark recesses.

The original *Mayflower* left Plymouth, England, on September 16 with 102 passengers and crew, and it arrived off Cape Cod 65 days later on November 19. The ship cruised up and down the coastline for a few weeks looking for a suitable place to land and live. The *Mayflower* finally dropped anchor in Plymouth Harbor on December 26, 1620, for four months before sailing back to England in April 1621. When its captain and co-owner died in 1624, the ship fell into disrepair and was probably sold for its scrap wood value. It disappeared from ownership records that year.

The ship has a number of costumed crew and passengers on board ready to answer visitors' questions. These people, employees of Plimoth Plantation, are trained to stay in character and to answer questions only as someone in 1621 would answer. They will not even respond to the term "Pilgrim," a term that was applied to them back in England as a derogatory description but which they did not use to describe themselves. The original settlers considered themselves Englishmen who were leaving their country in order to worship as they pleased. Self-government was first introduced to the Plymouth colony on November 11, 1620, when the colonists were still on board the *Mayflower*. The settlers drew up a simple document that called on all of the of-age male members of the group to form a "civill body politick." While still acknowledging King James as their leader, the colonists agreed to meet on occasion to "enacte lawes, ordinances, acts constitutions, & offices." Known since 1793 as "The Mayflower Compact," the document received little attention until after the American Revolution when the United States was struggling to write its own Constitution. The new Americans pointed to it as an example of how early colonists had always dreamed of self-determining government rather than forever remaining under the rule of a faraway king.

Pilgrim Hall Museum ★★★

75 Court St., Plymouth,
just west of the waterfront
T: 508-746-1620
pilgrimhall.org
February–December daily 9:30am–4:30pm
Admission: $6

This museum features artifacts from the Plymouth colony, including Governor William Bradford's Bible, chairs and chests, some weapons and armaments, and the only known portrait of a *Mayflower* colonist, Edward Winslow. The painting, completed nearly 30 years after the colony was established, shows Winslow in a somber black suit.

One of the more interesting artifacts in the museum collection are the wooden ribs of a small ship, just 40 feet long, that sailed from England for Plymouth in 1626. The ship was wrecked on Cape Cod, but most of the passengers were rescued by the residents of Plymouth. It may be the only surviving remnants of a 17th-century ocean-going vessel that made it to the New World.

The National Monument to our Forefathers ★★

Allerton St., near intersection with Court St., Plymouth
Admission: Free

Called the largest granite statue in the nation, this allegorical monument was first conceived in 1820 but not finished until 1889. It is 81 feet tall with a central female figure representing Faith standing 36 feet tall. This figure, holding the Bible in one hand and standing on Plymouth Rock, represents the inspiration that brought the settlers to Plymouth. Four other figures surround her: Morality, Education, Law, and Liberty. These figures represent the founding principles of the Plymouth colony. Its sculptor was Hammit Billings, a Bostonian whose drawings illustrated the first editions of *Uncle Tom's Cabin*. He died 15 years before his statue was finally erected in Plymouth. The names of all of the surviving members of the first colony are listed on plaques.

Alden House Museum ★★

105 Alden St., Duxbury
T: 781-934-9092
alden.org
Mid-May–mid-October Mon–Sat noon–4pm
Admission: $4

This house, built in 1653, is still owned by the Alden family. It is thought to be the only surviving original home in which any of the *Mayflower* passengers actually lived. The owners are descendants of John Alden and Priscilla Mullins, who are thought to be the third couple from the *Mayflower* to marry.

The courtship of John and Priscilla is one of the more endearing stories of the Plymouth Colony. Captain Miles Standish, a recent widower, sent Alden to the Mullins' household to inquire as to the availability of Priscilla, who was still living at home with her parents. This courtship

by messenger was not uncommon. Priscilla, acting unusually independent for a woman of the time, told Alden to speak for himself. Alden then asked her to court him instead of Standish.

One unusual feature of the house is its walk-in closet in the master bedroom. Closets were considered rooms in colonial times and the local governments taxed landowners on the numbers of rooms in their houses. Another unusual feature is the bonnet of Priscilla, which is on display in a glass case.

Plimoth Plantation ★★★★★

137 Warren Ave., Plymouth
T: 508-746-1622
plimoth.org/
April–November daily 9am–5:30pm
Admission: $24 for combination ticket to both Plimoth Plantation and *Mayflower II*, $21 for Plimoth Plantation only. Ticket is good for two consecutive days.

Founded in 1947 by Henry Hornblower II, a Bostonian who had spent his summer vacations in the family's Plymouth vacation home, Plimoth Plantation (the spelling favored by its Governor William Bradford) is actually two attractions in one. One is a living-history village where visitors will encounter the Plymouth colonists in 1627, seven years after the *Mayflower* had landed. The other is a recreation of a Wampanoag village where Native Americans in period dress do not assume 1600s personas. Instead, the Indians of today explain how their ancestors interacted with the Plimoth colonists. This village is recreated based on information from an Indian named Hobbamock, who lived adjacent to the colony for more than 20 years.

No modern concessions are made for visitors to the Plimoth Colony village. That means that visitors in wheelchairs may have a hard time visiting the village on their own because the path is sandy and rocky. There are no restrooms in the village. The only shelters are the same small houses that are used by the interpreters playing colonists. Once tourists leave the visitor center, they enter the 17th century, observing and talking to people in 1627.

The colonists are skilled actors as well as knowledgeable historians. They will ignore tourists' strange dress and accoutrements such as cameras, but they will not be tripped up by anyone trying to make them acknowledge the 21st century. They will not understand or respond to any questions about the American Revolution. As far as they are concerned, that is still 150 years in their future and their king is now Charles I, not George III of the American Revolution.

The residents of the Plimoth Colony's speech patterns, customs, dress, chores, songs, and beliefs are all typical of the early 17th-century colonists. Indeed, all of the interpreters have taken on the roles and names of real colonists. It is conceivable that visitors with ancestors dating back to the Plymouth Colony could even converse with someone posing as their own ancestor. It is not unusual for visitors to spend time listening and talking to a number of "colonists" to glean information about life in the 1600s.

Women are likely to be found cooking meals inside the houses or sewing in the front yard while the men are making shingles, tending gardens, or daubing on mud to seal holes in their homes. Both men and women are likely to break into song. Other interpreters may blow on hornpipes.

The Wampanoag village consists of several huts made of oak-tree bark. Sitting outside the huts and under shelters are Native Americans wearing deerskins. They are not in character but are knowledgeable and willing to speak about their ancestral

tribes. They know the geographical range of the Wampanoags, how the native society revolved around the eldest mother of the family, and how their tribe interacted with the first settlers. (The reason they do not adopt first-person techniques should be obvious—tourists would not know the Wampanoag language, though it still exists and the Indians can speak it.)

The visitor center has a permanent display titled "Thanksgiving: Memory, Myth & Meaning" that addresses and then dismisses the image of the November holiday that has been passed down through generations of school books and folklore. The holiday as we know it was not actually celebrated by the Plimoth colonists on an annual basis and the interpreters will not react to anyone asking about it. (Thanksgiving was not declared a national holiday until 1863 when President Abraham Lincoln called for a national day of thanksgiving. The holiday was not set as the fourth Thursday in November until President Franklin Roosevelt signed that into law in 1939.)

The Thanksgiving holiday itself does have its roots in Plymouth based on a few lines written by Governor William Bradford in which he mentions that the colony celebrated taking in the harvest in 1621. The Wampanoags did attend and stayed for several days. They contributed to the feasts by bringing hunted deer. There is no mention of the word "thanksgiving" nor turkeys, though wild turkeys did roam the woods. Instead of being a joyous feast with Native Americans and *Mayflower* settlers sitting around the same table, as often pictured in paintings through the years, the event was likely tense. The Wampanoags did not trust the settlers after some incidents of theft from Indian food caches so they kept their weapons within easy reach. There were no other "thanksgivings" mentioned in the records after 1621, so the colonists apparently did not make this an annual celebration.

Another Thanksgiving myth that the display addresses is the differences between Puritans and *Mayflower* settlers. The Puritans wanted to "purify" the Church of England in England while the *Mayflower* settlers were separatists from the Church of England. The *Mayflower* settlers came over in 1620 and were led by William Bradford while the Puritans came over in 1629 and were led by John Winthrop. The Puritans tended to wear black and white clothing on occasion while the *Mayflower* settlers wore much more colorful clothes, including hats for women. The only true commonality is that both sects looked to John Calvin for their teachings and both sects settled in Massachusetts. Somewhere in history's timeline, the story of the Puritans merged with that of the *Mayflower* settlers.

GETTING TO AND AROUND PLYMOUTH

Plymouth, Massachusetts, is about 40 miles south of Boston, and is reached by air via Logan International Airport. Logan has a good selection of rental car companies. People arriving at Logan will take the Ted Williams Tunnel and I-90/Mass Pike west to I-93 south via the new Exit 24. Take the left exit for Rte. 3 south after I-93 branches off to the right. Watch for Exit 6A to reach downtown Plymouth.

There is a mass transit option from Boston, as commuter trains and buses run between Boston and Plymouth. Consult the Massachusetts Bay Transit Authority at 800-392-6100 or their website at mbta.com for details. Keep in mind that one of the major attractions in Plymouth, Plimoth Plantation, may not be considered to be within walking distance of Plymouth Center. If arriving in Plymouth by train or bus, visitors should consider taking a bus or taxi from Plymouth Center to Plimoth Plantation.

Another air option for those wishing to avoid Boston traffic is to fly into Green Airport in Providence, Rhode Island, about 53 miles west of Plymouth. Those arriving at the Green Airport will take I-95 north to I-495 south to Rte. 44 east. The last 30 miles will be on two-lane roads through several small towns.

Plymouth may also be a boating destination for some travelers. There are marinas on the waterfront with restaurants and accommodations within walking distance. There is a harbor cruise on what looks like a Mississippi River boat called the *Plymouth Belle.* These tours operate May through October. The 90-minute tours leave the harbor starting at 11am and include historical information on the *Mayflower* settlers and the fishing industry based in Plymouth.

There is a 45-minute trolley tour of Plymouth Center that does not include going out to Plimoth Plantation. The tours leave Plymouth Rock starting at 9:30am on the half hour until 11:30am then start again on the hour at 1pm. Call 508-747-4161 for details.

ACCOMMODATIONS

Another Place Inn

240 Sandwich St., Plymouth
T: 800-583-0126 or 508-746-0126
anotherplaceinn.com
$100–$150

Another Place is an authentic 1860 half-cape, built by sea captain Hiram B. Sears. It has been accurately restored with original wide-board floors, antique furnishings, and decor.

Auberge Gladstone

8 Vernon St., Plymouth
T: 866-722-1890 or 508-830-1890
aubergegladstone.com
$90–$100

This 1848 Inn is a colonial-style manor house. It sits one block west of Plymouth Rock and the waterfront in the historic district. Pets are welcome for an additional charge.

1760 Peabody Bradford Homestead

6 River St., Kingston
T: 781-585-2646
1760bradfordhouse.com
$69–$125

In 1760, Peabody Bradford, great-grandson of Plymouth Colony's Governor William Bradford, built a five-room English colonial Cape house on the northern bank of the Jones River. Its dock, known as "The Landing," received and dispatched all of the goods and travelers leaving or coming by boat to Kingston, just four miles from Plymouth.

SOURCES & OTHER READING

A Little Commonwealth: Family Life in Plymouth Colony, James Demos, Oxford University Press, 1999

Of Plymouth Plantation, William Bradford, The Vision Forum, 1999

Plymouth Colony: Its History and People, Eugene Stratton, Ancestry.com, 1997

The Times of Their Lives: Life, Love, and Death in Plymouth Colony, James Deetz, Anchor, 2001

Websites:

http://pilgrims.net/plymouth/history/index.htm

rootsweb.com/~mosmd/

Fort Stanwix

New York

Fort Stanwix's moat and abatis

THE WAR YEARS

The reconstructed Fort Stanwix in downtown Rome would be an interesting, picturesque place to visit even before considering the fact that the original fort was saved by Benedict Arnold. Arnold would later betray the Revolution, but his help here ended the attempt by British forces to separate the northern colonies from the southern colonies.

Like Fort Ticonderoga to the east, Fort Stanwix was started by the British in 1758 during the French and Indian War as an outpost to keep the French at bay. Its role was to protect the Oneida Carrying Place, a land portage between the Mohawk River and Wood Creek, which eventually connected with Lake Ontario. This land bridge protected by the fort allowed passengers in vessels as small as canoes and as large as cargo-carrying flat-bottomed boats to travel by water from deep within Canada to the Atlantic Ocean at New York City. Both the French and the British knew the importance of these waterways, which allowed them great mobility, so the British rushed to erect a fort to guard against the French trying to use the Mohawk River to penetrate eastward.

Fort Stanwix was designed with flat walls facing out toward the Mohawk River with other walls pointing inward so that overlapping fields of fire could be concentrated on an enemy attacking any wall. Each side of the fort had a series of ditches, sloping dirt walls, and walls of wooden stakes. Most of the fort was actually below ground so that attacking forces had very little to shoot at with muskets or traditional cannons. Only mortars could be elevated enough to drop shells into the interior of the fort.

Any soldier making it close to the wall encountered wooden poles sharpened into stakes placed at head level. The fort actually seemed to bristle with log defenses like a porcupine, making it fearsome looking as well as virtually impregnable.

The fort served its purpose: The French never made the feared attack on New York City by inland waterway. In 1763, the fort was rendered useless when the British captured Quebec City in Canada and killed the French army commander, ending the French and Indian War. In 1768 the British signed a treaty with six Indian nations at the fort that ceded a vast amount of land to the south to the Crown. The Indians thought the treaty would limit the amount of land that the colonists would seek, while the British and their colonists thought of the treaty as the first step in a process that would open up vast stretches of land to colonial settlement.

In 1775, the Carrying Place again became strategically important. Patriots occupied the abandoned ruins and began to rebuild it as an outpost to stop the anticipated British invasion of the northern colonies from Canada. The ruins were renamed Fort Schuyler after a local commander.

One prong of the British invasion from Canada, under General John Burgoyne, began to march south along the Hudson River and Lake Champlain. A separate British force, including Mohawk and Seneca Indians, moved east from the Great Lakes region under British General Barry St. Leger. That force arrived at Fort Stanwix (then called Fort Schuyler by the Americans) on August 2, 1775. St. Leger surrounded the fort and demanded its surrender. The American commander, Colonel Peter Gansevoort, only

26 years old, refused. According to legend, in defiance he raised a flag bearing stars and stripes to signify that this was an American fort. (This was at least 10 months before the stars and stripes flag that legend claims Betsy Ross sewed in Philadelphia. Gansevoort may have raised a flag with red and white stripes that contained the Union jack in the upper corner, which was common at the time.)

The siege of Fort Stanwix lasted three weeks, and the British never made a full assault. During this same period, a Patriot relief column, including some Oneida Indians, tried to reach the fort, but it was ambushed by a force of Mohawks at a marshy ravine six miles to the east in what became known as the Battle of Oriskany. While that battle raged on, British attention was diverted and a force from the fort was able to raid some nearby Indian villages to get much-needed supplies, including a replenishment of gunpowder.

St. Leger eventually pulled away when he captured a courier carrying news of a huge relief force that was on its way to the fort. Arnold and others, employing some wartime psychology, wrote fake letters to the commander of the fort describing the large size of the supposed relief force. They then allowed the couriers to be "captured" by the British so that St. Leger would begin to worry about being caught in the open between the fort and a superior advancing column. When St. Leger's Indians believed the letters and left, he had little choice but to pull back his regular British soldiers as well. St. Leger's force actually outnumbered Arnold's force, and he could have taken the fort and then marched east to help Burgoyne, possibly changing the history of the war. Fort Stanwix/Fort Schuyler was not surrendered, nor starved out.

For the rest of the Revolution, the story of Fort Stanwix served as a morale booster and example of how the Patriots could successfully fight the British. Small, tenacious Patriot forces could outlast the larger, but more ponderous and tradition-bound, British forces. British forces were trained to decimate an enemy in open combat, but if the Patriots took up strong defensive positions, they could outlast the British. Fort Stanwix continued to be garrisoned by Patriots through 1781, but the British did not return to avenge their humiliating defeat.

In 1784, Fort Stanwix played a role in post-Revolution history when it hosted a treaty conference between the United States and the Iroquois Confederacy. The treaty was necessary because the Treaty of Paris of 1783 that officially ended the war between England and the colonies had not addressed hostilities between the Indian allies of the British and the Americans. The Confederacy may have thought that they had little choice but to trust the new Americans now that their British sponsors had left. In exchange for keeping Indian land heading north into Canada, the Iroquois signed away rights to land to the south and west that would later be settled by white men from Pennsylvania and would become Ohio. The Oneida, who had sided with the colonists, were told that they could keep their land. That promise was later broken, and the Indians continued to war with colonists through the 1780s and 1790s. Final control over the lands was not settled until after the War of 1812, when the British left the continent once and for all, and the Indians were overwhelmed by the ever-growing numbers of colonists.

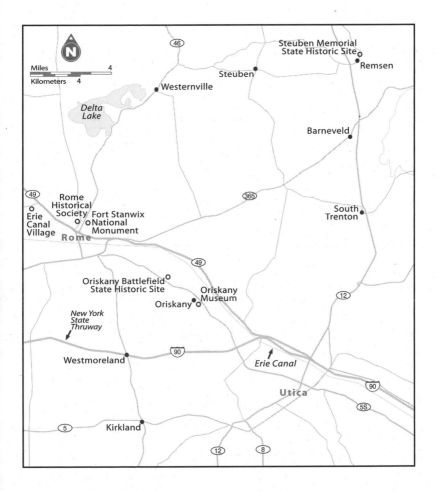

FORT STANWIX TODAY

The history of the reconstructed Fort Stanwix is almost as interesting as the history of the original fort, which long ago rotted away. By the 1870s, when the town of Rome was incorporated, the fort's site had been virtually forgotten and its place in history ignored. Then in the 1930s, a hardy lot of local historians came along with a vision of reconstructing the fort and making it a centerpiece of historic tourism for Rome.

It took more than 40 years of political wrangling and purchases of industrial property, but by 1976 a large portion of downtown Rome had been cleared of buildings. Archaeological research established the original outlines of the fort. Using old written accounts and drawings and making a few educated guesses, the fort was reconstructed on the same site that it occupies today. A small visitor center was built in one of the interior rooms of the fort.

Rome, a town of about 30,000, was originally built on the ruins of the fort, but the central business district now stretches to the west. There are restaurants near the fort, as well as a motel directly across the street from it.

The town itself is not especially picturesque, but it is located on the southwestern edge of the Adirondack Mountains. Side trips on the two-lane state roads to the northeast through the mountains make a pleasant diversion. It is advisable to check weather forecasts as winter can come as early as October.

POINTS OF INTEREST

Fort Stanwix National Monument
★★★★★

112 East Park St., Rome
T: 315-336-2090
nps.gov/fost
Daily 9am–5pm; closed January–March
Admission: Free

Fort Stanwix's new visitor center opened in July 2005 with exhibits focusing on the American Revolution, the importance of the Mohawk River Valley during both the French and Indian War and the Revolution, the relationships between Indian tribes and settlers, and the siege of Fort Stanwix itself. The story of Fort Stanwix is told through the eyes of four different people: a middle-aged Loyalist merchant; a young, enthusiastic Patriot soldier; a female Indian tribal leader; and the Patriot sister of the Loyalist. These characters are introduced in video presentations in the front of the museum. As visitors move through the exhibits, these characters reappear either on written panels or on videos to discuss his or her views on what happened to them over the years.

This multimedia presentation, augmented by traditional displays of maps and first-person accounts, as well as some artifacts, makes this site a great place to study the often-neglected, often-misunderstood action in western New York State. In fact, visitors should use the visit to Fort Stanwix to look beyond the specific time frame of the Revolution, as this historic site offers

tourists a chance to study the relationships between colonial settlers and
American Indians, and how two wars
changed those relationships.

What happened at and around Fort
Stanwix from the 1750s through the
1770s colored the relationship between
Indians and the United States government
for more than 150 years. The National
Park Service does not focus on the distant
future of Indian relations in their interpre-
tation here at Fort Stanwix. But the displays and videos make it clear that both
whites and Indians sensed that the con-
flicts that had occurred between the two
races in the past would pale in comparison to what would happen in the future. It
made no difference who won the French
and Indian War and the American
Revolution: The colonists and the Indians
would be at war until one party or the
other was defeated.

Fort Stanwix was isolated when the
American Revolution began. Most of the
rebelling colonials were gathered along the
coast and were more likely to have traveled to England than to the far reaches of
the Mohawk River. The rebels in Boston
and New York City had no understanding
of what life was like west of the
Adirondack Mountains and had no contact
with the frontiersmen who lived in those
remote settlements.

The city dwellers leading the Revolution
had never experienced the French and
Indian War, but the pioneering settlers of
western New York and the Indian tribes
who lived nearby had never forgotten it. In
fact, little had changed in their lives after
the French had lost the war. The American
settlers were still pushing westward; and
the same Indian tribes who had resisted
giving up their lands to those settlers were
still there.

The tribes did not welcome the idea of
another war. Twelve years earlier the tribes
had been forced to choose between siding
with the French and the British. Now they
would have to either align themselves with
American settlers and their promises to
contain their westward migration, or to
align themselves with British soldiers who
made the same promises. The tribes had
thought those questions had been settled
20 years earlier when the British had won.
Once again the tribes of Native Americans
would be forced to fight each other to settle a war between the whites. Peace
between the tribes after the French and
Indian War would be broken again.

Visitors to Fort Stanwix who expect to see
a Civil War–era brick fort or a Plains
War–era wooden stockade will be surprised
as they leave the visitor center and start
the quarter-mile walk to the entrance of
the fort. Fort Stanwix is almost invisible,
which is the genius of its design. There
are no tall walls that could be breached by
cannon fire. Most of the fort lies below
ground level so that any attacking cannon
fire has no targets. A bonus of this design
for visitors is that it means that the modern-day town of Rome virtually disappears,
making it easier for visitors to put themselves back into the 1700s. Another
aspect of the design that may be surprising is the sharpened poles protruding from
the walls. These were designed to slow
attacking soldiers, but this seemingly
effective means of protecting a fort's walls
had disappeared by the time the United
States government started its own round
of coastal fort construction in the 1830s.

There are often interpreters on hand inside
the fort who are practicing crafts common
to the 1700s. For instance, coopers may
be making barrels, and Native Americans
may be making trade goods. Everything
appears to be authentic, including the
poorly drafting fireplaces. On some days

smoke from the fireplaces fills the low rooms inside the wooden barracks because the original fort's chimneys were not tall enough to properly draft away the smoke. Look around the fort and note how its designers tried to be as practical as possible. For instance, the wooden rain gutters dump water collected from the roofs into large wooden barrels.

Allow at least two hours and maybe three to see all of the displays in the visitor museum and to experience the fort itself.

Rome Historical Society ★

200 Church St., Rome
T: 315-336-5870
when-in-rome.com/RomeHistorical
Tue–Fri 10am–5pm, Sat 10am–3pm
Admission: suggested donation

Located just a block from Fort Stanwix, this museum has exhibits on the area's forts and their importance in both the French and Indian War and the Revolution. The influence of the Indians, particularly the Iroquois, is also examined.

Erie Canal Village ★★★

5789 New London Rd., Rome (Rtes. 46 and 49 west of Fort Stanwix)

T: 315-337-3999
eriecanalvillage.net
Memorial Day Weekend–Labor Day
Wed–Sat 10am–5pm, Sun noon–5pm;
September Sat–Sun noon–5pm
Admission: $15

This living-history museum is located on the site where construction was first started on the Erie Canal in 1817. Rides are offered on the canal in authentic packets pulled by mule teams. There is also a steam-powered locomotive providing train rides. One building houses a museum on the canal and other buildings depict a village in the 19th century. Also on site are the ruins of Fort Bull, a French and Indian War outpost.

For much of the 19th century, the 363-mile long Erie Canal, stretching from the Hudson River in Albany to Lake Erie in Buffalo, was farmers' principal means of transporting goods in this area of New York state. As railroads were built, it declined in importance but later surged again in use as railroads increased their shipping rates.

Allow two hours to visit this site.

SITES NEAR FORT STANWIX

Oriskany Battlefield State Historic Site ★★★★

7801 Rte. 69, Oriskany, six miles east of Fort Stanwix
T: 315-768-7224
nysparks.state.ny.us/sites/info.asp?siteID=21
Mid-May–mid-October; Museum Wed–Sat 9am–5pm, Sun 1–5pm; Grounds open most days even when museum is seasonally closed
Admission: Free

Had there not been a siege of Fort Stanwix, there would not have been a Battle of Oriskany. On August 2, 1777,

when British General Barry St. Leger started his siege of the fort, word spread east by courier that the fort was under attack and it would have to be relieved by Patriot militia forces.

General Nicolas Herkimer assembled about 800 militiamen and a handful of Oneida Indian scouts and began a 30-mile march to break the siege. St. Leger learned of the approach of the relief column and sent a force of professional soldiers, Tory militia, and Mohawk and Seneca Indians east to ambush it. The Indians chose a ravine through which the

Patriot militia would have to pass on its way to crossing Oriska Creek as the point where they would stage an ambush. The Indians took up positions on top of the ridge behind trees, giving them the high ground so they could shoot down into the Patriot ranks.

At 10am on August 6, the first 600 Patriot troops were already in the ravine when shots rang out from three sides. During the first volley, General Herkimer was shot in the leg. After a few volleys, the Mohawk and Seneca left their hiding places to begin fighting hand to hand with axes and clubs. The 200 men in the Patriot rear guard retreated, but the Indians chased them down determined to wipe out the entire column. The slaughter that ensued was so intense that Blacksnake, a Seneca leader, later said, "The bloodshed made a stream running down on the sloping ground."

The battle raged for nearly six hours before the Indians left the field upon receiving a report that a force of soldiers from Fort Stanwix had found their camps and had carried away their supplies. The surviving Patriot militia took the opportunity to leave the field, leaving their dead behind. Of the 800 Patriot militiamen who walked into the ravine at Oriskany, only 150 walked away unscathed. Most of the 650 were killed by the Indians, making it one of the bloodiest and costliest battles for the Patriots. The British and Tory forces suffered fewer casualties.

A regular army force under General Benedict Arnold also headed toward Fort Stanwix. When the Indians heard of this force, which they believed to be even larger than the defeated militia force, they abandoned St. Leger. St. Leger, now denied most of his forces, retreated himself, breaking the siege.

There is a small museum (opening hours noted above.) The site itself is generally open for visitation even when the museum is closed. The ravine where the fiercest fighting occurred is below the museum. Visitors can stand on the same ground where the Mohawks loyal to the British fired their first volley, and look down toward the hopeless position occupied by the helpless Patriots.

The museum contains some artifacts from the battle. Allow at least an hour here if the museum is open; if not, a half hour is enough to tour the battlefield.

Oriskany Museum ★

420 Utica St., Oriskany
T: 315-736-7529
Wed–Sat 1–5:30pm
Admission: donation suggested

This museum has some artifacts from the nearby battle, as well as some artifacts and a jet aircraft from the USS *Oriskany*, an aircraft carrier named after the battle. Allow a half hour to see the museum.

Steuben Memorial State Historic Site ★

Starr Hill Rd., 2.5 miles west of Rtes. 12 and 28, Remsen (20 miles north of Rome)
Admission: Free

This site marks the gravesite of one of the most mysterious—yet important—men in the American Revolution. The true training and military background of Friedrich Wilhelm von Steuben is still in doubt, and many historians continue to wonder why he was discharged from the Prussian army in 1763 at the age of 33. After his dismissal, von Steuben tried to join the armies of France, Austria, and Baden, but all of them turned down this supposedly well-trained military officer.

Von Steuben did not find gainful military employment again until 1777, when he attended a party in Paris where he was introduced to Benjamin Franklin. Franklin, believing von Steuben to have some kind of superior military training that he rightly recognized could be of value to the mostly self-taught military leaders of the American Revolution, wrote a letter introducing him to General George Washington.

Von Steuben, finally a soldier again after more than a decade out of uniform, caught up with Washington at an opportune time. The Continental Army was entering winter quarters at Valley Forge in the winter of 1777–78. Recognizing, or at least believing, that von Steuben was a professional soldier, Washington assigned the Prussian the task of shaping his still-disorganized men into a real army. Washington wanted a force that would react with military precision to its well-trained British counterpart army.

During that winter, von Steuben, who spoke no English and only some French, developed a training regimen that became the standard method of basic training that is still used by the United States' military forces today. He trained 100 men to fight together as a company. Each company trained independently and then were assembled into regiments. Historian Douglas Southall Freeman, a biographer of George Washington, famously called Washington the father of the United States Army and von Steuben its first teacher.

Von Steuben never became an active field general as he had hoped to. Given 16,000 acres of land by the state of New York for his military service, von Steuben built a two-room log home on this land. He lived there in the summer and then wintered in New York City. He died on his property in 1794. In 1804 the large granite monument was erected over his remains (in defiance of his request to be buried in an unmarked grave).

Von Steuben may have been a soldier of fortune who exaggerated his real military resume. Or he may have been a true military genius who understood how to train and motivate fighting men. Either way, von Steuben became one of the most important men in the American Revolution for his role in transforming a rabble of undisciplined farmers and shopkeepers into the Continental Army that George Washington commanded in the northern colonies.

SOURCES & OTHER READING

The American Revolution in Indian Country: Crisis and Diversity in Native American Communities, Colin Callaway, Cambridge University Press, 1995

The American Strategy and French Role in the Fort Stanwix Treaty of 1784, Edward Ball, self-published, 1972

Days of Siege: A Journal of the Siege of Fort Stanwix in 1777, anonymous, Eastern Acorn Press, 1983

Fort Stanwix: A Brief History, Frederick Rahmer, self-published, 1976

The Other New York: The American Revolution Beyond New York City, 1763-1787, Joseph Tiedemann, State University of New York, 2005

The Treaty of Fort Stanwix, Henry Manley, Eastern National Park & Monument Association, 2003

Getting to and around Fort Stanwix

Fort Stanwix, located in downtown Rome, can be reached by flying into Syracuse Hancock International, which is served by nine airlines, seven rental car agencies, and several taxi and limousine services. Syracuse is about 44 miles from Rome. There are a half-dozen highways that lead into Rome, as well as a train terminal served by Amtrak and a bus terminal within a mile of the fort. That makes the reconstructed Fort Stanwix one of the most accessible national parks in the nation, even though it is in relatively remote upstate New York.

The highway corridor between Rome and Albany spans eight counties and is called the Mohawk Valley Heritage Corridor (mohawkvalleyheritage.com). The Corridor covers history dating back to the French and Indian War with a special concentration on that war and the American Revolution. There are a number of historical sites contained within the corridor.

Rome prides itself on being along the "great portage" between the Mohawk River and Lake Ontario, a region known to Indians, British and American soldiers, and fictional frontier trappers such as Natty Bumpo in *The Leatherstocking Tales* by James Fenimore Cooper.

One way to have reached Rome in the mid-19th century would have been to use the nearby Erie Canal. Visitors can take rides along the canal at several spots along the Heritage Corridor.

Accommodations

Hathaway Inn Bed & Breakfast

213 Main St., Oriskany Falls
T: 315-821-2762
hathawayinnbedandbreakfast.com
$110–$125

This Queen Ann Victorian home was built in 1882 by Harry Hathaway, a manufacturer of wool hats and scarves. It opened in 2001 as a B&B.

Quality Inn

200 South James St., Rome
T: 800-434-6835
$100

The best thing about this motel is that it is directly across from Fort Stanwix.

Rosemont Inn Bed and Breakfast

1423 Genesee St., Utica
T: 866-353-4907 or 315-790-9315
rosemontinnbb.com
$89–$155

This brick Italian-Victorian home, located in the historic district of Utica, was built in 1870 for Charles Miller, a wealthy Industrialist who owned the Utica Pipe and Gas and Water Pipe Foundries in Utica. In the Inn's history, it is said that Vice President Sherman, Thomas Edison, and President Taft have been guests.

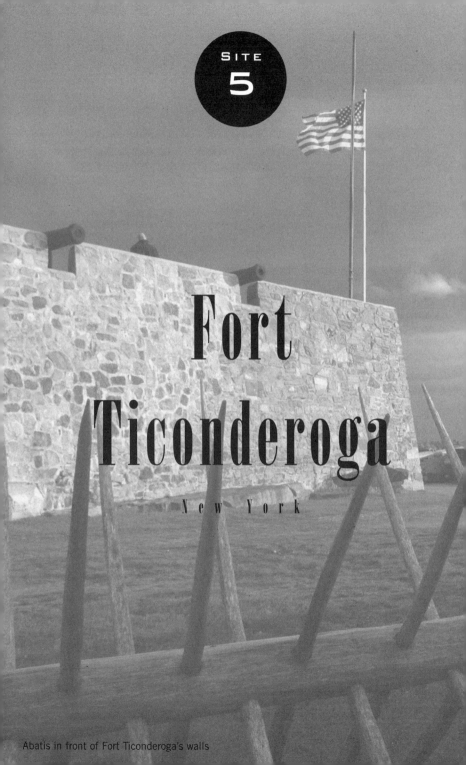

Fort Ticonderoga

New York

Abatis in front of Fort Ticonderoga's walls

THE WAR YEARS

Fort Ticonderoga, first named Fort Carillon, was started by the French during the French and Indian War in 1755 as an outpost to protect access to both Lake Champlain and Lake George. To make sure the fort was not attacked before it was finished, the French moved on the British-held Fort William Henry on the southern end of Lake George. (The siege resulting in the surrender of the British fort in April 1757 was made famous in James Fenimore Cooper's novel *Last of the Mohicans*.)

The British mounted a counterattack in July 1758 and headed toward Fort Carillon. The French, knowing their permanent fort was still not ready, threw together a dirt and log bastion, and awaited the British. The Battle of Fort Carillon took place west of today's stone fort and resulted in a bloody British defeat. The French eventually left a small force at the fort and pulled back to Canada, leaving the small force at the mercy of an advancing British army.

The British eventually captured the fort, then sent forces into Canada to attack the French at Quebec City. On September 13, 1759, British General James Wolfe successfully captured Quebec City, only to be mortally wounded, as was the French commander Montcalm. This marked the end of the French and Indian War. The British inherited Fort Carillon, renamed it Fort Ticonderoga, and improved it with native stone. However, with the French now back on their side of the Atlantic, the fort was of little use, and Fort Ticonderoga fell into disrepair during the 20-year peace that followed.

With colonists who were presumed to be loyal settling this area of New York, the British never dreamed that the growing discontent with the Crown 225 miles downstate in Boston would ever touch this area, but they were wrong. When word got around of the British attack on colonists at Lexington and Concord on April 10, 1775, two men, Benedict Arnold and Ethan Allen, realized the same thing: Fort Ticonderoga was a natural way station for anyone planning to invade the colonies from Canada since it was near both Lake Champlain and the Hudson River. They concluded that they needed to capture Fort Ticonderoga's store of heavy cannons and transfer them down to Boston where they could be used against the British before the British came down from Canada to retrieve them.

Arnold was a 34-year-old seafaring merchant, a very proper man with a learned background from New Haven, Connecticut. Allen was a 37-year-old giant of a man from the backwoods of what would become Vermont. He was already considered somewhat of an outlaw by the royal governor of New York because of his involvement in trying to create the new colony of Vermont. The two men found themselves thrown together in the common goal of capturing Fort Ticonderoga. Arnold allowed Allen to take charge of the adventure since all of Allen's Green Mountain Boys militia refused to serve under Arnold.

On May 7, 1775, Allen, Arnold, and a militia force of 200, most of them Green Mountain Boys, rowed across a stormy Lake Champlain and landed near the fort. They rushed the gates, unsure what to expect.

The fort was virtually undefended, garrisoned by fewer than 50 British soldiers, most of whom were sick and unable to stay in ranks. In addition to the soldiers, the fort contained a number of women and children. Remarkably, with the American Revolution about to erupt, the British commanders in Canada were caught utterly by surprise. Coming just a month after their embarrassing retreat from Lexington and Concord, it was the second time that the most powerful army on the planet underestimated the abilities of a ragtag bunch of disgruntled colonists.

Without firing a shot, the Patriots captured 78 cannons, six mortars, cannonballs, black powder, and a supply of flints once meant for British Brown Bess muskets that would do just as well for the Patriots' widely varying weapons.

Once the Patriots had the cannons, they had to get them to the places where the fighting was occurring. On December 5, 1775, a former bookseller by the name of Henry Knox arrived at Fort Ticonderoga charged with figuring out how to get the cannons back to Boston. He scoured the countryside for anything that could roll and any livestock that could pull. He finally settled on the construction of 42 sledges, or flat-bottomed boxes on runners, that would be pulled by teams of oxen confiscated from area farmers. In a remarkable feat of logistics, Knox transported the cannons and munitions more than 300 miles to the eastern outskirts of Boston at Dorchester Heights. There the Patriots were able to put the guns to use by besieging Boston, then held by the British. The British, frightened by the prospect of their own heavy guns being used against them, decided to evacuate the city on March 7, 1776. More than 11,000 British regulars evacuated the city. The Americans, now on Dorchester Heights with the guns from Fort Ticonderoga, did not fire on the retreating ships.

Because the Revolution so quickly centered around the population centers, the British did not immediately mount a major overland march down from Canada until July 1777, more than two years after the Americans had captured the fort. The small force of Americans holding Fort Ticonderoga had ignored a nearby hill, thinking it was too steep for the British to scale. But the British managed to move a force of cannons onto the hill that looked down on the supposedly secure fort. The American commander evacuated, leaving the fort to the British once again.

Fort Ticonderoga had fallen twice, once to the Americans and then back to the British. In both instances, not a shot was fired and not a life was lost. It would remain in British hands only until September when the Americans would defeat the British army at Saratoga, 60 miles or three days' march to the south.

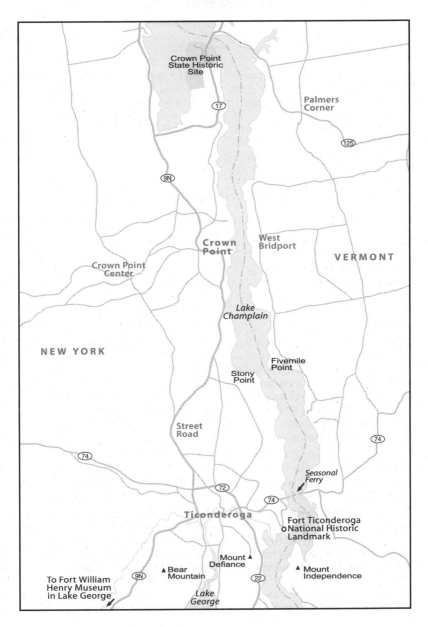

Crown Point
State Historic
Site

17

Palmers
Corner

125

9N

Crown
Point

West
Bridport

VERMONT

Crown Point
Center

Lake
Champlain

NEW YORK

Fivemile
Point

Stony
Point

Street
Road

74

74

Seasonal
Ferry

72

74

Ticonderoga

Fort Ticonderoga
National Historic
Landmark

Mount
Defiance

To Fort William
Henry Museum
in Lake George

9N

Bear
Mountain

Mount
Independence

22

Lake
George

Ticonderoga is a village of 5,000 people with all the basic amenities. There is one small motel in town, but the abundant bed-and-breakfasts scattered around the area are more pleasant for history-minded travelers. The fort is just north of the village. Surprisingly, signs in the village pointing to the fort are not that obvious. Once downtown, head north on Rte. 74 about 1.5 miles out of town. Watch for the entrance on the right.

This is a premier vacation area that has much more than history to offer tourists. The region is dotted with lakes surrounded by tall mountains. Water and winter sports are popular with residents and tourists, and Lake Placid is about an hour north of Fort Ticonderoga.

This area is also where literary history was made. James Fenimore Cooper, author of *The Leatherstocking Tales,* set *Last of the Mohicans* in this area.

POINTS OF INTEREST

Fort Ticonderoga National Historic Landmark ★★★★★

Rte. 74, Ticonderoga
T: 518-585-2821
fort-ticonderoga.org
May 10–late-October daily 9am–5pm
Admission: $12

Fort Ticonderoga is the most impressive fort in the nation based on its dedication to authenticity, its beautiful location, and its collection of artifacts. If tourists want to visit only one Revolutionary War fort, it should be Fort Ticonderoga.

The interesting thing about this fort is that this is not the original Fort Ticonderoga, or even a restoration of it. It is a complete reconstruction of Fort Ticonderoga.

The original fort was abandoned as a military asset almost immediately after the American Revolution. By the early 1800s, the residents in the area had begun dismantling the fort's walls to incorporate the stones into their own homes. By 1820 the fort was in ruins and was in danger of completely disappearing. Paintings of the

fort from the period show it to be a stark shell with crumbling walls, almost unrecognizable as the famous fort it had been at the start of the Revolution.

A New York merchant named William Pell, who had watched the disintegration of the fort while cruising on Lake Champlain, purchased the fort and the surrounding grounds to preserve them. He even built a summer home near the fort so that he could personally keep watch to make sure the fort was not totally lost to history.

In 1826 James Fenimore Cooper's novel, *Last of the Mohicans*, was published. Readers flocked to the region to see Fort Ticonderoga and Fort William Henry, which were both featured in the book.

In 1908, Pell's grandson Stephen and his wife, Sarah, began the process of rebuilding the fort based on plans that had been found in archives. Work continued for the next two decades. A foundation was established in 1931 to transfer ownership of the fort from the Pells, but they and family members remained active in its management. All through the first part of the 21st century, work continued on rebuilding the fort. By the fall of 2007, an extensive construction project should be completed that will hide modern infrastructure improvements in and under a newly constructed limestone section of the fort that will replicate how it looked in the 1750s. This $20 million construction project will allow the fort to become a year-round attraction. (In recent years it has opened on May 10, the anniversary of the day in 1775 that it was captured from the British. It has usually closed in late October when colder weather arrives in upstate New York.)

The setting of Fort Ticonderoga is incomparable in beauty to any other fort on the American continent. Once a visitor walks through the gift shop and toward the entrance to the fort, Mount Independence in Vermont, another important Patriot defensive position, looms on the horizon. Below the mountain is the very southern end of Lake Champlain, a narrow, 100-mile-long lake on which General Benedict Arnold built a fleet of small warships to protect this region from larger British warships. Visitors looking to the right see Mount Defiance.

Turn left through the gateway to enter the fort. There are two museums contained within the fort. One on ground level contains what is reputed to be the third-largest collection of colonial and precolonial weapons. On display are a number of pole arms or spears augmented by an array of tips that were used by soldiers before the invention of the firearm. Here too are the earliest forms of muskets, the wheel lock and the matchlock.

The display includes all of the firearms that were used by both sides in the French and Indian War, as well as later in the American Revolution, allowing firearms aficionados to study the subtle, but dis-

tinct changes that military inventors incorporated into their muskets. On the opposite wall are a number of swords and other edged weapons.

A second museum on the second floor of the fort covers the history of the fort through its early construction by the French right through its modern-day restoration. There are a number of interesting displays here, including the fanciful painting showing the Green Mountain Boys' commander Ethan Allen banging on the fort's door and demanding its surrender. Modern-day historians working at the fort explain that their research indicates that Allen was more of an opportunist and a historical blowhard than he was a Revolutionary War hero, pointing out that when Allen was captured by the British, George Washington refused the British offer to exchange him.

Among the rarer artifacts on display are some colonial-era drums that belonged to a fife and drum corps. (Today Fort Ticonderoga maintains its own fife and drum band made up of local teenagers who play daily in the fort during the summer months.)

One unusual museum exhibit is a large display of black powder horns. While the horns kept the powder dry for Patriot rifles, they also proved to be handy items on which to carve art. Some of the powder horns have maps carved into them. Others have elaborate carvings of elk, moose, and other game.

On the top floor of the museum are some displays dating from World War II through the 1990s. During World War II, the US Navy built an aircraft carrier named *Ticonderoga* that served right through the 1970s, when it recovered the Apollo spacecraft from the ocean. Other displays are dedicated to the Navy's first Aegisclass cruiser, also named *Ticonderoga*, which was just recently decommissioned.

Also on display in the museum is the original of *The Noble Train of Artillery*, a 1946 oil painting by Tom Lowell that depicts one of the most amazing military feats in American history. The painting accurately depicts the difficulty the men faced in moving the guns over the snow and ice-covered hills and mountains. (It was widely distributed as a print and school textbook illustration by the Dixon Pencil Company to promote its Ticonderoga brand pencils in the 1950s and 1960s. The painting is good history and advertising, but short of the truth. Ticonderoga pencils were never made anywhere near Fort Ticonderoga, but Dixon executives thought tying their pencils to such a dramatic historical event studied by schoolchildren made good business sense.)

Two surviving "Knox guns" (General Henry Knox captured and loaded a total of 59 cannons onto sleds, which were pulled by teams of oxen and taken to Boston) are now on display in the courtyard of the fort. These guns are not mounted as are most of the other cannons and mortars scattered around the fort. Although not among the largest cannons, they are historically significant in that their presence, along with 57 other captured cannons, contributed to the major embarrassment of the British army having to retreat from a disorganized "rabble" army.

The cannons at the fort are all original. These guns, ranging from six-pounders up to 24-pounders all had an effective range of around 1,200 yards.

Allow at least three hours to see the fort and its two museums. Allow at least four hours if visiting during tourist season in the summer when there may be living histories and fife and drum concerts.

Mount Defiance ★★★★★

Part of Fort Ticonderoga National Historic Landmark. Follow road signs from downtown Ticonderoga
Daily 9am–5pm
Admission: Free

Mount Defiance, now owned by the Fort Ticonderoga Foundation, was the downfall of American occupation of the fort in 1777. The hilltop to the west of the fort was deemed too steep to scale and too steep for cannons by the inexperienced American officers who garrisoned the fort after it had been captured in May 1775. So the Americans at Fort Ticonderoga made no effort to fortify the position, which looked right down on the fort.

Several military men, including Generals Benedict Arnold and Polish-born artilleryman Thaddeus Kosciusko, warned the commanders at the fort that any mountain could be scaled by determined men. They further warned that any cannons that made it to the top would have height and gravity on their side and all of the fort would be easily within the mountain's range, but they were ignored.

In July 1777, the Americans woke to see artillerymen under British General John Burgoyne placing cannons on top of the mountain. Burgoyne, marching south from Canada in a campaign to cut off the northern colonies from the southern colonies, had simply cut a road to the top of the mountain. Rather than wait for the British to open fire, the Americans abandoned Fort Ticonderoga on July 5, 1777.

Mount Defiance offers a spectacular view of Lake Champlain and the fort. Cannons are mounted here to demonstrate how they could have bombarded the fort. The road leading to the top of Mount Defiance is on the original roadbed cut into the mountain by Burgoyne's men.

SITES NEAR FORT TICONDEROGA

Crown Point State Historic Site ★★★

739 Bridge Rd., Crown Point. 10 miles
north of Fort Ticonderoga
T: 518-597-4666
nysparks.state.ny.us/sites/info.asp?siteID=6
Museum: May–October Wed–Mon
9am–5pm
Admission: $3

This site, first called Fort St. Frédéric
when it was built by the French in 1734
more than 20 years before they went to
war with the British, was once the center
of French power in the American northeast. It was occupied by the French for
more than 25 years until they abandoned
it to the British in 1759. It was the
British who built the stone fort that
remains in ruins here today.

The day after they captured Fort
Ticonderoga, the Americans captured
Crown Point. The cannons that could be
salvaged here were taken down to Fort
Ticonderoga to be taken to Boston. The
British recaptured this fort in 1777 when
Burgoyne marched past it on his way
south toward his eventual defeat at
Saratoga. Despite that loss, the British
didn't surrender their presence at Crown
Point until 1784 when they moved back
into Canada.

There was no true battle of Crown Point
during the American Revolution, but the
remaining walls of the fort and the
redoubts demonstrate the military technology of the day. More important, this site
represents the last measure of French
colonial power in New York before the
French retreated into Quebec City during
the French and Indian War.

Fort William Henry Museum ★★

Canada St., Lake George
T: 518-668-5471
fwhmuseum.com/index.html
May–October daily 9am–6pm
Admission: $12

Though the fort existed less that two
years—late 1755 through the summer of
1757—Fort William Henry was made
famous by James Fenimore Cooper's 1826
book, *Last of the Mohicans*. It was built
by the British to protect the land bridge
between Lake George and Lake
Champlain.

In the summer of 1757, 5,600 French
soldiers and 1,700 Indians besieged the
British fort, and the British agreed to surrender. Once they left the safety of the
fort, the British came under repeated
attacks from the Indians, who had been
told by the French that they had rights to
goods left behind in the fort by the
British. Reliable numbers on what has
been termed a massacre by the Indians on
the surrendered British column have never
been fully tallied, but British deaths after
they surrendered were at least 200. The
French denied any responsibility in their
failure to control the attacks by the
Indians, and did help the British obtain
the release of some British soldiers,
women, and children who had been taken
captive by the Indians.

Today's wooden stockade is built on the
same ground as the original Fort William
Henry. Programs at the fort are geared
toward schoolchildren, but the fort does
give adult visitors an idea of what the original fort and its soldiers looked like during
the French and Indian War.

GETTING TO AND AROUND
FORT TICONDEROGA

Fort Ticonderoga is served by Burlington International Airport in Vermont, 55 miles away. To reach the fort, visitors cross a narrow portion of Lake Champlain by a ferry that operates from May through October. In winter months, visitors should come into Albany International Airport, 100 miles to the south.

The Champlain ferry starts at 8am and stops running at different times depending on the season. Call 802-897-7999 for details on how to reach it. The crossing is only seven minutes. Those coming from Vermont should check their road maps carefully to see whether they could save time by taking the ferry rather than driving around the bottom of Lake Champlain.

Public transportation is nonexistent in this area of the state. There is no real way to reach the fort other than by car (or by watercraft, as the town and the fort are located where Lake George virtually touches Lake Champlain.) Watch carefully for the signs pointing to the fort. Since it is not a national park, the signs are not always well placed.

Fort Stanwix and Fort Ticonderoga could be visited in one day, but only if visitors start early. The two forts are separated by a three-and-a-half hour drive on two-lane roads through the Adirondack Mountains. Visitors can choose to travel between the two forts by sticking to the major north-south and east-west highways, of course, but passing through the small towns is a pleasant experience. Just be aware that some roads hug lake coastlines so the roads can be curvy and slow.

Fort Ticonderoga is in a remote part of New York state, where winter snows often come early. Consult the fort's website or call in advance to make sure it is open. At press time, the fort was undergoing renovations that will allow it to stay open during colder months.

SOURCES & OTHER READING

Benedict Arnold, Revolutionary Hero: An American Warrior Reconsidered, James Kirby Martin, New York University Press, 2000

Ethan Allen, Stewart Holbrook, Binford & Mort Publishing, 1988

Ethan Allen and the Green-Mountain Heroes of '76, with a Sketch of the Early History of Vermont, Henry W. De Puy, Heritage Books 2004

Fort Ticonderoga: A Short History, Steven Pell, Fort Ticonderoga Museum, 1975

Henry Knox: George Washington's Confidant, General of Artillery, and America's First Secretary of War, Thomas Lonergan, Pictan Press, 2003

Websites:

u-s-history.com/pages/h1270.html

ACCOMMODATIONS

Emerson House Bed and Breakfast

3826 Main St., Warrensburg, NY
T: 518-623-2758
emersonhousebandb.com
$90–$150

The Emerson House is a Greek Revival
home built in 1830 that was restored in
2000, and opened as a B&B in 2001. It
is listed on the National Register of
Historic Places.

Silver Spruce Inn Bed & Breakfast

Rte. 9 P.O. Box 426, Schroon Lake, NY
T: 518-532-7031
silverspruce.com
$90–$120

The earliest part of this inn dates back to
the 1790s. Part of the inn was a
speakeasy during Prohibition and the bar
is from the original Waldorf Astoria in New
York City.

Whitford House Inn

912 Grandey Rd., Addison, VT
T: 800-746-2704 or 802-758-2704
whitfordhouseinn.com
$110–$250

A 1790s renovated country home,
Whitford House Inn overlooks rolling
meadowlands and is framed by the
Adirondack range. It is located near Lake
Champlain and the Green Mountains.

Saratoga

New York

American artillery looking down on the Hudson River

THE WAR YEARS

I f the British had not been so stubborn about wanting to wear down the colonists, the Revolution might have been won by the Americans only two years after it started. In the fall of 1777, British General "Gentleman Johnny" Burgoyne lost two battles that would collectively be called Saratoga. After his defeat, he surrendered his remaining force of nearly 6,000 soldiers. Burgoyne's surrender boosted colonial morale and hardened the British will to destroy the Americans, making this isolated battlefield a major turning point in the Revolution.

During the first two years of the war, the British clung to their notion that once the rebels viewed a red-coated army moving into the colonies from Canada, the rebellion would fold.

British General John Burgoyne continued to pursue that strategy in the summer of 1777. Instead of breaking his army in Canada into smaller units that could have pursued smaller bands of rebels, he held his army together, believing that its size alone would frighten the rebels into submission. As his 8,000-man army ponderously made its way south, its men spent weeks building bridges and roads to support their movements.

Burgoyne was focused on capturing Albany, New York. He intended to join forces with one British army under General Barry St. Leger, marching toward him from the west, and with a second force under General William Howe, who Burgoyne assumed would come up from New York City. But Howe had other ideas. Instead of joining Burgoyne, he wanted to pursue George Washington and capture the rebel capital of Philadelphia.

Burgoyne was in a quandary by the end of July. He had a large army with long supply lines stretching back into Canada, so long that he could no longer count on the security of that line. Smaller British forces had been defeated east of him at Bennington, Vermont. St. Leger had been stopped by stubborn resistance at Fort Stanwix. Indian scouts, on whom Burgoyne counted to guide him along the maze of cow paths toward pockets of civilization, were deserting.

Finally, on September 16, 1777, Burgoyne's remaining scouts discovered the tracks of a Patriot army. At last, Burgoyne thought, this was a chance to display the might of the British redcoats and destroy the enemy with the bayonets of the Brown Bess muskets that had won so many other battles for England.

Burgoyne then did something that was uncharacteristic. He divided his forces into three columns north of a community called Stillwater and south of a community called Saratoga. Worse, he allowed those three columns to advance out of sight and contact with each other.

Though the columns started marching before dawn, it was past noon before Burgoyne's center column made contact with the Patriots on Freeman's Farm. Lying in wait was a force of riflemen led by a tough, bullet-scarred man with a grudge to settle. That was six-foot-tall, 200-pound Colonel Daniel Morgan, a 41-year-old Virginia frontiersman whose cousin was Daniel Boone. Morgan had hated the British ever since he had been whipped for striking an officer during the French and Indian War.

The first contact between British muskets and Morgan's rifles was no contest. The British .69-caliber smoothbore muskets were designed for mass firing, but their range was no better than 100 yards. Morgan's riflemen had .45 caliber rifles with a range of at least 300 yards. In the first volley, Morgan's men dropped every British officer in the front rank. As the British column crumbled, Morgan's men pursued them. The attack stalled when the Americans ran into Burgoyne's main line.

Burgoyne doggedly moved forward in classic British style with long lines of men in tight formations. The Americans, including a force under General Benedict Arnold, hid in the woods and lined up the British in their sights and fired into their lines. For a long time the strange battle raged—proper British tactics of stand-up fighting against the insidious Americans who would not show themselves. As darkness fell, the British held the field, making them the technical victors of the battle, but at the terrible cost of 350 British soldiers and Colonial losses of 319 men.

For some reason, the commanding American General Horatio Gates did not move more forces down into the field to finish off the British. Gates's lack of action enraged Arnold, who believed Burgoyne's force could have easily been wiped out at that point.

The battle went into a two-week lull with the British in the field and the Patriots in the woods until Burgoyne, tired of waiting for the reinforcements that he had requested from New York, decided to send a small force of 1,600 men to test the American defenses dug in on Bemis Heights. It was a foolish mission. Burgoyne's entire force now numbered just 6,000 while the Patriots had more than twice that number.

First Morgan's riflemen attacked, followed by a charge led by Arnold, who was wounded. The British fell back to their own fortifications pursued by the Americans. On October 12, Gates maneuvered his army between Burgoyne and the Hudson River, blocking what would have been the quickest and safest route back to Canada and bringing the battle to an end. Gates could have demanded unconditional surrender of Burgoyne's crushed forces, but instead, he allowed Burgoyne to suggest the terms under which he would surrender. Burgoyne suggested that his army be allowed freedom to return to England with the agreement that none of the men fight again in North America. Gates agreed.

The Patriot victory at Saratoga had global effects. Not only had the supposedly ragtag colonists defeated a British army, it had driven them from the continent. As a result, France decided to get into the fight. It declared war on England, opening up a new front that would help keep the English occupied elsewhere while the colonists continued to fight in America. Burgoyne returned to England and was never given another command.

Gates tried to use his victory at Saratoga to his advantage. For awhile, he tried to undermine Congress's confidence in George Washington and get Congress to name him supreme commander of colonial forces. Instead Congress sent Gates south where the British were winning some battles. He was pounded in the Battle of Camden, South Carolina, on August 16, 1780, and ran from the field. Gates, exposed as a coward, never commanded again. Meanwhile, Benedict Arnold brooded over how he did not receive the proper credit for winning Saratoga and promised to get even—somehow.

SITE
6

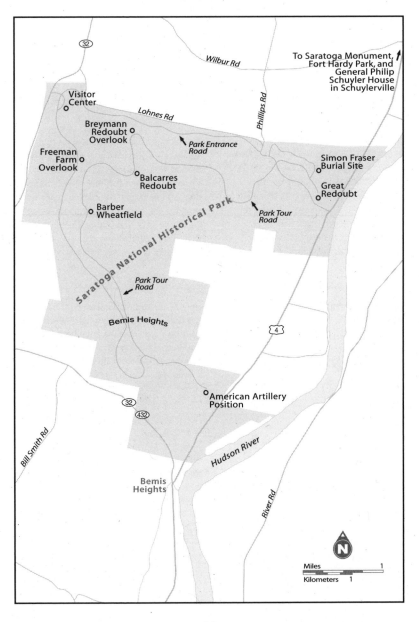

32

Wilbur Rd

To Saratoga Monument, Fort Hardy Park, and General Philip Schuyler House in Schuylerville

Visitor Center

Lohnes Rd

Phillips Rd

Breymann Redoubt Overlook

Park Entrance Road

Freeman Farm Overlook

Simon Fraser Burial Site

Balcarres Redoubt

Great Redoubt

Barber Wheatfield

Park Tour Road

Saratoga National Historical Park

Park Tour Road

Bemis Heights

4

32
432

American Artillery Position

Hudson River

Bill Smith Rd

Bemis Heights

River Rd

N

Miles 1
Kilometers 1

As noted in "Getting to and around Saratoga," finding Saratoga can be confusing. The Saratoga National Historic Park is 17 miles from Saratoga Springs, and signs for the Park within Saratoga Springs are clustered around Interstate 87 and can be easily missed. The Saratoga monument commemorating the surrender of the British is in the tiny town of Schuylerville, which used to be called Saratoga until the village's name was changed in recognition of hometown hero General Philip Schuyler. The Battle of Saratoga was actually fought closer to the village of Stillwater than it was to the village of Saratoga. Saratoga got the battle honors because it was where Burgoyne formally surrendered—eight miles away from where he was defeated.

The park itself is off Rte. 32, south of Victory Mills. Be sure to purchase gasoline or food before leaving Victory Mills as there are no such facilities anywhere near the battlefield, and the park is isolated from the main road. The National Park Service reports that the park receives more than 350,000 visitors each year, which is remarkable given the park's remoteness.

POINTS OF INTEREST

Saratoga National Historical Park
★★★★★

648 Rte. 32, Stillwater, five miles south of Schuylerville
T: 518-664-9821x224
nps.gov/sara/
Visitor Center daily 9am–5pm
Admission: $5

British General John Burgoyne, nicknamed "Gentleman Johnny," had the right tactical idea when he wrote in 1775, "I have always thought Hudson's River the most proper part of the whole continent for opening vigorous operations. Because the course of the river, so beneficial for conveying all the bulky necessaries of an army, is precisely the route that an army ought to take for the great purposes of cutting the communications between the Southern and Northern provinces, giving confidence to the Indians, and securing a junction with the Canadian forces."

Burgoyne's strategy worked right up until the Battle of Saratoga, fought beside the Hudson River. Had his anticipated support from General Barry St. Leger to the west and General William Howe to the south arrived, no colonial force could have stopped Burgoyne from going anywhere he wanted in the northern colonies.

But that support never arrived. Instead, Burgoyne found his army isolated here at Saratoga, far from Canada with many Americans ahead. The Hudson, the river Burgoyne once considered an advantage, now blocked his retreat to the east, and there was nothing but hostile territory to the west. He had no choice but to fight. Eventually, he had no choice but to surrender his entire army.

The visitor center has an electric-map program that outlines the battle's movements. On display are two British 24-pounder cannons. Most museums have the more common—and smaller—six- and 12-pounder cannons. These 24-pounders were among the largest the British ever carried into land battles. It is quite a rare sight to see such large cannons in a colonial display.

The tour road encompasses two different battles, one fought on September 19 and one fought on October 7, that are collectively called the Battle of Saratoga. Since the battles were fought on virtually the same ground both times, it is difficult to sort out on the tour what happened in which battle. The following descriptions do not include all of the stops suggested by the National Park Service, but point out the major highlights.

Stop 1 ★★★★★ is Freeman Farm Overlook, the spot where Daniel Morgan's riflemen opened what has been called the First Battle of Saratoga, or the Battle of Freeman's Farm, on September 19, 1777. The battle, in which just one of the three British columns was engaged, may have been decided in the first volley, as Morgan had instructed his riflemen to concentrate their fire on the British officers (who stood out due to their shoulder epaulets).

When the British turned and retreated, Morgan's men rushed after them in a disorganized charge that was broken up when they ran into a larger force of British. Morgan at first believed that his entire force had been destroyed, but when he called for an assembly, most of his riflemen appeared from the woods.

Most were unhurt, simply surprised at blundering into another British column. The unnerved British soldiers started firing without orders in an attempt to cut down the Americans. Some British were shot by their own men in the confusion. Burgoyne called in other reinforcements, including some Hessians who rushed west from the river. At the end of the day, the Patriots retreated, as their ammunition was used up. The British were in command of the field, which technically made the Battle of Freeman's Farm a British victory. But it did not feel that way to Burgoyne who saw that his men had folded in the face of fire from a bunch of frontier farmers.

Before Burgoyne's men had even reached Freeman's Farm, their general had made his first and biggest mistake, dividing his army in the face of an enemy whose strength he did not know. By this time most of Burgoyne's Indian scouts had abandoned him. He had no real idea where the Americans were, or how many they numbered. Military protocol says that an army that does not know the strength of its enemy should fight as a single entity. Had Burgoyne kept his army together, he would have rolled right over Morgan and advanced on to Bemis Heights. He would pay dearly for that mistake.

Burgoyne, still unsure how many Patriots were in front of him, stopped his army in this vicinity to wait for reinforcements from New York City that he believed would be coming to help him. That force, commanded by General Henry Clinton, left the city and began an advance up the Hudson River, but eventually turned back when General Howe asked for help in attacking Philadelphia. Burgoyne waited three weeks for help that never came.

Today, visitors will find a field with signs describing what took place here.

Stop 2 ★★★★★ is Bemis Heights, or the Neilson Farm, high ground that was the headquarters for American General Horatio Gates. The American reinforcements left from this area. A recreated farmhouse stands on the high ground where Gates and Benedict Arnold continually argued over how to conduct the battle. Arnold's principal complaint was that Gates had more than enough men held in reserve here that could have been used to rush into battle at Freeman's Farm and destroy that isolated British column. Gates had refused. Arnold was so enraged that he threatened to resign. Gates's subordinates, knowing that Arnold was a better general than Gates, persuaded him to stay.

The Second Battle of Saratoga is sometimes called the Battle of Bemis Heights, though the actual fighting was somewhat north of this position.

The high ridge gives a good view of the topography of the battlefield.

Stop 3 ★★★★ is an American artillery position that looked down onto the Hudson River and the flat land beside it that Burgoyne had hoped to march past. These guns were too high for Burgoyne's own guns to reach. Had he tried to get past, his men would have had shots and shells raining down on them. These cannon positions are a little walk from the parking lot, but the view from the guns is instructive.

Stop 5 ★★★★, the Barber Wheatfield, is where the British advance of October 7 was first discovered and beaten back.

Stop 6 ★★★, Balcarres Redoubt, was a British earthwork that had been thrown up in the event that their troops had to retreat toward the Hudson. After being hit at the Barber Wheatfield, this redoubt offered some measure of safety. The earthworks here have been reconstructed.

Stop 7 ★★★★★, Breymann Redoubt, was a German-held fort until the Americans took it from them. There is a monument to General Benedict Arnold, who was wounded while leading a charge to capture the earthwork. The monument is unusual in that it shows only his boot, not his face. The monument was erected long after the war by Patriots who wanted to honor Arnold's heroism at this battle, but

not recognize a man who would eventually betray the Revolution and go over to the British side. The monument draws criticism from some historians who maintain that the capture of Breymann Redoubt was already going in favor of the Americans when Arnold showed up to lead what may have been an unnecessary charge.

Stop 9 ★★★, the Great Redoubt was a fort Burgoyne built just in case he would need it to cover a retreat. The earthworks have been reconstructed.

Stop 10 ★★ is a one-mile trail leading down to the burial site of British General Simon Fraser. Note that it is quite steep. Fraser, a Scot, spoke fluent French with a French accent. During the French and Indian War, he used his language skills to help the British get past French pickets protecting Quebec City in Canada. Once that city was captured, the war was essentially over and the French presence in America began to wane.

With the death of Fraser for the British and the wounding of Arnold for the Americans, the Battle of Bemis Heights, or the Second Battle of Saratoga, was over. Burgoyne had suffered around 600 killed and wounded compared to 150 for Gates.

Burgoyne began a retreat march back north, heading for Canada. Weighed down with wounded, his march was so ponderous that Gates was able to get ahead of him, cutting off all land roads and access to the Hudson River, where Burgoyne had hoped to board boats. Now outnumbered almost three to one, exhausted, and defeated twice by a rebel army, Burgoyne knew he had only one choice—surrender.

Gates met with Burgoyne under a tree in the village of Saratoga and did an incredible thing. He allowed Burgoyne to dictate what the surrender terms would be. Together they drew up the "Convention of

Saratoga" which allowed Burgoyne and his surviving 6,000 men to return to England if they promised never to return to fight again "during the present contest." The two generals even exchanged toasts at dinner with Burgoyne lifting his glass to Washington and Gates toasting King George III.

Historians still disagree over Gates's conduct in defeating Burgoyne. Gates was the commanding general, but his subordinates chaffed under his command. Most of the battlefield decisions were made by Arnold, who had been barred from even showing up at Gates's headquarters. But, in the end, the world saw that Gates had not only forced a British army to surrender, he had forced it to return to England.

The Saratoga Monument ★★★★★
Near Rtes. 4 and 32, Victory
Dawn to dusk
Admission: Free

The cornerstone was laid in 1877 on the centennial of the battle. The 155-foot-tall monument is open for stair climbers from Memorial Day to Labor Day Wed–Sun from 9:30am–4:30pm. There are three statues in recesses of the monument: Gates, Schuyler, and Morgan, and an empty spot for a missing fourth statue. That symbolizes Benedict Arnold, whose statue was never cast because of his treason in going over to the British side in 1780.

Fort Hardy Park ★
Broadway Street, Schuylerville
Dawn to dusk
Admission: Free

To the east of the Saratoga Monument is now an athletic field. During the war it was where the British formally stacked their arms. There are several iron markers scattered around the town commemorating the surrender. One is near the spot where Burgoyne offered Gates his sword as a symbol of the formal surrender of his army.

General Philip Schuyler House ★★★★,
Rte. 4 at Fishkill River Bridge,
Schuylerville
June–Labor Day Wed–Sun
9:30am–4:30pm

Next to Rte. 4 and southeast of the Saratoga Monument, this house was built on the foundation of the original house that was burned by Burgoyne's forces on their march south. Costumed interpreters describe what life was like in the house and in the surrounding countryside in the period immediately after the Revolution.

The Schuyler name is very famous in this area of New York, as he was one of only four major generals in the Continental Army. In reality the general did very little of a military nature other than plan a failed invasion of Canada in an attempt to draw the British armies out of the northern colonies.

The Surrender of Burgoyne, by painter John Trumball, now hangs in the rotunda of the United States Capitol, an indication of how important the two battles fought at Saratoga were to American history. When France and the other, older European countries heard reports about how Burgoyne's 6,000-man army had returned to England from the colonies in defeat, they realized that the ability of England to defeat its rebellious colonies was in doubt. The loss at Saratoga was a disaster from which the British army never recovered.

Visitors should plan to allow at least three hours to see the battlefield.

GETTING TO AND AROUND SARATOGA

Saratoga Battlefield is 17 miles east of Saratoga Springs, a famous horseracing town that has nothing to do with the battlefield. The Battle of Saratoga was fought close to a town now named Schuylerville. The site where the British surrendered and the site of the Saratoga Monument are in Schuylerville. It can be confusing, so know where you are going before you make travel arrangements.

Saratoga Springs is the nearest town with accommodations and restaurants, but it is crowded and expensive during the racing season. If you are visiting in the summer, last-minute accommodations might be impossible to get. Some hotels double the price of their rooms during racing season, which runs from July through September.

The nearest airport is Albany International Airport, about 35 miles south of Saratoga Springs. That airport is served by nine airlines, rental car agencies, and taxis.

Amtrak also has a station in Saratoga Springs, making it accessible to any other city with similar Amtrak connections. There are at least three rental car companies in Saratoga Springs, meaning that visitors could arrive by train and then rent a car to reach both Fort Ticonderoga and Saratoga Battlefield.

Anyone who makes the journey to see this remote Revolutionary War battlefield will likely want to linger awhile in Saratoga Springs, which is focused on "health, horses, and history." This is a center for spa treatments, racing, and strolling along quiet, small-town sidewalks to see the Victorian houses that were built during racing's golden age at the end of the 19th century. Numerous carriage ride companies offer rides downtown with drivers who can describe the city's long fascination with horses and racing.

SOURCES & OTHER READING

Battle of Saratoga, Rupert Furneaux, Stein & Day, 1983

Battles of the Revolutionary War: 1775-1781, W.J. Wood, DeCapo Press, 2003

Decisive Battles of the American Revolution, Joseph Mitchell, Westholme Publishing, 2004

The Generals of Saratoga: John Burgoyne and Horatio Gates, Max Mintz, Yale University Press, 1992

Saratoga 1777: Turning Point of a Revolution (Campaign Series 67), Brenden Morrissey, Osprey Publishing, 2000

Saratoga: Turning Point of America's Revolutionary War, Richard Ketchum, Owl Books, 1999

ACCOMMODATIONS

Saratoga Arms

497 Broadway, Saratoga Springs
T: 518-584-1775
saratogaarms.com
$150–$595

The 1870 Second Empire brick hotel located in the heart of the historic downtown district of Saratoga Springs is ideal for business or leisure travelers.

Wayside Inn B&B and Meeting/Education Center

104 Wilton Rd., Greenfield
T: 518-893-2884
waysidein.com
$85–$205

Built in 1786 by Captain St. John, a veteran of the American Revolution, this former stagecoach stop is alive with history. The longest continuously running Masonic Lodge in America was founded on the top floor of the Inn in 1802. The Inn was commandeered by British officers during the War of 1812. Before and during the Civil War, the Inn was a stop on the Underground Railroad. Early in the 20th century, the property became one of the largest dairy farms in the area (Hall Dairy Farm—Brookside Dairy). It has operated as an inn since 1988.

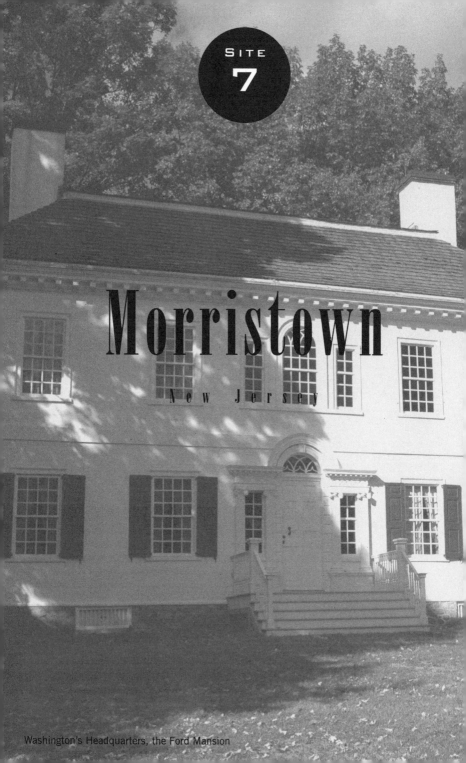

Morristown

New Jersey

Washington's Headquarters, the Ford Mansion

THE WAR YEARS

I mmediately after the Battle of Princeton on January 3, 1777, Washington took stock of his army. In less than 10 days, they had fought three major battles and won all of them. But his army was totally exhausted. He feared they would mutiny if he asked much more of them. He had wanted to march on to New Brunswick, New Jersey, a British camp stocked with an army payroll, but Washington doubted his men could make the one-day journey without collapsing on the road. He remarked that with 6,000 fresh soldiers he could have captured New Brunswick, taken the money and military supplies, and "put an end to the war." However, instead of marching another 17 miles east and going into battle, Washington headed 44 miles northeast toward Morristown, a peaceful village on a plateau that backed up to a mountain. That plateau was surrounded by swamps, and the campground at Morristown was high ground. If necessary, the Continental Army could fight defensively—and decisively—if Cornwallis decided to press a winter offensive. If necessary, Washington would be able to use the network of roads connecting Morristown with New York state to move against any British movement into the interior of the state. In addition, Morristown was in a farming area that had so far been untouched by foraging raids from either side, which meant the farmers' grain bins were full, and Washington would be able to supply his men with food through the winter.

Washington stationed his troops at Morristown from January 6 through May 28, 1777. Every day he worried about the future of the revolution. The militia who had promised to reenlist were deserting daily. Some of his troops were being struck down with smallpox. In a desperate move to stop the disease, Washington tried inoculation of a few of his soldiers with a mild form of the pox. It seemed to work, and one of the first examples of mass inoculation in the history of the world was performed on the army.

What worried Washington most was that the British would get wind of his depleted condition and move on his winter quarters. That was a distinct possibility, especially since the 200 residents of Morristown had not been pleased to see a few thousand starving, diseased men move into their midst. It was not unthinkable that a disgruntled farmer would make his way to the British winter camp at New Brunswick to tell them about the starving army. At one point, Washington had just 1,000 regular colonials and around 2,000 militiamen who were fit to take the field. Only two days' march away were more than 10,000 British redcoats.

"The situation here is by no means favorable to our views ... though I confess I do not know how we shall procure covering for our men elsewhere," Washington wrote to the President of Congress John Hancock.

In order to keep the British from attacking him in winter quarters and to help feed his men, Washington sent raiding parties out to harass the British foraging parties. This was a somewhat counterintuitive means of keeping the British off balance, as Washington's strategy of picking at the British in small raids could have just as easily resulted in the British attacking his winter quarters in retaliation. The British were irritated, but they never acted on that impulse. Attacking an enemy in winter was simply not the gentlemanly thing to do, and the British officers considered themselves gentlemen above all else. British General William Howe wrote a letter complaining, "We have been boxed about in Jersey, as if we had no feelings ... and in short, the troops harassed beyond measure by continual duty."

By mid-May 1777, new recruits began trickling back into Washington's camp, drawn by the glow of good feelings left over from the earlier victories at Trenton and Princeton. More important, the French were beginning to think that the Americans might win their revolution. While not yet ready to send troops, the French did start sending supplies, including hundreds of .69-caliber Charleville muskets. Many of Washington's men had been using their own hunting rifles and varying types of arms. Equipped with the Charleville, it would be much easier to standardize the distribution of ammunition. By the time Washington pulled out of his winter quarters on May 28, 1777, to defend Philadelphia, he had more than 8,000 troops.

After two more years of fighting, Washington and his army returned to Morristown on December 1, 1779. They stayed through June 22, 1780. Washington chose Morristown for the same reasons he had the first time. New York City was still occupied by the British, and he could keep watch on them from this defensible position.

Winter came early that year and many of the Continental regiments had to march through cold and snow in order to reach Morristown. While the winter quarters at Valley Forge, Pennsylvania, had been cold the previous year, this year was even worse. Some reports call the winter of 1779–80 the worst winter on record. When Washington's army first came to Morristown two years earlier, they had stayed in houses in town. This time they erected more than 1,000 log huts, denuding the forests for miles around. In order to avoid drafts, the huts were built without any windows.

Still the men suffered, mostly from lack of food. The local townspeople were not very sympathetic, as they had little means of supplying such a large number of men, and they had yet to see any proof that Washington was winning the war. And even if he was, they did not understand what difference it would make in their lives. The king in England was demanding taxes and the Congress in Philadelphia was trying to figure out new ways to tax them. Both sides were trying to take their money, food, and property, giving the people of Morristown little inclination to help either side.

One visitor who came to Morristown who was appalled at what he found was a young Frenchman named Lafayette who had pledged that he would do all he could to help the Americans. Lafayette wrote, "An army that is reduced to nothing, that wants provisions, that has not one of the necessary means to make sare [soup], such as the situation wherein I found our troops. However prepared I could have been to this unhappy sight by our past distresses, I confess I had no idea of such an extremity."

Washington moved his men in June 1780.

SITE
7

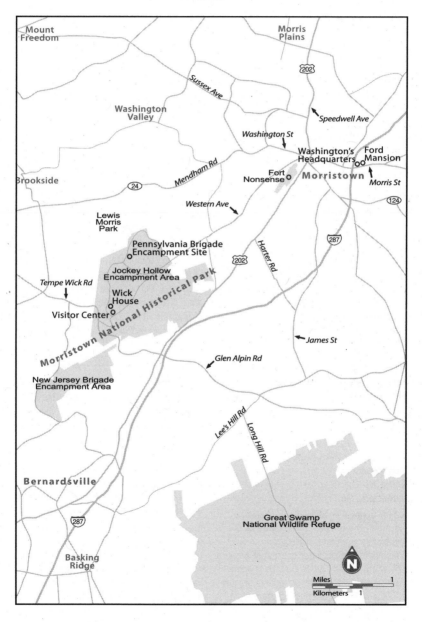

Mount Freedom

Morris Plains

202

Sussex Ave

Washington Valley

Speedwell Ave

Washington St

Washington's Headquarters

Ford Mansion

Mendham Rd

Fort Nonsense

Morristown

Brookside

24

Morris St

124

Western Ave

Lewis Morris Park

287

Pennsylvania Brigade Encampment Site

Harter Rd

Jockey Hollow Encampment Area

202

Tempe Wick Rd

Wick House

Morristown National Historical Park

Visitor Center

James St

Glen Alpin Rd

New Jersey Brigade Encampment Area

Lee's Hill Rd

Long Hill Rd

Bernardsville

Great Swamp National Wildlife Refuge

287

Basking Ridge

N

Miles   1
Kilometers   1

MORRISTOWN TODAY

In colonial days when it was the site of two different winter encampments by Washington's army, Morristown had only about 200 people, but it also boasted two churches and two schools. It was a vibrant and established village when Washington brought his army here to establish winter camps in January 1777 and then again in December 1779.

Morristown today is still a small town of 18,000 people, with many of them commuting to jobs in the larger cities surrounding it. Most of the town's Revolutionary history actually took place in the country to the south, but the town has an interesting statue commemorating an often-forgotten figure from the Revolution. In Burnham Park is a statute of Thomas Paine, the English-born pamphleteer who some consider one of the best writers of the American Revolution. Paine's statue commemorates the writing of his pamphlet *Crisis*, which starts, "These are the times that try men's souls."

After the Revolution, two more historic events occurred in town. In 1838, the first public demonstration of the telegraph was held here. In 1929, the Seeing Eye, the international foundation that trains guide dogs for the blind, was founded here. Dogs in training are a common sight in downtown Morristown.

There are only a handful of hotels and motels in Morristown, but plenty of restaurants, so visitors wishing to spend the entire day exploring the winter encampment site as well as the Victorian homes of Morristown will find at least several hours' worth of touring to keep them busy.

POINTS OF INTEREST

Morristown National Historical Park
★★★★★

Exit 36 off I-28 onto Morris Ave., Morristown
T: 908-766-8215 (Washington's headquarters); 973-543-4030 (Jockey Hollow); nps.gov/morr/
Daily 9am–5pm
Admission: $4

Valley Forge, Pennsylvania, has always captured the public's imagination as the winter encampment of George Washington's fledgling Continental Army in the winter of 1777–78. Countless elementary school texts portrayed Valley Forge as a place of great suffering, where the soldiers' sacrifice was portrayed as an example of how the Revolution succeeded despite hardship. This image of Valley Forge so captured the public's imagination that many have no idea where the Continental Army hunkered down for its other five winters.

In reality, the winter Washington's men spent at Valley Forge was mild compared to what they experienced in Morristown.

It was here about 90 miles to the north of Valley Forge, where the men suffered through a period of record-breaking cold weather. While the temperature around Valley Forge rarely dipped below freezing in the winter of 1777–78, the temperature at Morristown in 1779–80 fell below zero on some days and snowfall was measured in feet rather than inches. Men could not get out of their huts to go on duty and those who did go into the open sometimes died of exposure.

Morristown was an important encampment twice during the Revolution. Immediately after fighting at Trenton and Princeton in January 1777, Washington marched his 5,000-man army here to establish a winter encampment. That was a routine military exercise for 18th-century armies when muskets did not perform well in cold, damp weather and the men were not issued heavy winter coats.

Whoever had chosen Morristown for Washington was well skilled in reading the importance of landscape in maintaining an army. The British stronghold in New York City, just 30 miles to the east, could be watched from numerous mountain passes. The same mountains also gave Washington's scouts the height to watch for any movement of the British forces in New Brunswick or Trenton to the south. The farms surrounding Morristown had not been touched by the war, and their grain storage bins were full. There was even a small mill nearby that made gunpowder for the farmers.

Washington made the decision to keep most of his men in and near the town so that spies could not determine how few men he actually had (which would have been possible had he built a winter camp). Instead, Washington took advantage of the existing homes and put two to four men in the houses of residents. The townspeople were not happy about having to share their homes with these soldiers. In addition to being the same grievance the colonies had filed against King George III about billeting soldiers in private quarters, Washington's men carried smallpox. One

study found that up to a quarter of the citizens of Morristown came down with the disease during the army's stay in 1777.

Two years later, Washington returned here in early December 1779 with a much larger, more experienced, and hardened army than had camped in Morristown in 1777. Great Patriot victories had been won at Saratoga, New York, and Monmouth, New Jersey. But, the British still had New York City and the coastal Southern cities in a stranglehold. The future of the American Revolution was still cloudy. More immediately, old timers in the region predicted that this would be a cold winter. Washington heeded their warnings.

Because his army was at least twice the size it had been in 1777, now 12,000 men, Washington did not have the option of billeting his men in the existing houses in the village, and he began building a large camp five miles south of town (Jockey Hollow). He started the camp in December, as soon as he arrived, on a day of blowing snow and ice. The men lived in tents while they threw up the log cabins.

The museum located next to the Ford Mansion, which served as Washington's headquarters, has a number of interesting artifacts, including a pocket sundial. Before leaving the park headquarters, ask for a sheet with directions for visiting the other sites of the park. Allow two hours to see this portion of the park, which includes the museum and Ford Mansion. All of the following sites are within the national park:

Ford Mansion ★★★★★

The Ford Mansion, at stop 1 on the outskirts of Morristown, was rented by Washington as his headquarters. This house can be visited only by guided tours led by rangers. Among the original artifacts still in the house is a stand-up desk at which Washington wrote orders to his generals.

The Ford Mansion was brand new when Washington asked to rent it from the widow of Jacob Ford, a local Patriot leader, who had built the fine house in 1774 but who had died early in 1777 from the rigors of serving in the field. Mrs. Ford and her five children moved into two rooms of the house to accommodate. Washington, his wife Martha, who frequently stayed with the general in the field, and Washington's military staff. It was in this house that Washington and his chief aide, Alexander Hamilton, laid out their plans for the rest of the war. A number of other famous people, including the Marquis de Lafayette, and Generals Nathaniel Greene, Henry Knox, and Benedict Arnold, spent time here. The house stayed in the Ford family until 1874 when a foundation was formed to preserve it for future generations. The National Park Service took over ownership in 1933 when the Morristown National Historic Park was formed.

The Morristown National Historic Park was the third park focusing on history to be added to the National Park Service and the first in the system to be specifically labeled a "national historic park."

Washington Statue ★
Across from Ford Mansion

This is a large, impressive statue of Washington, though it is not an exact likeness. Note that the general is dressed for winter, an important aspect of his time in Morristown.

Jockey Hollow Encampment Area ★★★★★

Five miles southwest of Morristown on Western Ave.
T: 973-543-4030
Visitor center daily 9am–5pm

Jockey Hollow is part of the national park headquarters at Morristown, but it will require driving to get there. Once at Jockey Hollow, it is possible to walk to the following sites, though it is really more practical to drive.

The best time to visit Jockey Hollow, site of the second winter encampment, is after a good snowfall, which enables visitors to get an idea of what it must have been like for the soldiers (but note that the National Park Service warns that heavy snows may require closing the park). Leaving the Ford Mansion, get on I-287 south and take Exit 30B for the Jockey Hollow Encampment Area. Follow signs to the Jockey Hollow visitor center, where a room is set up as if a soldier had just left it. The life-size diorama demonstrates how dark and dreary life was inside the winter huts and gives a sense of what the soldiers endured for months at a time.

There are more than 20 miles of hiking trails at Jockey Hollow. Although there is a road, the best and shortest route to reach the New Jersey Brigade Encampment Area is by walking south from the visitor center.

Before leaving the visitor center at Jockey Hollow, take another look at the mock interior of the hut. Already experienced from building the log huts at Valley Forge the previous winter, the soldiers threw themselves into building a log city of more than 1,000 huts. Each hut was 14 feet by 15 feet and housed 12 men. Each hut had a door and a fireplace. There were no windows. At least 600 acres of trees were cleared to build the log city.

The men finished the huts just in time. When they arrived, there was already a foot of snow on the ground. Within days, another six feet of snow had fallen in a storm described by a local resident as being so powerful that, "no man could endure its violence for many minutes without endangering his life." One study of local records found that 28 distinct snow storms fell on Morristown in that one winter.

The snow drifts were so deep—up to 12 feet tall—that no one could get out of or into the camps to bring fresh food. Some men resorted to eating the bark from trees and boiling their shoes in soups in hopes of getting some taste and nourishment from the cow hides. One of Washington's officers wrote after the winter was over that he remembered that the ink he used to write reports had frozen in its ink well while it was sitting in front of a fire. Things became so desperate for Washington's officers that they finally resorted to killing and eating one officer's pet dog.

Wick House ★★★★, in Jockey Hollow, is a New England–style cottage that was the home of farmer Henry Wick, who was the unwilling host of the winter army. Most of the trees that were cut down for the cabins came from his forest. The still-stylish Wick home can be compared to the quickly thrown-together cabins to show what can be done with house construction when an impending winter is not forcing a person to rush building. The house is open for touring daily 9:30am–4:30pm.

There are five cabins on display at the **Pennsylvania Brigade Encampment Site ★★★★★**. These houses are not entirely authentic, as the original cabins had no windows. Still, these cabins likely look much like those built by the men.

Allow at least an hour and a half to see Jockey Hollow.

Fort Nonsense ★★★

Western Avenue north of Jockey Hollow

When Washington's army arrived, he adhered to the old military adage of "take the high ground and hold it." The hill on which these old earthworks were built looked down on the village of Morristown. Had any British attacked, this hill would have been a strategic defensive position.

It is unclear if the colonial soldiers who dug the trenches here dubbed the position Fort Nonsense, or if the name was created later by wry historians. The local story goes that the fort got its unusual name from soldiers who thought they were ordered to dig the entrenchments just to keep them busy. (That is unlikely, as Washington surely would have been more interested in having the men build more cabins, or repair poorly constructed cabins.) The trenches were likely dug because Washington and his officers understood, better than their soldiers, that any hill overlooking one's camp would be very dangerous should an enemy take it.

Morristown is just 25 miles west of Newark Liberty International Airport, which is served by all of the domestic airlines and some international carriers. It has all of the national rental car chains. The town is also serviced by commuter trains operated by New Jersey Transit. It is best seen by car.

Visitors arriving in town without their own vehicles could take taxis from the Morristown train station to the separate units of the national park. The site of the winter quarters is just a few miles southwest of downtown. Once there, visitors without cars could walk to all of the exhibits, but it would be a lengthy walk to see the entire park. The reconstructed huts where they spent the winter are about a half mile from the visitor center.

Directions to Morristown's Revolutionary War Sites can be tricky for the first-time visitor traveling I-287. Drivers wanting to go directly to the Continental Army's 1779–80 winter quarters rather than start at Washington's Headquarters in downtown Morristown should take Exit 30B from I-287 at Bernardsville, which is south of Morristown. The interstate sign for this portion of the Morristown National Historical Site is labeled Jockey Hollow Encampment Area.

Washington's Headquarters are in downtown Morristown, Exit 36. After visiting this unit, which was under extensive renovation in 2005, visitors should ask the rangers for a sheet of directions. The directions show visitors how to reach the winter encampment at Jockey Hollow and Fort Nonsense.

Rangers warn visitors to leave town before 3:30pm since I-287 "becomes a six-lane parking lot" in the late afternoon because of its proximity to major population centers in New Jersey and New York.

SOURCES & OTHER READING

Encyclopedia of the American Revolution, Mark Boatner, Stackpole Books, 1966

First American Army: The Untold Story of George Washington and the Men Behind America's First Fight for Freedom, Bruce Chadwick, Sourcebooks, 2005

Morristown: A History and Guide, Morristown National Historical Park, New Jersey, Russell Weigley, National Park Service, 1985

Morristown: A Military Headquarters of the American Revolution (Making of America Series), John Rae, Arcadia Publishing, 2002

New Jersey in the American Revolution, Rutgers University Press, 2005

Rebels & Redcoats, George F. Scheer, and Hugh F. Rankin, De Capo Press, 1957

ACCOMMODATIONS

The Pillars of Plainfield Bed and Breakfast Inn

922 Central Ave., Plainfield
T: 888-745-5277 or 908-753-0922
pillars2.com
$114–$250

This is a restored Victorian Georgian mansion on a secluded acre of trees and gardens in the Van Wyck Brooks Historic District of Plainfield. It is located 12 miles west of Newark Airport.

The Whistling Swan Inn

110 Main St., Stanhope
T: 973-347-6369
whistlingswaninn.com
$99–$219

Located in the Skyland region of New Jersey, just 13 miles from Morristown, the Whistling Swan Inn was built in 1905 by Justice of Peace Daniel Best for his wife, Sarah. After being passed through six families, this Victorian house was restored to its turn-of-the-twentieth-century splendor.

Trenton &
Princeton

New Jersey

Guarding Trenton from the Old Barracks Museum

THE WAR YEARS

H ad George Washington failed to surprise the Hessians at Trenton's barracks on Christmas night 1776, his threadbare, exhausted Continental Army would have found itself with its back to the Delaware River facing an angry British army with a reputation for its cruelty. The war for independence might have ended that night with the death or capture of the future first president of the United States.

The Patriots' early victories were a dim memory by the end of 1776. The euphoria after the capture of Fort Ticonderoga, the harassment of the British army at Lexington and Concord, the near victory at Bunker Hill outside of Boston, and the abandonment of Boston by the British, which had all taken place back in 1775, were not helping them make further headway toward victory. Ever since the bold Declaration of Independence had been issued on July 4, things had gone badly for the colonials. The British had shifted their military attention from Massachusetts to New York state and they had been successful in rolling over the fledgling Continental Army on every front.

George Washington was out-thought and out-fought first on Long Island, then on Manhattan, and then at White Plains. But from each defeat, he learned a bit more about British tactics and each time he was able to escape with his army intact. Still, the British victories were emboldening them and devastating American morale. If the British could capture the infant nation's largest city, how much longer would it be before they captured Philadelphia and then returned to retake Boston?

Washington retreated into the interior of New Jersey, crossing the Delaware River on December 7, 1776. He then thoughtfully burned the boats he could find along the river so that British General Cornwallis would not follow him. General Charles Lee, Washington's second-in-command, was captured by the British on the 13th by a British patrol, indicating how closely the main British army was pursuing Washington. Lee's army marched on without him to join Washington.

On December 16, essayist Thomas Paine wrote a famous essay in a pamphlet that summed up the state of the rebellion, at least as it applied to George Washington's role as commander in chief. Paine wrote, "These are the times that try men's souls. The summer soldier and sunshine patriot will, in this crisis, shrink from the service of his country, but he that stands it now, deserves the love and thanks of man and woman."

Who knows if Washington himself was inspired by Paine's writings, but just before Christmas, Washington presented his generals with a bold plan. Instead of waiting for Cornwallis to come after him, they would launch a preemptive strike. It was perhaps reckless, but Washington had little choice. On January 1, 1777, the enlistments of most of his army would expire, and he had no confidence that the men, who had been beaten three straight times over the last several months, would reenlist.

On Christmas night, Washington found some boats that he had not destroyed and crossed from the west bank of the Delaware back to the east bank at a spot nine miles above Trenton. The river was full of ice and flowing swiftly. By early morning on December 26, some 2,400 colonials and militiamen had landed. The force was smaller than it should have been, as two other columns had not yet crossed the river.

Hours behind schedule, Washington pushed toward Trenton, arriving at dawn. The German-born Hessians who were barracked in Trenton were taken by surprise, as their officers had never expected that an American force could cross the raging river. In the ensuing battle, more than 100 Hessians were killed, including their commander. Not a single American lost his life.

Washington determined that he did not have enough men to withstand an attack from the British forces who were camped at nearby Princeton, so he withdrew back across the Delaware. When he asked his men to extend their enlistments by six more weeks so that they might deal with the enemy just across the river in New Jersey, the regiments agreed. In fact, according to records, these reenlistments were unanimous.

On January 2, Washington recrossed the Delaware and formed south of Trenton with the intention of attracting the attention of Lord Cornwallis, who had vowed to "bag Washington like a fox." He defeated that British force. Washington then pulled a ruse in which he left a small force in the trenches at Trenton to feed campfires while the bulk of his army headed toward Princeton. Cornwallis saw the fires and decided against a nighttime attack. There would be time enough the next day to bag Washington. But the next day, he discovered that Washington had escaped.

As the first elements of Washington's army reached Princeton, they ran into a strong force of British who fired a deadly volley into them. The Americans were beginning to panic when Washington himself arrived on the scene. Washington's calm battlefield manner worked its charm. The men rallied to his side and their retreat turned into an attack. The British retreated. Washington pondered chasing down the fleeing British, but he feared he would not be able to destroy them before they made it to the safety of Cornwallis's larger army coming from Trenton. Instead, Washington marched into Princeton, mostly to allow his men to experience the joy of retaking an American city.

Washington never intended to attack Cornwallis's main army. He knew that his men had done all of the fighting they could do that winter. They had embarrassed the Hessians at Trenton and some British at Princeton, but his men were near total collapse. Washington had seen the bloody footprints in the snow and knew that many of his men had fought barefoot. They had to go into winter quarters so his men could rest.

But Cornwallis did not know any of this. All he knew was that Washington had defeated two different British forces at Trenton and Princeton. Instead of pressing on after Washington and taking him at his chosen winter quarters of Morristown, New Jersey, Cornwallis went into winter quarters himself.

Had Cornwallis pressed on for another two months and continued trailing Washington, he might have fought that one crushing battle that would have totally defeated the main colonial army. Washington's men had kept their promise to extend their enlistments by six weeks, but when that time was up, most of them refused to enlist again. Had Cornwallis understood how the colonial enlistment system worked, he could have waltzed into Washington's winter camp and taken the general himself, in which case the war might easily have been over by the early spring of 1777.

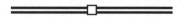

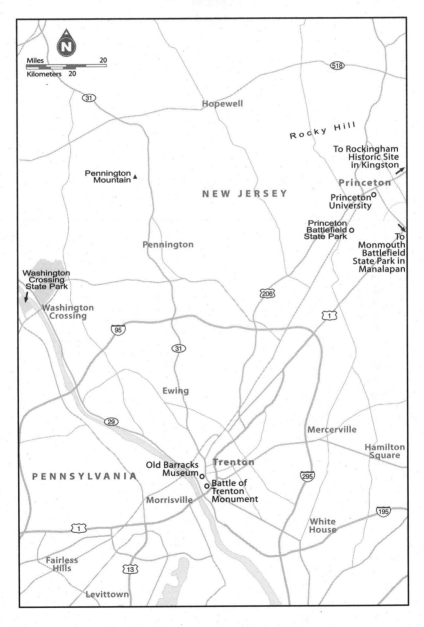

The capital of New Jersey with a population of just 85,000, Trenton is a small city beside the Delaware River. Today's visitors can offer thanks to residents who realized decades ago that their hometown played a pivotal role in keeping the American Revolution alive during one critical 10-day period spanning December 1776 and January 1777. Had those residents not preserved the Old Barracks, there would be little visual evidence of the events that changed the course of American history.

Most of the town's focus is on state government rather than colonial history, but with a city map, one can find where the Battle of Trenton took place.

Princeton, just 13 miles east of Trenton, is an even smaller town, with just 14,000 permanent residents, and home to Princeton University. Though it played a pivotal role in George Washington's comeback as a military leader, Princeton is mainly a college town and little attention is given to its wartime history.

POINTS OF INTEREST

Old Barracks Museum ★★★★★

101 Barrack St., beside the state capitol
T: 609-396-1776 weekdays;
609-777-3599 weekends
barracks.org
Daily 10am–5pm
Admission: $6

It may be difficult to step back in time in the middle of New Jersey's state capital, but the historical interpreters of the Old Barracks Museum do a good job of erasing modern intrusions. The Old Barracks is part original and part reconstructed. One portion of the crumbling barracks was purchased by local preservationists in 1902, and the state purchased another portion in 1914. The center portion was then built to restore what the original building would have looked like in 1758, which was the year the British built the barracks to house soldiers fighting the French.

The British didn't occupy the barracks until December 1776. Chasing the retreating Continental Army, they took the city after Washington had crossed over the Delaware River. Hessians, soldiers of German descent and hired by the British for the duration of the war, were assigned to live in the barracks.

During the French and Indian War, when the barracks were regularly occupied, about 300 British soldiers were garrisoned here. They lived 12 to a room, which was crowded, but likely better than living in the field in tents. These rooms all had fireplaces and bunks and would have been quite comfortable in the winter. One room is furnished just as it would have been for the average soldier.

The officers lived in somewhat larger quarters in the same building. One interesting artifact in the officers' quarters is what appears to be a set of white dominoes with the figures of soldiers painted on each block. These were used for young officers to practice forming military formations.

A museum on the top floor of the Old Barracks displays artifacts and weapons. Among the displays is a manikin showing a Hessian soldier in full uniform and carrying his weapons.

One story about the Battle of Trenton that has grown to mythological proportions is that the Hessian soldiers were still drunk and lying in their beds after celebrating Christmas when Washington and his army attacked on the morning of December 26. The written accounts and the subsequent battle show that the soldiers may have been unprepared and surprised, but they were probably not drunk and disorderly.

Battle of Trenton Monument ★★★

348 South Warren St., southeast of Old Barracks Museum
(ask for directions from staff)

There was no fighting at the Old Barracks during the Battle of Trenton. All of the fighting took place several blocks to the south along Warren (wartime King) Street and Broad (wartime Queen) Street. The Battle of Trenton Monument was erected in 1893 on the spot where American artillery was placed to rake the street on which the Hessians were attacking. The granite monument, designed by John H. Duncan, the same man who designed U.S. Grant's Tomb in New York City, is 150 feet tall. George Washington is the figure at the top of the Doric column.

The key to the Battle of Trenton was Washington's audacity in crossing the Delaware River despite the large ice chunks flowing down it. Because it was Christmas and the weather was so cold, the Hessian commander, Colonel Johann Rall, had opted not to mount patrols along the Delaware since he did not believe any general would order his men to cross the river in such poor weather.

Rall, finally convinced by his men that an American attack was taking place, sent his troops up both King and Queen Streets, but American artillery decimated them. Rall and his second in command were both fatally wounded in these attacks. The Hessians tried to rally in an orchard near the Delaware, but they were quickly surrounded. More than 100 Hessians were killed and 900 surrendered after a battle that lasted only two hours. Only four Americans were wounded.

Because the morning was so cold and damp, historians report that muskets played little role in the battle. Accurate American artillery, commanded by men like Lt. James Monroe, who would become the fifth president of the United States, killed most of the German soldiers. The American cannons kept the Hessians from getting close enough to use their bayonets.

SITES NEAR TRENTON & PRINCETON

Washington Crossing State Park ★★★★

1112 River Rd., Washington Crossing
T: 215-493-4076
cr.nps.gov/nr/travel/delaware/was.htm
Tue–Sat 9am–5pm, Sun noon–5pm
Admission: $5

This park is administered by both Pennsylvania and New Jersey as it is split by the Delaware River. It was from the Pennsylvania side of the river that George Washington and 2,400 men successfully crossed an ice-choked river on Christmas night 1776 to the New Jersey side. The attack was supposed to be three-pronged, but the two other columns found the river so treacherous that one column never did cross and the second crossed so late that it was unable to give Washington any assistance in the attack.

This is a popular park for bicycling and hiking so expect to find a lot of people using it on warm days. Though there are trails on both sides of the river, the Pennsylvania side is the most interesting.

The iconic 1851 painting by Emanuel Gottlieb Leutze, *Washington Crossing the Delaware,* showing Washington standing up in a rowboat, is inaccurate. The painting shows Washington crossing in what looks like a rowboat that would have been used by an ocean-going ship for transferring men to shore. He is standing in the bow of the rowboat, bracing himself with one foot on a gunwale while other men are rowing and pushing away ice floes. The Continentals actually crossed the ice-choked river in flat-bottomed Durham boats, which were designed to haul iron ore. The Durham boats in 1776 looked more like large modern kayaks with their forward and aft sections covered. If Washington stood up at all he would have been well back of the bow.

The McConkey Ferry Inn, where Washington reputedly spoke to his men just before they entered the water, still stands beside the Delaware, though it is unused. Today it is the only Revolutionary War building in the park.

Note that the steel bridge crossing the Delaware is extremely narrow. There is a small café on the New Jersey side that gives a good view of the crossing site. On Christmas Day each year, weather permitting, a reenactment of the crossing is staged by Revolutionary War reenactors using the Durham boats that are normally stored in the sheds at the park.

Allow an hour of walking time to see the Pennsylvania side of the park, visitor center museum, and Durham boats in their sheds. There is little of historical value to see on the New Jersey side.

Princeton Battlefield State Park ★★

500 Mercer Rd., Princeton
T: 609-921-0074
state.nj.us/dep/parksandforests/parks/
   princeton.html
Wed–Sat 10am–noon and 1–4pm,
Sun 1–4pm
Admission: Free

The battle here on January 3, 1777, marked the third victory in 10 days for George Washington's Continental Army, and the first time that his men successfully stood up to regular British troops. All during the summer, fall, and winter of 1776, Washington and his generals had made one blunder after another in Brooklyn and on Manhattan Island. Defeat followed defeat as his army retreated across New Jersey and into Pennsylvania. Only after winning two battles at Trenton against mostly Hessian troops, and then here at Princeton against regular redcoats, did the Continental Army begin to gain confidence that it could successfully fight the British.

The Battle of Princeton was small compared to other battles, and confusing to both sides. The battle began with a ruse to fool the British. On the night of January 2, Washington lit fires around his former position at Trenton, then quietly moved his army toward Princeton. (Lord Cornwallis, the British commander, had moved from Princeton to Trenton.) The two forces virtually passed each other in the night.

Early on the foggy morning of January 3, Washington's column marching on Princeton ran into a British column leaving Princeton on its way to Trenton. The battle was on. Unable to determine the strength of their enemy in the fog, the British column panicked and rushed on toward Trenton while Washington marched into Princeton where he captured a large number of British supplies. He scooped up the supplies and rushed out of town toward Morristown where he finally went into permanent winter quarters.

Americans suffered 40 killed and wounded compared to the British with 28 killed, 38 wounded, and an unusually high number of 187 missing. While the casualties were light, this additional victory and the supplies they captured from the British camp gave the Americans a morale boost.

The Thomas Clarke House, which can be visited on the 86-acre battlefield, is where Continental General Hugh Mercer died nine days after his wounding under the Mercer Oak, a famed landmark that finally died in 2000. Mercer was a Scot-born, Indian-fighting veteran of the French and Indian War who lived in Fredericksburg, Virginia, before the Revolution. Four counties and one town are named after him including Mercer County, of which Trenton is the county seat. Some historians credit Mercer with coming up with the bold plan

to attack the Hessians at Trenton on Christmas Day. He was present at both battles around Trenton.

Monmouth Battlefield State Park ★★

347 Freehold-Englishtown Rd., Manalapan
T: 732-462-9616
state.nj.us/dep/parksandforests/parks/
 monbat.html
Daily 8am–4:30pm
Admission: Free

The Battle of Monmouth, a two-day battle, is interesting in several respects. This was the first battle in which General George Washington was able to try out his newly trained army after leaving winter quarters at Valley Forge. Here, too, Washington finally rid himself of his second in command, General Charles Lee, a British-born general who had thrown his lot in with the Patriots. And a Patriot legend of a woman fighting on the battlefield was created.

The set-up for the battle began when Washington got word on June 16, 1778, that British General Henry Clinton had left Philadelphia and was in the open in New Jersey. Washington began a pursuit, reluctantly allowing General Lee to plan the attack since Lee was his chief lieutenant. Lee bungled the attack and Washington's army began a retreat that ended only when Washington himself rode onto the battlefield to rally his men. After Monmouth, Washington relieved Lee of command for making the battlefield mistake of breaking up his attack into small pieces rather than keeping his army intact.

Emanuel Gottlieb Leutze, the same man who painted the more famous *Washington Crossing the Delaware*, captured the scene in a painting called *Washington Rallying the Troops at Monmouth*. According to legend, the painter had to repaint his original work because his sponsor thought Washington appeared too angry. In the finished work, Washington appears oddly unconcerned about the battle raging around him.

During the battle, a woman named Mary Hayes McCauley watched in horror as her husband was cut down while he was firing a cannon. Mrs. McCauley had been carrying water to the troops, a job that was so common among women traveling with armies that they were called Molly Pitchers. Mrs. McCauley supposedly put down her water bucket and took over her husband's place loading the cannon. Several paintings have portrayed the incident, including one showing General Washington personally congratulating Mrs. McCauley for her heroism and service. One of the bronze reliefs on the Monmouth Battle Monument shows Mrs. McCauley at her cannon.

Allow an hour at Monmouth to see the battlefield and monument.

Rockingham Historic Site ★★

Laurel Ave., Kingston
T: 609-683-7132
rockingham.net/index.htm
Wed–Sat 10am–noon and 1–4pm,
Sun 1–4pm
Admission: Free

This was Washington's last headquarters. He was here in October 1783 when he learned that the Treaty of Paris officially ending the war had been accepted and signed by the British. Before leaving the house, he penned his Farewell Orders. Speaking of himself in the third person, Washington ended his lengthy address with these words to his troops: "May ample justice be done them here, and may the choicest of Heaven's favors both here and hereafter attend those, who under the divine auspices have secured innumerable blessings for others: With these Wishes, and this benediction, the Commander in Chief is about to retire from service. The Curtain of separation will soon be drawn and the Military Scene to him will be closed for ever."

Washington had no idea that the office of president would be offered to him after the United States Constitution was drafted and approved.

The house is staffed with volunteers in period clothes describing what life was like for the Washingtons, who were anxious to return home to their Virginia farm.

SOURCES & OTHER READING

The Day is Ours!: An Inside View of the Battles of Trenton and Princeton, November 1776-January 1777, William Dwyer, Rutgers University Press, 1998

Decisive Battles of the American Revolution, Joseph B. Mitchell, Westholm Publishing, 2004

General George Washington: A Military Life, Edward Lengel, Random House, 2005

Iron Tears: America's Battle for Freedom, Britain's Quagmire: 1775-1783, Stanley Weintraub, Free Press, 2005

New Jersey and the Revolutionary War, Alfred Hoyt Bill, Rutgers University Press, 1992

Washington Crossing Historic Park: Pennsylvania Trail of History Guide, John Bradley, Stackpole, 2004

Washington's Crossing, David Hackett Fischer, Oxford Press, 2004

The Winter Soldiers: The Battles for Trenton and Princeton, Richard Ketchum, Owl Books, 1999

GETTING TO AND AROUND
TRENTON & PRINCETON

Both Princeton and Trenton are served by Trenton Mercer Airport about 20 miles from Princeton. The only commercial flight coming into this airport connects with Boston's Logan Airport. There are rental cars at Trenton Mercer.

Another choice with better flight connections to Trenton may be to fly into Newark Liberty International or Philadelphia International Airport. Philadelphia is 40 miles south of Trenton and Newark is 60 miles to the east. Both are linked to Trenton by interstate highways and both have the standard rental car agencies.

Another choice for those coming from a larger city like New York is to take a train to Trenton or Princeton and then use taxis to reach the historic sites. Commuter trains run from Philadelphia and New York City to Trenton with a stop in Newark near the airport. The trip by train from New York City to Trenton is about an hour and a half. From Philadelphia to Trenton is about an hour. From Trenton to Princeton is a 40-minute trip by train.

The best historic site in Trenton, the Old Barracks, is right next to the state capitol, and the area where the fighting actually took place is a few blocks away. That means a taxi ride from the train station could easily take visitors to the most important sites in the city. If arriving by car, parking is convenient near the capitol.

One interesting site near Trenton, Washington's Crossing, is a considerable distance from downtown and may not be worth the price of a taxi ride compared to the experience found at the Old Barracks.

ACCOMMODATIONS

Fernbrook Bed & Breakfast

142 Georgetown Rd., Bordentown
T: 609-298-3868
fernbrookbb.com
$100–$150

This 1750 Georgian estate home is set in the countryside and opened as a B&B in 1995 upon restoration. Enjoy the charm of the gardens and the nursery. It is located 15 miles southeast of Princeton.

Inn at Glencairn

3301 Lawrenceville Rd., Princeton
T: 609-497-1737
innatglencairn.com
$195–$235

The Opdykes, a Dutch family from New York, were the first recorded settlers on the site of Glencairn in 1697. The present stone wing of the manor house was likely built in the early 1700s. In 1776, while the British army was quartered in Princeton, Glencairn was believed to have been confiscated as British quarters. It served as a Hessian Hospital for a brief period during the American Revolution.

Philadelphia

Pennsylvania

Independence Hall

THE WAR YEARS

P hiladelphia was founded in 1644 as the site of a church 37 years before Pennsylvania was even granted its status as a colony, Philadelphia is tied closely to the influence of Quaker William Penn. Penn arrived in 1682 to create the colony on land given him by King Charles II to repay debts the king had run up with Penn's father. Penn, who moved back and forth between his colony and England, granted the city's charter in 1701.

Located on the Delaware River, which feeds into the Atlantic Ocean, Philadelphia grew steadily for 90 years before the Revolution as a major port for the colony. Sheltered from oceanfront storms that sometimes affected bay ports like Boston, the city's river port boomed. At one time, its shipping wharves stretched more than two miles along the riverfront. More residents arrived to set up shop to take advantage of the growing shipping industry. With a growing population came increased demands, and the city was often cited by other colonial cities for its "firsts": first public school in 1689, first statewide newspaper in 1719, first public library in 1731, first fire department in 1736, first hospital in 1755, first fire insurance company in 1752. By the mid-1700s, it was one of the largest cities in the colonies with a population of more than 25,000.

By the late 1760s, discontent had begun to spread among the colonies after the end of the French and Indian War and the imposition of taxes on the colonies by the Crown. Colonial leaders began to talk about sending King George III a unified message from all 13 colonies. Because Philadelphia was a major city geographically far from Boston and New York City, both of which were coastal cities already under British domination, it was chosen to host the First Continental Congress in September 1774. This Congress sent a conciliatory message to the king, while still complaining about taxation without representation. The message gently threatened a boycott of British imported goods.

When violence flared the following April with the British raid on Lexington and Concord, the Second Continental Congress met in Philadelphia on May 10, coincidentally the same day that Patriots captured Fort Ticonderoga's cache of cannons in New York state. This Second Continental Congress was not as conciliatory as the First. It appointed George Washington to command the Continental Army and authorized an invasion of Canada in hopes that the French living there would join the 13 American colonies to revolt against English rule.

The Second Continental Congress stayed in session for nearly two years. On July 4, 1776, it issued the Declaration of Independence. It moved to York, Pennsylvania, in September 1777 when the British, under commander in chief Lord William Howe, threatened to take the city.

The occupation of Philadelphia by Lord Howe's redcoats turned out to be a hollow victory. Instead of focusing on destroying Washington's fledgling and still barely trained army that had been trying to protect Philadelphia, Howe had focused on capturing the city itself, thinking that bagging it like the British had done with Boston and New York City would deal the Revolution a death blow.

Paradoxically, though Philadelphia was where all of the documents that were considered treasonous in the eyes of the British were written, it was also a city with strong Loyalist tendencies. The Quakers who had founded the city were not happy with the rebellious Congress because they valued peace at any cost. Philadelphia merchants were also more concerned that trade with England, the source of their wealth, continue than they were with establishing a new nation.

So instead of the occupation's demoralizing the populace, the people seemingly went right on about their business. While the British were taking control, the Continental Army and the Continental Congress both had time to escape. Benjamin Franklin, then in Paris encouraging the French to come to American aid, recognized that the capture of Philadelphia actually had little impact on the war when he responded to the news with "Philadelphia has captured Howe!"

American and British historians have long questioned Howe's strategy of sailing and marching on Philadelphia instead of linking up with a British force under the command of General John Burgoyne coming south from Canada. Burgoyne expected Howe to meet him so they could create an overwhelming force that would cut off the New England colonies. Instead, Howe went to Pennsylvania, which left Burgoyne's force under-manned. He was defeated at the two battles of Saratoga—New York in September and October 1777—both early turning points in the war that demonstrated that the Patriots were able to defeat full British armies on a battlefield without resorting to sniping from behind fences, as had been done at Lexington and Concord two years earlier.

Lord Howe and his army remained in Philadelphia until May 1778 when word came from England that France had entered into an alliance with the Americans. Fearing that the French fleet would bottle up the mouth of the Delaware River, the British made plans to return to New York. At the same time, Howe finally received word that his resignation, submitted the previous fall, had been accepted by King George III. Howe was replaced as commander in chief by General Henry Clinton.

Once the British left the city, so fast that one bitter Tory claimed they "vanished," Congress returned. The city effectively served as the home of the federal government until 1800 when the buildings in the District of Columbia were finished. The city was never considered for a permanent capital of the United States because the newly adopted United States Constitution called for the establishment of a federal district that would become the District of Columbia.

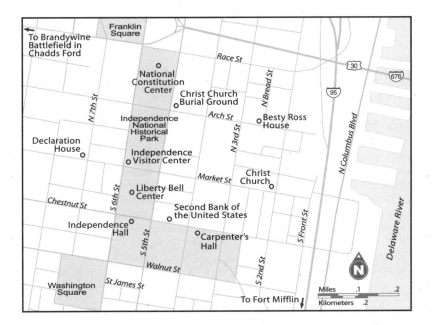

To Brandywine Battlefield in Chadds Ford

Franklin Square

Race St

N 7th St

National Constitution Center

Christ Church Burial Ground

Arch St

N.Bread St

N 3rd St

30

676

95

Independence National Historical Park

Declaration House

Independence Visitor Center

Besty Ross House

N Columbus Blvd

Market St

Christ Church

Chestnut St

S 6th St

Liberty Bell Center

Second Bank of the United States

Independence Hall

S 5th St

S Front St

Carpenter's Hall

Delaware River

Walnut St

S 2nd St

N

Washington Square

St James St

To Fort Mifflin

Miles   .1   .2

Kilometers   .2

SOURCES & OTHER READING

First City—Philadelphia and the Forging of Historical Memory, Gary Nash, University of Pennsylvania Press, 2001

Independence Hall in American Memory, Charlene Mires, University of Pennsylvania Press, 2002

Lives of the Signers of the Declaration of Independence, Benson Lossing, Wallbuilder Press, 1985

Philadelphia, a 300-Year History, Russell Weigley, W.W. Norton, 1982

The Philadelphia Campaign, Stephen R. Taaffe, University Press of Kansas, 2003

Websites:

teachingamericanhistory.org/convention/

usconstitution.net/const.html

ushistory.org/philadelphia/

PHILADELPHIA TODAY

With more than 1.4 million people living within its city limits, Philadelphia ranks as the fifth-largest city in the nation. During the Revolution, it was ranked the third-largest city after New York and Boston.

Though it is a modern city with a diverse range of businesses, Philadelphia has preserved the landmarks of its early colonial history. All of the important sites of interest to tourists are within a five-by-five-block area near Penn's Landing, the location where William Penn landed in 1682. (That site today is a waterfront park that includes some interesting exhibits, including the USS *Olympia*, a US Navy cruiser from which Admiral Thomas Dewey gave his famous order, "You may fire when ready, Gridley" during the 1898 Battle of Manila Bay against the Spanish fleet in the Philippines. This may be the only United States Navy vessel from the Spanish American War still floating.)

This historic area of Philadelphia is popular with visitors so be forewarned that both interstate and surface street traffic is heavy and parking difficult. There is underground parking at the Independence Visitor Center, but if that is full, visitors will have to try nearby public parking garages attached to office buildings.

POINTS OF INTEREST

Independence National Historical Park
★★★★★

143 South Third St.,
exits off I-95 and I-676
T: 215-965-2305
nps.gov/inde
Visitor center daily 8:30am–5pm
Admission: Free

Independence National Historical Park is different from the nation's other national parks since it is in an urban setting. The park encompasses 21 buildings on 11 city blocks so prepare to do a lot of walking. The park attracts heavy visitor traffic from around the world every day of the week, and it could easily take more than a day to see all of the sites here. Visitors who want to see every building in the park should consider setting aside at least two days.

If a shorter time frame is necessary, visitors should plan on arriving early in the morning and staying through late afternoon. This is particularly true when trying to get in to see the two most famous attractions: the Liberty Bell and Independence Hall. Both of these attractions require visitors to obtain time-specific tickets and pass through metal detectors. The tickets are free and available at the visitor center. Note that one will not even get close enough to take decent photographs of either of these attractions without a ticket.

The following are sites found within or near the park:

Independence Visitor Center ★★★★

Corner of Sixth and Market Sts.
T: 800-537-7676 or 212-965-2305
independencevisitorcenter.com

Visitors must stop at the visitor center before continuing on to see either the Liberty Bell or Independence Hall. Free tickets to both attractions are obtained here, and they are stamped with a suggested time to go through the metal detectors located in the building housing the Liberty Bell.

The visitor center may be considered an attraction in itself as it has costumed characters roaming the hall as well as static exhibits. Visitors wanting someone to lead the way will find guided walking tours of the park beginning here. The 75-minute tours cover 15 historic sites, including the Liberty Bell and Independence Hall. Cost is $15 for adults.

There is a café here with a variety of snacks and sandwiches. An indoor mall with an extensive food court can be found about a block away on Fourth Street.

Note that the visitor center has bathrooms whereas the building housing the Liberty Bell and Independence Hall do not.

Liberty Bell Center ★★★★★

Across street from Visitor Center
Daily 9am–5pm
Ticket required

The bell started humbly enough, a 1751 replacement for the bell then in Independence Hall. At the time it was ordered, an inscription was placed on it, "Proclaim LIBERTY throughout all the Land unto all the inhabitants thereof," which is a Bible verse. At that time, it was meant to recognize William Penn, who insisted that religious freedom be part of the colony's foundation.

The bell was rung on numerous occasions, including July 8, 1776, when the Declaration of Independence was read in public for the first time. By the 1830s, it had become a symbol for abolitionists who were pressing for the end of slavery. In 1846 the bell cracked when it was rung. A repair was attempted, but the crack only widened. It has not been rung since. The bell today is encased in a large plastic case. It weighs about one ton.

Independence Hall ★★★★★

Chestnut and Sixth Sts.
Hours vary during the season but generally daily 9am–5pm
Ticket Required

Construction started on the Pennsylvania State House in 1732. The colonial government's finances ebbed and flowed, so it was not completed until more than 20 years later. The building underwent many updates through the years, but was restored to its 1776 look in 1950.

The First Continental Congress did not meet here in 1774, as ties to the Crown were still strong and the delegates thought better of challenging authority by meeting in the same building where much of the colony's business with England was conducted. By the next year, however, relations with England had deteriorated and the delegates thought it symbolically important to meet in a building dedicated to government.

The most important room in Independence Hall is the assembly room. There, Washington was appointed general of the Continental Army in 1775, the Declaration of Independence was debated in 1776, the Articles of Confederation were debated in 1781, and the United States Constitution was debated in 1787. This room was essentially the center of United States government from 1775 through 1783 with the exception of the winter of 1777, when the British occupied the city. Most of the furniture in the room is appropriate to the period. The rising sun chair in which Washington sat while the Constitution was being debated is original. Records indicate that Washington said little during debates over the Constitution out of concern that his opinion would unduly influence the other delegates.

Carpenter's Hall ★★★★

320 Chestnut St.
T: 215-925-0167
ushistory.org/carpentershall/
Hours vary by season but generally
Wed–Sun 10am–4pm
Admission: Free

While Independence Hall gets most of the attention, the first steps toward colonial freedom were taken in 1774 in this private building where the First Continental Congress met. This Congress did not make demands for freedom, but was organized to show England that the colonies could present a united voice in asking for concessions from the Crown. It convened after England shut down the port of Boston after the Boston Tea Party. The most important item of business was passing a Declaration of Rights and Grievances that was sent to the King.

Carpenter's Hall consists of one large room; one corner is set up with the desks and chairs that were used in 1774.

Second Bank of the United States ★★★★★

Chestnut St. between Fourth and Fifth Sts.
Wed–Sun 11am–4pm
Admission: Free

The contentious history of establishment of national banks by the United States government is not the main focus of this building. Instead, visitors can find a wonderful collection of period oil paintings of virtually every person who played a role in the American Revolution. Many of the paintings are by Charles Wilson Peale, the preeminent artist of his day. Each painting is accompanied by a short biography of the person. Visitors might consider making this their first stop in the park (after get-

ting their tickets for the Liberty Bell and Independence Hall). By viewing these portraits, visitors may get a better sense of the people who formed the nation.

National Constitution Center ★★★

Race and Fifth Sts.
Daily 9:30am–5pm
Admission: $9

While the admission may seem steep, this attraction offers good value for the money. One free thing to do before paying the admission is to inspect an exact replica of the Liberty Bell.

After paying admission, visitors move to a theater where an actor gives a presentation on the themes of the Constitution. Visitors then exit into a huge exhibit hall where static displays and multimedia presentations run continually on the history of the Declaration, its meaning, and how it has been tested through the years.

Many of the exhibits are designed to engage schoolchildren, including one in which they can superimpose themselves into the inauguration of the President of the United States. Computer stations are available so that visitors can quiz themselves on what they know about their states and their own rights guaranteed in the Constitution.

One interesting experience is walking among the statues of all the Constitutional Convention delegates. The statues are all positioned in a hall debating with one another, so visitors can stand beside them to analyze their facial expressions.

Declaration House ★★★

7th and Market Sts.
Wed–Sun by tour only (meet at Visitor Center desk at 1pm)

This house is actually a reconstruction from 1975, but it claims to be an accurate reproduction of the house in which

Thomas Jefferson wrote the Declaration of Independence. Jefferson had rented rooms on the second floor. Preserved here is the lap desk on which Jefferson penned the document. Although just two blocks away from Independence Hall, back in 1776, the house was on the edge of town. (Apparently a stable across the street drew horseflies that bothered Jefferson as he was trying to write.)

Christ Church ★★
(not part of Independence Park)

Second and Market Sts.
Mon–Sat 9am–5pm, Sun 12:30–5pm
Admission: $2 donation suggested

Started in 1727, this church was the first Anglican church in the colonies and is considered the home church for the - American Episcopal Church. Many of the early colonial leaders, including George Washington and Benjamin Franklin, worshipped here.

Christ Church Burial Ground ★
(not part of Independence Park)

Arch and Fifth Sts.,
two blocks west of the church
Mon–Sat 10am–4pm, Sun noon–4pm
Admission: $2

Benjamin Franklin's grave can be seen from the Arch Street sidewalk, so visitors may want to save their time and money. On the other hand, this burial ground dates back to the 17th century and is rich with interesting tombstones.

Betsy Ross House ★
(not part of Independence Park)

239 Arch St.
T: 215.686.1252
betsyrosshouse.org
April–September daily 10am–5pm;
October–March Tue–Sun 10am–5pm
Admission: $3

Although modern historians now discount the 100-year-old legend that George Washington and a congressional committee came to the widow Ross with the request that she create a national flag for the fledgling nation, the Betsy Ross House still serves as an excellent tour of a typical home of the period.

The main source of the story was Mrs. Ross's grandson, who was no older than 11 when any meeting would have taken place. Most critical to historians is that they can find no mention in journals or letters of what would be assumed to be a momentous meeting to create a national flag. The Betsy Ross website addresses the issue by saying that as an elderly lady, Mrs. Ross entertained her grandchildren with the story of how she sewed the first flag after showing the visiting officials how easily a five-pointed star could be created by folding and snipping some cloth.

SITES NEAR PHILADELPHIA

Fort Mifflin ★

Fort Mifflin Rd., Exit 15 off I-95
T: 215-685-4167
fortmifflin.com/pn
May–November Wed–Sun 10am–4pm
Admission: $6

This fort, which is restored to the way it looked in the 1830s, played a key role in keeping the British from defeating Washington's weary army in the fall and winter of 1777. After Washington was defeated at the Battle of Brandywine, nearly 20,000 British soldiers marched into Philadelphia without any opposition. But that large number of soldiers had to be resupplied if they were going to march after Washington before the winter came.

Blocking that plan were three forts situated south of Philadelphia on the Delaware River. The closest to Philadelphia, and the only one in Pennsylvania, was Fort Mifflin. Fort Mifflin was defended by only 450 men, but it took a siege of six weeks before the British ships were finally able to capture all three forts.

By then, however, it was late fall and cold weather was coming early. Ice was already forming in the Delaware. Instead of pushing west toward Valley Forge, where Washington had set up a winter camp, the British hunkered down in the houses of Philadelphia to wait out the winter themselves. Had Fort Mifflin's defenders not been so stubborn in their defense, the sorely needed supplies would have been delivered to the British army much sooner in the fall. Rested, fed, and with their equipment replenished, the British would have been able to move on Washington's exhausted army before winter. The Revolution might have ended in the fall of 1777 but for Fort Mifflin.

The fort has occasional Revolutionary War programs and demonstrations.

Brandywine Battlefield ★

US 1, Chadds Ford
T: 610-459-3342
ushistory.org/brandywine/brandywine.htm
Tue–Sat 9am–4:30pm, Sun noon–4:30pm
Admission: $5

Most of the Brandywine Battlefield has disappeared under urban development, but this small state park preserves the headquarter houses of both George Washington and the Marquis de Lafayette. Both houses can only be visited by guided tours. There is a small museum on site. A 6.4-mile driving tour of surviving battlefield structures and features is available.

On September 11, 1777, Washington met Cornwallis here in a battle that would leave some Continental leaders wondering if Washington should be replaced as army commander. Acting without intelligence or scouting, Washington made multiple wrong decisions about where the British would attack. Over and over, the redcoats took him by surprise. Finally, after fighting all day, Washington withdrew after losing 1,300 of his 11,000-man force. The British lost only 577. The British also captured 11 of Washington's cannons.

Over the next two weeks, Washington fought smaller engagements west of Philadelphia, losing each one. On September 20, more than 150 of his men were bayoneted in their camp in what was later called the Paoli Massacre. On October 4, Washington was defeated again at Germantown when he attacked an unsuspecting British column.

Tired and defeated, Washington pulled his men west toward the winter quarters he had chosen at Valley Forge. Morale was low, but French observers who had attached themselves to his army were impressed with his bold dawn attack at Germantown. They realized that an army that had been defeated so often, but which still had the élan to attack again, had to be dedicated to its cause. More important, its officers had to believe in their commander. The French observers realized that the Patriots had not yet lost the American Revolution.

From a strategic standpoint, Washington's actions defending the Philadelphia area had kept Cornwallis from moving north to link up with John Burgoyne's army marching south out of Canada. Once Washington's army moved out from nearby Valley Forge in the spring of 1778, the army was rejuvenated.

Getting to and around Philadelphia

The historic area of Philadelphia is easy to reach. Philadelphia International Airport is just seven miles from downtown, and I-95 runs right past the historic area. The historic area can also be reached from the west by I-676, which connects to I-76, which connects to the Pennsylvania Turnpike at Valley Forge.

Visitors arriving by air or train and only wanting to see Independence Park will not need a rental car. There are accommodations near the park, and visitors can walk to the sites. Some hotels near Independence Park even have shuttles from the airport.

There are several tour options, including the Philadelphia Trolley Works, which offers a $25 90-minute tour with 20 stops that allows free on and offs, and the Big Bus Company, which operates double-deck buses for a $27 tour that goes out to the Philadelphia Zoo and returns. Brochures for both are available at the visitor center.

Carriage rides can be picked up along Fifth Street. These rides vary from 20 minutes for $30 up to an hour for $80.

Another option is tour by duck. A duck is an amphibious truck that was developed in World War II to land troops on beaches and then keep advancing inland. Philadelphia's ducks tour the city's historic sites, then go into the Delaware River to demonstrate what made these trucks so important to the marines and the army. Tickets are $23 for an 80-minute ride. The ducks run March through November.

Accommodations

The Columns on Clinton

922 Clinton St., Philadelphia
T: 215-627-7598
$85–$135

The Columns is a Georgian house built between 1854 and 1856. The house is just one block from Philadelphia's historic Antique Row.

Cornerstone Bed and Breakfast

3300 Baring St., Philadelphia
T: 215-387-6065
cornerstonebandb.com
$100–$275

This B&B is a restored 1870s church-stone mansion with a spacious wrap-around porch and seven lovely stained-glass windows. It is within walking distance of the Art Museum, Philadelphia Zoo, University of Pennsylvania, and Drexel University.

Morris House Hotel

225 South 8th St., Philadelphia
T: 215-922-2446
morrishousehotel.com
$159–$249

This colonial-style house was built in 1787. The hotel is two blocks from the Liberty Bell and Independence Hall.

Trade Winds Bed and Breakfast

943 Lombard St., Philadelphia
T: 215-592-8644
tradewindbedandbreakfast.com
$60–$110

Trade Winds was built in 1795 and is furnished with art and antiques from all over the world. The Liberty Bell is an eight-block walk from the B&B.

Valley Forge

Pennsylvania

Cannons that protected winter quarters cabins in the rear

THE WAR YEARS

I f one place can evoke the suffering and desperation of the American cause and how close the American Revolution came to failure, it would be Valley Forge. By mid-1777, the war had been dragging on for two full years. Washington and his army were still a viable force after the victories at Trenton, New Jersey, on Christmas 1776, followed by Princeton on January 3, 1777. But one army barely staying alive did not mean that the colonies were any closer to winning their independence.

Washington decided to stay on the defensive by waiting to see what British General William Howe, who had wintered his troops in New York City, would do. In 1776, Howe had threatened to take Philadelphia, believing that if the colonies lost their largest cities, they would give up the rebellion. Winter had closed in before that mission could be accomplished, and Washington had unexpectedly struck back at Trenton.

Howe was slow to leave New York, so slow that by early summer, Washington moved his army toward New York in order to coax the British into making some kind of move. For the rest of the summer and early fall, Howe played cat and mouse with Washington. Howe moved his men in ships out of sight of land so that Washington had no idea from which direction Howe would eventually attack.

Finally on September 11, 1777, Howe made clear his intention to capture Philadelphia. He moved his men toward Brandywine Creek, just 25 miles southwest of Philadelphia. Inexplicably, Washington did not order his own reconnaissance and ignored local reports of British movements. Howe easily outflanked Washington, forcing the Continental Army to retreat under cover of darkness.

The eventual capture of Philadelphia was almost assured, but Washington was not going to give up. He maneuvered in front of Howe's army for several days until September 21, when a large force of British surprised the sleeping force of General Anthony Wayne. More than 300 Continentals were killed and wounded by bayonets in what would be called the Paoli Massacre. A shaken Washington then misinterpreted a Howe maneuver and marched in the opposite direction, rather than moving to face the British. On September 26, Howe marched his men into Philadelphia with no opposition at all. On October 4, Washington attacked a British outpost northwest of Philadelphia, but the fog confused his men and the British won the Battle of Germantown.

With winter coming, Washington tried to find a battlefield on which he could defeat Howe, but Howe refused to give battle and he and his army retreated back into the warm houses of Philadelphia. Finally, Washington scouted out areas for his own winter quarters, settling on Valley Forge, an area 20 miles northwest of Philadelphia. It really was not a valley, but a series of wooded hills between a creek and the Schuylkill River that gave Washington high ground to protect should the British leave their winter quarters and launch a surprise winter attack.

Washington arrived with 10,000 men, including 2,000 who were so sick that they could not make roll call. While Valley Forge was good, defensible land, it was a poor choice logistically. There were few farms around from which to draw food. There were few existing houses in which to make headquarters. There were no wells, meaning men had to carry water from the creeks more than a mile to their camps.

Washington set his men to building log huts, 14 feet by 16 feet, in each of which 12 men would live. The huts were spartan at best, but they kept the men from the wind. Food was a major problem. The commissary was unable to find fresh meat and vegetables. By early January 1778, the men were living on nothing more than fire cake, a biscuit or bread made from flour and water paste and baked as best a soldier could.

Rather than simply seize what provisions local farmers had, Washington tried to glean food from as far south as Virginia and as far north as New York. He was hampered by the failing remnants of a once-successful quartermaster department that had been dismantled earlier in the war by a Continental Congress who had little idea themselves of what it took to keep a fit army in the field. Eventually General Nathaniel Greene was appointed quartermaster and he targeted food and cattle in New Jersey and Delaware, two colonies with high numbers of Loyalists.

Forced to take what he needed, Washington learned through spies and other reports that many in the colonies were not inclined to help his army survive the winter. While the troops in Valley Forge were starving, civilian farmers on the east side of Philadelphia were selling their produce to the British in the city. The grain markets in New York City were selling to civilian customers in New England while ignoring buyers for the army.

In late February, a man calling himself Baron von Steuben arrived in Washington's camp with the offer of training the army in European army tactics. Von Steuben claimed to have been a general with Frederick the Great. Washington believed him, though historians would later discover he was little more than a traveling soldier of fortune who may have never met Frederick. Still, von Steuben wrote out a drill manual in French that his 17-year-old assistant translated into English. For weeks, von Steuben drilled Washington's men until they finally resembled the force of the British. The drilling not only made the men into soldiers, but kept them busy and their minds off the lack of food.

Early historians described the winter in Valley Forge as one of the worst on record, but later historians compared temperature readings in Philadelphia, less than 20 miles away, and found those temperatures to be within normal ranges for winter. What was not exaggerated, however, was the suffering of Washington's men. In addition to erratic, inadequate food supply, what food did get to the soldiers was often moldy or insect-ridden grains. Besides food problems, there was no system for supplying uniforms, heavy coats, and shoes. Many of the men had worn out their shoes in summer and fall marches and had little choice but to wrap their feet in rags.

By March, the temperatures began to moderate and supplies began to flow into the camp more regularly. Troops began to pick up a military spirit thanks to von Steuben's regular daily drilling. In May, Washington sent out newly trained units to harass the British. Leading one of the first raids from Valley Forge was a young Frenchman who had thrown his lot with the Americans, the Marquis de Lafayette.

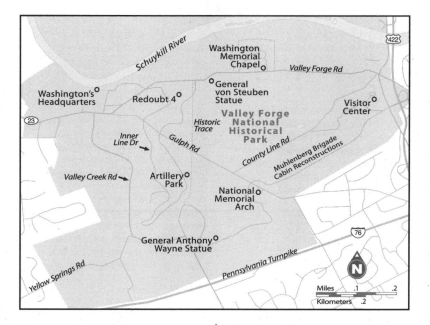

SOURCES & OTHER READING

Campaign to Valley Forge, July 1, 1777–December 19, 1777, John Ford Reed, Pioneer Press, 1980

The Road to Valley Forge—How Washington Built the Army that Won the Revolution, John Buchanan, Wiley, 2004

Valley Forge: Making and Remaking a National Symbol, Lorett Treese, Pennsylvania State University Press, 1995

Valley Forge: Pinnacle of Courage, John W. Jackson, Thomas Publications, 1996

The Valley Forge Winter, Wayne Bodie, Pennsylvania University Press, 2002

Websites:

ushistory.org/march/index.html

valleyforge.org/

VALLEY FORGE TODAY

A small, unincorporated community, Valley Forge today is not much more than it was in 1777.

That does not mean that Valley Forge is not a vibrant community. Montgomery County, the county in which the village is located, has branded the name Valley Forge to attract visitors to the county's accommodations, restaurants, and meeting facilities scattered around the Valley Forge National Historical Park. (Note that the Valley Forge Convention and Visitors Bureau is actually located in Plymouth Meeting, Pennsylvania.)

The Valley Forge that visitors are here to see is the Valley Forge National Historical Park. Visitors leaving the visitor center and riding along the first ridge past the reconstructed huts will soon realize why this particular ground was favored by Washington for his army's winter quarters. The ridge is high and faces southeast, the direction of Philadelphia, where the British troops were wintering in 1777. Any movement of redcoats in the direction of Valley Forge would have been spotted in plenty of time to man the lines. Such an attack did not happen, perhaps because the British too realized that the American position on the ridge was such a good one.

POINTS OF INTEREST

Valley Forge National Historical Park
★★★★★

Exit 326 from Pennsylvania Turnpike
Junction of Rte. 23 and North Gulph Rd.
T: 610-783-1000
nps.gov/vafo/
Welcome Center daily 9am–5pm
Admission: Free

The Valley Forge visitor center has some displays, an expansive book store, and an 18-minute movie that runs every 30 minutes that describes why Washington brought his army to this ridge in the winter of 1777–78. The movie addresses and discounts one of the great myths of Valley Forge, that the winter experienced by Washington's army was the worst on record. Temperature recordings taken in 1777 in Philadelphia, just 20 miles away, show that the winter that year was normal,

maybe even mild. Still, rangers here get questions as to how the men survived.

One question pondered by historians today, and not really addressed in the movie, is how Valley Forge was chosen as winter quarters. It was not near any major town that might have supplied the army with provisions. Some of Washington's own officers questioned his reasoning for selecting such remote winter quarters.

But what Valley Forge lacked in civilization, it made up for in availability of trees. Vast forests surrounded the ridges and valleys. When Washington's men arrived at Valley Forge on December 19, 1777, Washington put them to work immediately building shelters. That accomplished several purposes: It cemented the principle of teamwork that was so important in the army, it kept the men busy, and the physical labor kept them warm. The standard cabin built to hold 12 men was 16 feet by 14 feet. Each one had a fireplace and wooden bunks built against the wall. Within a few weeks, more than 2,000 cabins occupied the ridges.

Allow at least three hours to see the exhibits and cabins. This is a sprawling park of 3,500 acres with a driving tour, but a paved trail also encourages walking.

The first reconstructed cabins encountered in the park at **Stop 2 ★★★★★** are those built by General Peter Muhlenberg's Brigade of Virginians. Muhlenberg was an Anglican minister living in the Shenandoah Valley, far from the fighting, when he felt the calling to join the Revolution. The story is that he was reading the third chapter of Ecclesiastes to his congregation that begins, "To every thing there is a season." When he got to the line "a time for peace and a time for war," he took off his clerical robes to reveal his uniform. Muhlenberg and his Virginians fought well in several major battles, and he later fought at Yorktown. He returned to the pulpit after the war and is buried near Valley Forge.

Of the 10,000 men who wintered here, more than 2,000 died. Most of them died of the traditional army diseases of flu, typhoid, and dysentery furthered by the lack of sanitation and the closeness of living quarters with sick men. Further proving that the men did not die of cold, records indicate that two-thirds of the men died in the spring, long after the snow and coldest weather had passed.

No graves of colonial soldiers have ever been found on national park property. Historians believe sick men were likely moved to makeshift hospitals surrounding the camp, which could mean that they are buried on private property.

Across from the cabins, facing Philadelphia, is a typical three-pounder cannon. Cannons in those days were much smaller and less deadly than the cannons that would be used 80 years later in the Civil War. In most Revolutionary War battles, cannon fire did not have a major effect on the outcome of the action.

Stop 3 ★★★ is the National Memorial Arch, erected in the park in 1917. The arch is meant to honor George Washington and is inspired by arches seen in both France and Rome. A European arch honoring American soldiers seems somewhat out of place at Valley Forge, but when it was dedicated in 1917 it was deemed to be a great expression of patriotism.

Some of the explanation as to why Americans believe the army suffered so greatly here might be found in Washington's quote from the early spring of 1778, which is carved inside the arch, "Naked and starving as they are we cannot enough admire incomparable patience and fidelity of the soldiery." (Contemporary historians and linguists often point out that "naked" in colonial days usually meant poorly clothed rather than the literal idea that the men were without any clothes.)

Stop 4 ★★★★ is a massive, impressive statue of General Anthony Wayne, who sometimes is forced to bear the nickname of "Mad Anthony." The nickname has nothing to do with any accusation that Wayne, a Paoli, Pennsylvania, native was insane, but that he was often bold in combat. The statue faces the direction of his home, just a few miles to the east. It was Wayne's force that was surprised by a British bayonet attack at Paoli, resulting in the bloody deaths of many American soldiers. Most of those men died in their tents from a nighttime attack.

Wayne's greatest contribution to the colonial army was that he saw the need to organize basic training, a concept not generally accepted at the time, even by Washington. Wayne started working with a Prussian soldier of fortune named Friedrich Wilhelm von Steuben in February 1778 to mold the men into more of an army than they had been previously. Rather than groan at drilling, the men actually welcomed the chance to be trained by Wayne, who was a self-taught soldier, and von Steuben, who had spent his life in the army.

Wayne survived the war and took command of the US Army when he was appointed by President Washington.

Stop 5 ★★★★ is the Isaac Potts House, Washington's headquarters. It is open daily from 9am–5pm and can be toured for $3. The house was owned at the time by a Quaker, but it was being subleased to a woman who then leased it to Washington. Martha Washington, the general's wife, arrived here in February of 1778 and took over the duties of running the house. She organized meals, assigned laundry chores, and managed other things that she thought would ease the general's burden in keeping track of his army.

Stop 6 ★★★ is Redoubt 4, a small fort that anchored the northern end of the camp. It never came under fire.

Stop 8 ★★★★★ is Artillery Park, the glade where most of Washington's artillery was massed. This is a rare sight: massed Revolutionary War cannons. Most national parks and museums have at most one or two cannons on display—usually inside the museum and those are usually three-pounder "grass hoppers"—while these guns are six-pounders.

While putting all of an army's guns in one spot is normally not a good idea, Washington reasoned that this centrally located field was close enough to any part of the line that the guns could be rushed

into service if necessary. The British never attacked, so the gunners spent the winter cleaning their cannons of black-powder residue, and repairing the wooden carriages that might be splitting after the abuse of firing and being towed over rough, rutted roads.

Cannons were made either of iron or bronze. Bronze was much lighter, but a six-pounder made of this alloy had a range of 1,200 yards compared to an iron gun's range of 1,500 yards. Heavier guns were manufactured, but they were used in forts. The largest caliber gun most often used by the mobile artillery was the six-pounder. By the Civil War, cannon technology had increased to allow guns as big as 30-pounders to be towed by horses.

Stop 9 ★★★★ shows the statue of General von Steuben. The American Revolution made von Steuben a success because until he met Benjamin Franklin in Paris, the former Prussian soldier had been unemployed. Though von Steuben had never risen above the rank of captain in that army, Franklin got the idea that he had been a lieutenant general. The minister to Paris wrote a letter endorsing von Steuben to Washington and arranged passage for him to America.

Von Steuben made his way to Valley Forge where he introduced himself in French, a language that some of Washington's officers spoke. With the help of Alexander Hamilton, Nathaniel Greene, and Anthony Wayne, von Steuben wrote a drill manual for the Continental Army. Von Steuben trained companies as one unit, a concept that is still used in basic training today.

Stop 10 ★★ is Washington Memorial Chapel. Though it looks old and is made of stone, this Episcopal church dedicated to Washington's service was built in the early 20th century. It is an active church with a membership of more than 350 from the Valley Forge area. It is not part of the national park.

On May 6, 1778, word reached Valley Forge that France had decided to recognize the United States and to come into the war as an ally. When the same news reached the British in Philadelphia, they mobilized their army and quickly left out of fear that a French fleet would soon be sighted on the Delaware River. On June 28, Washington caught up with the fleeing British and defeated them at the Battle of Monmouth, New Jersey.

After Valley Forge, the American Revolution in the northern colonies turned in favor of the Americans.

GETTING TO AND AROUND VALLEY FORGE

Visitors flying into Philadelphia International Airport should plan to rent a car to reach Valley Forge, located 20 miles northwest of Philadelphia. However, if visitors are staying in downtown Philadelphia near a bus line, SEPTA bus route 125 makes a stop at the visitor center. (Note that the loop trail is ten miles long if you plan to walk from there.) Consult SEPTA to find out when the bus makes a stop to return to Philadelphia.

If arriving by car from Philadelphia, take I-76—the Schuylkill Expressway—and exit before the toll plaza. If arriving on the Pennsylvania Turnpike, take Exit 326 (also called old Exit 24) and follow the signs. Drivers should pay close attention. This is a very confusing intersection of roads that turn and double back on themselves.

Visitors can drive to all of the sites on a 10-mile loop trail. Cassette tape and CD tours are available from the gift shop. This park also has a six-mile sidewalk that is parallel to the driving trail, so hikers and bicyclists may wish to consider that option. There are some bathroom and water stops along the walking trail, making this one of the friendliest walking trails in any of the national battlefield parks.

Be forewarned if driving. This national park seems to be overrun with deer that can be seen grazing virtually up to the visitor center.

In the fall the park offers a motorcoach tour through the park with departure times at 11am, 1pm, and 3pm. The cost is $10. The tour takes 90 minutes and might be a good choice for someone who knows little about the war, Valley Forge, or who wants someone knowledgeable to ask questions of during the tour.

ACCOMMODATIONS

The Great Valley House of Valley Forge

1475 Swedesford Rd., Malvern
T: 610-644-6759
greatvalleyhouse.com
$95–$120

Built by an original Welsh settler prior to 1720, the house was completed in 1791. Title deeds can be traced back to William Penn in 1681.

The Manor House at Valley Forge

210 Virginia Ave., Phoenixville
T: 610-983-9867
$60–$85

This 1927 English Tudor house is located just three miles from Valley Forge.

SITE
11

Mount Vernon

Virginia

George Washington's house

THE EARLY YEARS

Ge orge Washington always claimed that he never wanted to be the commander in chief of the Continental Army, nor president of the United States, nor leader of the committee that drafted the Constitution. All he wanted to do was farm.

His farm, 8,000 acres outside of Alexandria overlooking the Potomac River, was centered around a relatively modest, white wooden house he called the Mansion. The farm itself, assembled from an initial 2,000 acres acquired by his great-grandfather, was nearly 100 years old when Washington inherited title to the entire estate upon the death of his half-brother's widow in 1761. The house itself was only four rooms wide on the first floor with three bedrooms on the second, and not at all grand compared to other Virginia homes of planters who were growing wealthy from crops such as tobacco.

Washington had begun leasing Mount Vernon in 1754 from the widow of his half-brother Lawrence, but he spent most of the French and Indian War in the field away from his new home. He returned to the house in 1758. The war had sharpened his military instincts, but had left him frustrated with the haughty British officers under whom he had served.

Home from the war, Washington threw his energy into making his farm the best it could be. He began experimenting with crop rotation to keep his acreage viable. He subscribed to numerous agricultural journals to learn of new planting and harvesting techniques. He experimented with more than 60 crops so that his parcels would always be either producing or regenerating their ability to grow the best cash crops.

Mount Vernon was not a lonely place for long. In 1759, he wooed and won a young widow, Martha Dandridge Custis, who moved into the house with her two grandchildren. Not long after Martha and the children moved in, George began to expand the house, including adding a veranda overlooking the Potomac.

For 15 years, Washington split his time between Mount Vernon and Williamsburg, living quietly as a gentlemen farmer and making occasional forays to the colonial capital after being elected to the House of Burgesses in 1758. He was a quiet delegate, rarely leading the increasingly fiery speeches that took place as tensions with England grew. Still, Washington was highly regarded as a legislator because he helped find compromise. He was selected as one of Virginia's delegates to the First Continental Congress. To his surprise, the Congress named him commander of the Continental Army in June 1775. He was surprised because he had failed at some of his ventures in the French and Indian War. Even more surprising was that he had commanded only a few men at a time and all of his experience had been on the far frontier. He had no experience in organizing logistics support, forming large bodies of men, or even developing strategy and tactics—all of the skills that a general needed to command an army.

For the next eight years, Washington only dreamed of Mount Vernon as he fought—and frequently lost—battles in New York, New Jersey, and Pennsylvania. Along the way, his army survived two severe winters and numerous crises of confidence in his leadership.

Finally, in September 1781, Washington marched past Mount Vernon and onto the Virginia peninsula, where he joined with French soldiers to force the surrender of Lord Cornwallis's British army at Yorktown, Virginia. Though it would be another two years before treaties officially ended the war, Washington's fighting was done. He stayed in uniform another two years, but finally resigned his commission in December 1783 and returned for good to Mount Vernon—or so he thought.

Washington, concerned that the nation was rudderless under the Articles of Confederation that were supposed to guide its development, left Mount Vernon again in 1787 to head the Constitutional Convention in Philadelphia. His goal was to write a constitution that would survive the test of time. He thought once that was accomplished that again he would retire quietly, but the Constitution called for the election of a president and every single man appointed to the electoral college voted for him.

Once again Washington was forced to go on the road, splitting time between the major cities of the day, New York and Philadelphia. The nation had no permanent capital and would not have one during Washington's two terms as president. All during the Revolution the government had shifted from one city and town to another to avoid capture by pursuing British forces. Now that the British threat was over, maneuvering began among several cities all wanting to be designated the official capital. It was not until 1790 that an agreement was reached to put the new capital district on the Potomac in exchange for the Southern states' voting to have the federal government assume all of the debts the individual states had incurred in fighting the British.

Though Washington never used any of the government buildings planned for the new District of Columbia, he helped select both the specific site of the new capital district and the man who would lay the city out, Pierre L'Enfant. It was no coincidence that the land Washington helped select was less than a few hours ride from his own vast holdings at Mount Vernon.

After serving two terms as president, Washington refused a third. He insisted that he was now too old to serve any longer at age 67. The presidency fell to Washington's Vice President John Adams. Washington retired to Mount Vernon where he finally was able to do what he had always wanted to do—concentrate on his farming. The first president lived another three years, finally dying in his bedroom in the Mansion on December 14, 1799, after being caught in a sleet storm while riding his acreage two days earlier.

Alexandria, the closest town to Mount Vernon and where the family shopped and worshipped, was founded in 1749, when Washington was 17 years old. The town grew quickly and its location along the Potomac, which links to the sea, made it an active, profitable port with goods moving directly to England. In 1753 Washington drilled the Virginia militia in the downtown's square. Though located directly across the river from the capital city, its growth was already assured more than 40 years before the decision was made to build the national capital there.

SITE
11

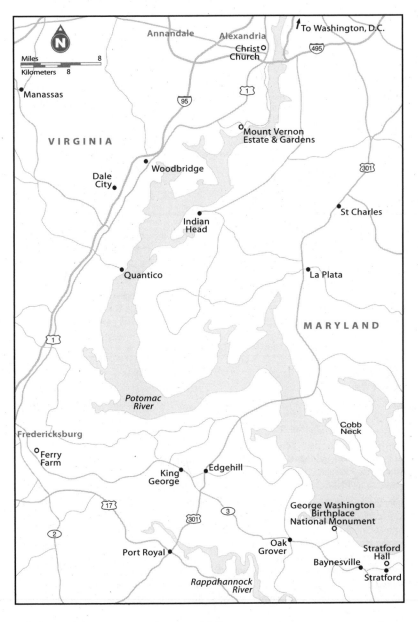

MOUNT VERNON TODAY

Mount Vernon is like an oasis in a desert of development. Visitors walking out the back door of George Washington's home see only the Potomac River and distant woods. Walk down a dirt path and one sees teams of oxen, goats, and colonial-era crops, such as corn, cabbage, and flax. Walk along a wooded path and one finds other tourists gazing respectfully on the tomb of the first president of the United States. Continue walking through woods that have not been cut since Washington roamed through them. Fewer than eight miles away but well out of earshot is an intersection of two of the most crowded interstate highways on the eastern seaboard called Spaghetti Junction. Nearby are malls with acres of parking lots. Fifteen miles from Mount Vernon is the nation's capital, filled with gleaming white monuments and countless office buildings.

Mount Vernon, owned by the Mount Vernon Ladies Association, the oldest historical preservation society in the nation, is the shrine it is today thanks to Ann Pamela Cunningham of South Carolina. In 1853 her mother was aboard a ship on the Potomac when the captain tolled the ship's bell as it passed the home where Washington had died in 1799. Mrs. Cunningham was shocked at the dilapidated condition of the home. She founded an association that bought the estate for $200,000. To this day no public funds are spent on its upkeep.

Old Town Alexandria is about 10 miles to the north. George Washington Parkway passes through the center of town.

POINTS OF INTEREST

Mount Vernon Estate and Gardens
★★★★★

3200 Mount Vernon Memorial Pkwy.
T: 703-780-2000
mountvernon.org/index.cfm
April–August daily 8am–5pm; March, September, and October daily 9am–5pm; November–February daily 9am–4pm
Admission: $13

Located just a half-hour from downtown Washington, D.C., Mount Vernon, named after a British admiral, is one of the most visited private homes in the nation. Plan on spending two to three hours roaming the house and grounds. Just behind the current entrance to the estate, a large new museum complex showing two movies and exhibits dedicated to Washington's life is scheduled to open in 2007.

There is always a line waiting to tour the mansion, but it moves quickly as the tours continuously snake through the rooms. Once visitors enter the outbuildings on the left of the mansion that were used as plantation offices, it takes approximately 20 to 30 minutes to exit from the main house. Docents in each room give visitors explanations of what they are seeing. No photography is allowed inside the house.

The exterior of the mansion is interesting in that it appears at first to be made of rock. In reality it is "rusticated" pinewood with sand thrown against the building after fresh coats of paint had been applied to create the look of stone. While Washington could have afforded a brick home, he preferred the modest look of wood. Washington expanded the four rooms of the original house in the 1770s into its current configuration. Visitors who have an interest in historic wood buildings should note that the front of the house bulges outward.

Visitors enter the home through what Washington called the **"new room,"** ★★★★★ as it was the last room he added to the original house. Washington even took time out of his war planning during the Revolution to send letters to Mount Vernon's manager directing him as to how to design the room. It was not finished until two years before Washington's death. Washington's vision of himself as a farmer is evident in the plasterwork and fireplace mantel, which depict farm scenes. The room is set up as if a dance were about to take place. Washington's body lay in this room for three days before its interment in his tomb.

Visitors exit onto the veranda that Washington had built. There are rocking chairs in which visitors are encouraged to sit to enjoy the view of the Potomac.

The **second entrance** ★★★★★ into the house from the veranda goes into the house's original hallway. Prominent in this room is the key to the Bastille prison in Paris, a gift from the Marquis de Lafayette after the French Revolution, which he believed was inspired by Washington and the American Revolution.

Off the hallway are **two parlors** ★★★ and the **small dining room** ★★. On a table is Washington's personal traveling liquor cabinet. The dining room is painted an intensely deep green, which Washington described as "grateful to the eye," though modern-day visitors may think it too bright of a color for a dining room.

There is one **bedroom on the lower level** ★★, a feature some historians consider to have been common and others call rare during colonial days. In the room is a chair said to be Martha's favorite, in which she sat to sew.

The second floor has five bedrooms. The second room is one in which Lafayette stayed on his visit to Mount Vernon in 1784. The other rooms saw a varying procession of important guests as the Washingtons frequently entertained people who would stay for several days.

Washingtons' bed chamber ★★★★★, over the downstairs study, contains the bed in which Washington died on December 14, 1799. This was also Mrs. Washington's office. Her desk is in the corner. Washington took to his bed on Friday, December 13, after becoming chilled the day before while attending to improvements on the property during a snowstorm. He woke in the middle of the night feeling ill, but he refused Martha's request that the servants be wakened to seek a doctor. The doctor was called in the morning, but Washington died on Saturday, the day after he fell ill.

The last room to be visited is the **downstairs study** ★★★★★, where Washington spent most of his daylight hours running his plantation. An interesting feature is a fan chair in which Washington sat, with his feet moving pedals attached to a wooden fan over his head. The large globe was made in England and delivered in 1789, the first year of Washington's presidency. In the bookcases are a number of Washington's books, which once numbered more than 900. He wrote his name on the front piece of each of them.

Outside the mansion are the well-appointed **kitchen** ★★ and slave cabins aligned along North Lane.

Walking down the lane, visitors can find **Washington's original tomb** ★★ and the **newer one** ★★★★★ built in 1837. The United States Congress originally intended for Washington to be buried under the Capitol, but his descendants refused. Washington had requested that he be buried on Mount Vernon's grounds. His sarcophagus is topped by a seal of the United States. This seal shows both eagles' claws gripping a shield.

On a quiet spot overlooking the Potomac is the **slave burial ground** ★★★★★ where at least 75 graves have been found. At Washington's death, there were 316 slaves living on the plantation. His will provided for a fund to be paid out to support elderly slaves.

Beyond the slave burial ground is a field with the types of crops that Washington once grew here. At one end of the field is a round barn he designed to act as a means of using horses walking in a circle to process wheat.

Christ Church ★★

118 North Washington St., Alexandria (George Washington Parkway)
T: 703-549-1450
historicchristchurch.org
Mon–Sat 9am–4pm, Sun 2–4pm
Admission: donation suggested

Finished in 1775, this Episcopal church is where Washington often worshiped when he was in Alexandria on business and still operates as a church today. As was the custom, he rented a pew to help provide income for the church. The Washington pew, the only one preserved in its original box configuration, is still in place. The silver nameplate bearing Washington's name was stolen by a Union soldier during the Civil War. In the church office next door, a display intended for visitors from the North politely asks for the return of the missing nameplate, as well as the communion service, also stolen by occupying Union soldiers.

SITES NEAR MOUNT VERNON

George Washington Birthplace National Monument ★★★★★

Rte. 204 off Rte. 3, 38 miles east of Fredericksburg
T: 804-224-1732
nps.gov/gewa
Daily 9am–5pm; closed major holidays
Admission: $4

This site may be considered off the beaten path by many tourists, but this site has two of the most valuable Washington artifacts in existence. The George Washington Birthplace is situated next to a large creek and is quiet, as relatively few tourists find their way here.

The actual house where Washington was born burned down long ago, but the foundations of the house remain. Behind it is a fine brick house that National Park Service Rangers freely admit looks nothing like the humble home in which Washington was born. This house was built in the 1930s when the site was turned into a national monument and Washington's admirers built a house they felt that he would have liked to have been born in. The house is interpreted as an example of what a wealthy colonial home might have looked like in the early 1700s. Washington's start in life was much more humble in a wooden house.

Inside the visitor center, where a good film of Washington's life can be viewed, are two swords worn by Washington. The first is actually a cutlass, a curved sword normally worn by sailors. Washington wore this cutlass during the American Revolution. When he returned to Mount Vernon after the war, he found he needed a pruning saw. Realizing that one was not readily available, he had his plantation blacksmith turn his cutlass into a pruning saw. Rangers agree that a man turning a priceless military artifact into a pruning saw demonstrates his humble and unassuming nature. It never occurred to Washington that his sword, the symbol of a general who won American independence from England, would be a historic artifact. He needed a pruning saw and his sword was handy.

On display below the pruning saw/cutlass is the dress sword Washington wore on the day he was sworn into the Presidency.

The walk from the visitor center to Washington's supposed birthplace and then back to the visitor center skirts a beautiful creek, goes through some woods, and then past a small colonial-era farm. It makes for a pleasant stroll. Plan on spending at least an hour here.

Stratford Hall ★★★★★

485 Great House Rd., Stratford
(Rte. 214 from Rte. 3, six miles from
Washington's Birthplace)
T: 804-493-8038
stratfordhall.org
Daily 9:30am–4pm; tours of house on the
hour; closed major holidays.
Admission: $10

While widely known and promoted as the birthplace of Confederate General Robert E. Lee, Stratford Hall had a rich colonial history long before Lee was born. Two signers of the Declaration of Independence, Richard Henry Lee and Francis Lightfoot Lee, were also born here. They were the only two brothers to sign the Declaration. They were also both

cousins to Henry "Light Horse Harry" Lee, Robert's father.

Built in the 1730s and designed by an unknown architect, Stratford Hall is a rare colonial example of a house shaped like a capital H. In colonial days, most houses were Georgian blocks. Stratford Hall has a total of eight chimneys and 16 fireplaces. In its day, it was one of the largest houses in the colonies.

Guided tours are limited to 20 people at a time. No photography is allowed in the house. The cradle in which family legend says Richard, Francis, and Robert were all kept as babies is in the **master bedroom ★★★★★**. One family story about Robert is that just before the family was about to leave Stratford to move to Alexandria, four-year-old Robert went missing. When he was found, he told his mother that he had gone back into the house to say good-bye to the angels in his room. In his room is an iron fireplace insert. Embossed on it are angels that only small children can see at their eye level.

Another magnificent room is the **great hall ★★★★★**, which features original paintings of the Lees from the 1700s. Guests are encouraged to sit in chairs pushed against the walls, just as they were when a dance was held.

After leaving the house, visitors are encouraged to roam the grounds. A modern museum details the Lee family, with particular focus on Lee and his father's cousins, Richard and Francis, who were considered leaders in the American Revolution. Displays recount their writings and statements that encouraged other members of the Continental Congress to call for freedom from England.

Plan on spending at least two hours at Stratford Hall.

Ferry Farm ★★★

268 Kings Hwy., Fredericksburg
(Rte. 3 just east of the city)
T: 540-370-0732
kenmore.org/ferryfarm/visiting_ferryfarm.html
Daily 10am–5pm; closed major holidays
Admission: $5

If George Washington ever really threw a penny or a silver dollar across the Rappahannock River, or chopped down a cherry tree and then admitted the deed to his father, it happened here at Ferry Farm. Those stories, staples of the legend of Washington, were related in early biographies of Washington by a man named Parson Weems. Weems was interested in creating an image of Washington as a strong, honest man so that future generations of schoolchildren would admire him. Washington himself never mentioned the two incidents that supposedly took place in his youth.

Washington and his family moved to Ferry Farm in 1738 when George was six years old. Washington's father died here when George was a teenager. He helped his mother and slaves run the farm. George lived here until 1752 when he left to make his way in the world as a surveyor.

The house in which young George lived burned down on Christmas Eve 1740 when he was eight. The house was rebuilt, but burned again in 1862 when Union forces occupied the property before the Battle of Fredericksburg. They also burned most of the trees that were on the property for campfires. (It is not known whether the forces occupying the land knew that it was the childhood home of Washington.)

No colonial structures currently exist at Ferry Farm, but the foundation that owns it is embarking on an ambitious plan to recreate the Washington farm as it may have existed. There is a visitor center detailing Washington's early life, a garden containing colonial crops, and riverside walking trails.

SOURCES & OTHER READING

General George Washington: A Military Life, Edward Lengel, Random House, 2005

George Washington's Mount Vernon, At Home in Revolutionary America, Richard Dalzell, Oxford University Press, 1999

His Excellency: George Washington, Joseph Ellis, Knopf, 2004

Historic Alexandria, Street by Street, A Survey of Existing Early Buildings, Ethelyn Cox, EPM Publications, 1989

Mount Vernon, Wendell Garrett, Monacelli, 1998

Washington, Douglas Southall Freeman, Scribner, 1995

The World of George Washington, Richard Ketchum, American Heritage Publishing, 1974

Websites:
mountvernon.org

Getting to and around Mount Vernon

Ronald Reagan Washington National Airport is less than five miles from Mount Vernon. The airport is served by 14 airlines and numerous rental car companies. Best of all, George Washington Parkway, a highway ending at Mount Vernon, is next to the airport. Just head east on the parkway. Taxis are plentiful and are often used by out-of-towners to reach the attraction. Visitors usually arrange a time for the taxi driver to meet them in front of the gift shop for a return trip.

If staying in downtown Washington without a car, take the yellow Metro subway line to Huntington Station in Virginia. Then take a Fairfax Connection bus to the front gate of Mount Vernon. Call 202-637-7000 or consult wmata.com/default.cfm for details. The bus ride is about 20 minutes to Mount Vernon.

The *Potomac Spirit* is a boat that leaves from Pier 4 at 6th and Water Streets, SW in Washington, on a six-hour cruise of the Potomac, including a stop at Mount Vernon. Cruises leave Tue–Sun from March 13–September 5 and Fri–Sun from September 10–October 2. The boat departs at 8:30am, arrives at Mount Vernon at 10am, then departs for Washington at 1:30pm. It arrives back at the dock at 3pm. The fare, including admission to Mount Vernon, is $35.

Gray Line offers a four-hour tour leaving from Washington's Union Train Station every day at 8:30am. Free pickups are made at many of the city's major hotels. Fare is $30, which includes admission.

Hardier tourists may want to walk or cycle via the Mount Vernon Trail, which parallels the George Washington Parkway for 18 miles, starting at Roosevelt Island, near Rosslyn. This asphalt trail is crowded on weekends, but it is flat and scenic.

Accommodations

Aaron Shipman House

Q St. NW near 13th St., Washington, D.C.
T: 877-893-3233 or 413-582-9888
aaronshipmanhouse.com
$75–$225

Built in 1887, this Victorian home features original wood paneling, stained glass windows, antique chandeliers, and a Victorian-style lattice porch. It is 10 miles from Alexandria.

Chester A. Arthur House B&B

13th and P Streets, NW (Logan Circle), Washington, D.C.
T: 877-893-3233 or 413-582-9888
$115–$165

This Victorian house was built in 1883. It features a mahogany-paneled staircase spiraling up three stories and double parlors.

Inn at DuPont Circle

1312 19th St. NW, Washington, D.C.
T: 866-467-2100 or 202-467-6777
theinnatdupontcircle.com
$95–$215

The inn is an 1885 Victorian townhouse. It is a half-block from the DuPont Metro station and the Circle, surrounded by outdoor cafes, restaurants, and embassies.

Relais & Chateaux Morrison House

116 S. Alfred St., Alexandria, VA
T: 866-834-668 or 703-838-8000
morrisonhouse.com
$150–$400
The Morrison House is in the heart of the historic district of Alexandria. Ronald Reagan Washington National Airport is three miles from the house.

Jamestown

Virginia

John Smith looking out over the James River

THE EARLY YEARS

The first successful English colony in the New World is located adjacent to a recreated living-history village. Visitors to the original site can watch archaeologists uncover real history, while next door reenactors depict living history.

After Queen Elizabeth's death in 1603, her successor, King James I, was not immediately interested in setting up colonies. James even beheaded Sir Walter Raleigh, the man who had organized the first failed English colonies in the 1580s, as a means of discouraging other dreamers interested in the New World.

But rumors of gold in North America and knowledge of gold coming from Mexico, Central America, and South America in Spain's treasure fleets finally won King James over. He warmed to the idea that England should colonize again. In 1606, King James authorized the creation of the Virginia Company and the Plymouth Company, two private enterprises that would fund new colonies—and develop vastly different ideas about how colonization should work.

The Plymouth Company took much longer than the Virginia Company to organize itself. Eventually, it changed its charter name and found a group of colonists to send over in 1620. These hardworking religious separatists sailed from Plymouth, England, in search of a land where they could practice their religion without fear of government intervention. They landed in what would become Massachusetts and named their colony after the town they had left. History remembers them by a name they never used: Pilgrims.

The Virginia Company started on its venture 20 years earlier than the Plymouth Company. This colony's backers had no concerns about religious freedom. What interested them was a big return on their investment. Their plan was to send colonists to the New World with two major objectives: to find gold and to develop a cash crop that would support the colony when gold became scarce. Many of the men who volunteered for this colony were noblemen who were entitled to land in England, but who had no access to property because all land titles had been issued by previous kings. While the men were adventurous, they had few of the skills necessary to survive in the wilderness—a flaw in the company's colonization plan that haunted the colonists for years.

After a rough Atlantic crossing during which more than 40 men died, three ships sailed up a river they named the James in May 1607. On board were 101 men and four boys. No women made the voyage as the colony was not supposed to be a family venture. The men named their new home Jamestown, and it would become the first successful English colony in the new world (founded 30 years after three colonies on Roanoke Island had failed).

Bad luck dogged the Jamestown colonists from the beginning. One ship carrying a few experienced outdoorsmen was stranded by a storm in Jamaica, leaving the first settlers without leaders who were knowledgeable about hunting, fishing, and farming. It took several months for those men to make their way to Jamestown. By August 1609, more colonists had arrived, but Jamestown still suffered from a lack of leaders who had the necessary survival skills. When colony leader Captain John Smith was injured and returned to England to recover, Jamestown was left to fend for itself.

The colony virtually collapsed in Smith's absence. Though it had been established for more than two years, Jamestown still was not self-sufficient. Its settlers still depended upon supplies being brought in from England. Scores died in the winter of 1609–10, now remembered as the Starving Time. Only 90 of the original 214 settlers were alive by the spring of 1610. At least some of the survivors became cannibals, murdering each other or eating the bodies of the buried dead.

The colony limped along for another two years with no clear sense of purpose. It became clear that there was no gold in Virginia. Their second purpose of developing a cash crop had also failed. The tobacco the Indians grew and smoked had been promising as a crop, but its flavor was rejected by English gentlemen as too harsh.

Finally, in 1612, a colonist named James Rolfe began to grow a milder-tasting tobacco from seeds he had obtained from South America. A young Indian woman nicknamed Pocahontas helped Rolfe cultivate his new seeds. She helped Rolfe crosspollinate his South American tobacco with the native Indian leaf. They then worked together to develop the process to dry and grind the leaves so that it could be smoked in pipes.

In 1614, Rolfe and Pocahontas were married. They sailed to England to sell their first crop. The milder tobacco was instantly popular among the wealthy, who demanded more from the Jamestown colony. Over the next several years, tobacco became the gold that the settlers in Virginia had set out for. Growing tobacco became so popular and profitable that Jamestown's leaders had to force colonists to set aside acreage to grow food so that they would never again find themselves in the dire straits of 1609.

In 1619, the colonists decided to form their own government. In July of that year, the colony's settlers met to discuss forming a representative form of government that would establish laws for all of Virginia. While the significance of what they were doing escaped the settlers, it was the first time in the history of the New World that people were establishing their own laws separate from those of their king back in England.

In the summer of 1619, a Dutch trading ship sailed up the river with a cargo of blacks from Africa. Some were exchanged for food. For the first few decades that blacks were in Virginia, they were treated the same as white indentured servants. They and their master agreed on a length of time that they would work, usually seven years. After that, they were free men. However, within 50 years of the arrival of the Dutch ship, the concept of indentured servitude faded and was replaced by the institution of slavery.

Life along the James River swamps never got any easier for the settlers of Jamestown. While they never made the exact connection between mosquito bites and malaria, eventually the colony's leaders began to associate the swamps with poor health. When the Jamestown courthouse burned in 1668, the leaders of the colony took the opportunity to move the colony's residents inland, away from the river that brought both illness and the possibility of raiding ships from other countries. The tiny settlement that they chose to move to was then called Middle Plantation, as it was halfway between the York and the James Rivers. The settlement had been established as an early warning way station to protect Jamestown from Indian raids. They renamed it Williamsburg.

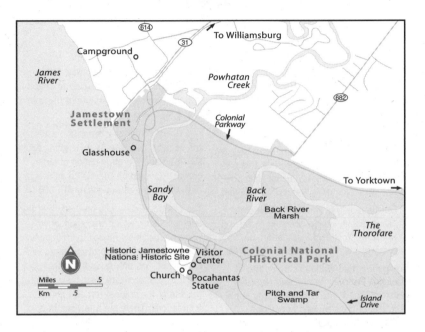

SOURCES & OTHER READING

A Land as God Made It: Jamestown and the Birth of America, James Horn, Basic Books, 2005

The Jamestown Adventure, Accounts of the Virginia Colony 1605–1614, Ed Southern, editor, John F. Blair Publisher, 2004

Jamestown and the Virginia Colony (Seeds of Change in American History), Daniel Rosen, National Geographic Society, 2004

Jamestown, Virginia: The Town Site and its Story, Charles Hatch, National Park Service, 1957

Love and Hate in Jamestown: John Smith, Pocahontas, and the Start of a New Nation, David Price, Vintage, 2005

Websites:

tobacco.org/History/Jamestown.html

JAMESTOWN TODAY

Jamestown is really two different places coexisting side by side. They are easily confused with each other. There is Historic Jamestowne, the site of the original colony, which is now within the confines of the Jamestown National Historic Site administered by the National Park Service. To make it even more confusing, this park is part of the Colonial National Historical Park, which includes Yorktown Battlefield.

Then there is the Jamestown Settlement, a living-history village operated by the Jamestown-Yorktown Foundation, an agency of the commonwealth of Virginia.

If coming from Williamsburg on the Colonial Parkway, Jamestown National Historic Site is reached by turning left at the end of the parkway. Jamestown Settlement, the attraction hosted by historical interpreters, is reached by turning right at the end of the Parkway. National Park Service Rangers are used to directing visitors from the original site of the colony to the recreated colony.

The visitor center at Historic Jamestowne, the national park site, is undergoing extensive renovation in anticipation of large crowds expected on the 400th anniversary of the founding of the colony in 2007.

There is no modern city on the site of the original colony, which was abandoned when the colonists moved to Williamsburg. Evidence of Jamestown disappeared over time and it has only been in recent decades that archaeologists have found the site of the original fort and house foundations. There are a few scattered houses and a marina at Jamestown, but no true "downtown" Jamestown.

POINTS OF INTEREST

Historic Jamestowne National Historic Site
★★★★★

East end of Colonial Pkwy.
T: 757-229-1733
nps.gov/jame
Entrance Station daily 8:30am–4:30pm
Admission: $8 for Jamestowne only or $10 for a joint ticket to also see the Yorktown Battlefield. If already holding a ticket from Yorktown, the charge will be $5 for admission to Jamestowne

Historic Jamestowne, the first permanent English settlement in America, must be one of the few—perhaps only—historic sites in the nation where visitors can watch archaeologists uncovering history on a daily basis. Visitors can walk up to the edge of an excavation hole and watch the work being done by archaeologists employed by the Association for the Preservation of Virginia's Antiquities. Volunteers with the APVA will describe what is being done and show visitors maps of the sites at Jamestowne that have already been excavated and photographs of what has been found.

Archaeology is not exciting to watch (it consists largely of men and women spooning and brushing away dirt from their latest find). But what they are working on is tremendously exciting. In 2004, a well that the colonists apparently used as a trash pit once it ran dry was excavated. Items found in it give evidence of what life was like in the early 17th century. One unhappy soldier tossed his chest armor in the well.

At the end of 2005, the archaeologists were working on what may be the foundation of the house occupied by the famous John Smith, the professional soldier who was one of the first leaders of the colony. In earlier years, archaeologists uncovered evidence of Jamestown's original wood palisade, which had long been thought to have washed away into the James River. Archaeologists now believe that most of the Jamestown colony is buried several feet below the surface of today's ground level. A new exhibit building that will focus on archaeology at Jamestown is under construction.

Jamestown's archaeology can create more mysteries than it solves. For instance, several years ago a fragment of skull was unearthed that showed signs of blunt-force trauma. The man had been hit from behind with a club. The skull also showed signs that a doctor had tried to alleviate pressure on the man's brain by drilling holes into the skull. The archaeologists determined that the doctor stopped his operation before penetrating the victim's skull. It is guessed that the man died. The identity of the man is unknown. It is also unknown if he was murdered by a fellow colonist, or attacked by an Indian.

The only building to see at Jamestowne is the Jamestown Church. It was built in 1907, but is behind a church tower dating to 1647 that was added to a church built in 1639.

Near the church is a bronze statue of Pocahontas erected in 1922. It was cast with little regard to what clothes she might really have worn. She is depicted with a single feather in her hair, a fashion that might have been more common to the Plains Indians. Near the river is a statue of Captain John Smith, erected in 1907 on the 300th anniversary of the founding of the colony.

There are quiet walking paths that lead away from the bustle of the archaeological zone into the New Towne area of Jamestown, where houses were erected in the 1660s. Brick construction became more common in this time period after settlers realized that they could lessen the fire danger to their homes. None of those houses survive. Only replica brick foundations remain.

Upon leaving the original site of Jamestown, visitors can a take three- or five-mile **driving tour** ★★★ of the marshy Jamestown Island. This wetland demonstrates why the settlers never enjoyed living here.

On a side note, Jamestown Island was vital to the Confederate cause during the Civil War. Because it was so far removed from civilization, Confederate Lt. John Mercer Brooke used it for a proving ground for the cannon that he invented. He also used it as a testing ground for armor plating that would eventually be installed on the ironclad CSS *Virginia*. Brooke fired round after round from cannons into various thicknesses of iron plating backed by varying thicknesses of wood planks. He wanted to determine both the thickness necessary to stop Union cannon rounds from piercing the iron plating, as well as the angle the armor should be mounted to cause the cannon balls and shells to ricochet harmlessly away. Exhibits encountered on the drive explain Brooke's experiments on the island.

Jamestowne Glasshouse ★★★

To the right after passing through entrance to the park

The original Jamestown settlers included two glass blowers, but they were never able to establish a viable venture. It was not until several decades later that glass blowing became a common activity in Jamestown. The remains of the original glass works were discovered in 1954 and recreated here. While the glass blowers wear colonial period clothing, their fire is heated by natural gas rather than wood. Glass pieces that look like they are from the period are for sale, but the artisans warn that they are not to be used for anything other than ornamental purposes.

Allow at least two to three hours to see the site of the first successful colony.

Jamestown Settlement ★★★★★

Just to north of Historic Jamestowne
T: 757-253-4838
historyisfun.org/jamestown/jamestown.cfm
Daily 9am–5pm;
mid-June–mid-August 9am–6pm
Admission: $17 for combination ticket to both Jamestown Settlement and Yorktown Victory Center

Jamestown Settlement opened in 1957 as Jamestown Festival Park on the 350th anniversary of the founding of Jamestown. Its name was changed to Jamestown Settlement in 1990. This living history village located within a wooden stockade is a faithful recreation of what Jamestown must have looked like when it was founded in 1607.

While everything looks period in this recreated Jamestown, the interpreters speak in modern-day language in order to explain to 21st-century visitors what life was like in a 17th-century colony. The house roofs are thatched with river reeds. The houses and church walls are made of wood coated with mud. The church, where settlers gathered twice a day to hear worship services, is at the center of the colony. The first representative government in the colony was established in 1619 in a building similar to this.

Historical interpreters roam the site encouraging visitors to ask questions about life in Jamestown. When they are not talking to tourists, the interpreters do chores just as the original settlers would have done. For instance, in late 2005, several interpreters were building a new guardhouse using tools that would have only been available to the original settlers.

The settlement depicts life around 1620, at least 13 years after the colony was firmly established. The date can be assumed because female interpreters are employed. The first 90 unmarried women arrived in Jamestown in 1620, a year after the first Africans arrived. (Coincidentally, 1620 was the same year that the Plymouth colony in what would become Massachusetts was established. Women had always been a part of that colony's plans, while it took 13 years for the first women to arrive in Jamestown.)

One difference between this living-history settlement and most museums with static displays is that military interpreters dressed in breastplate armor can demonstrate the weapons of the day. Particularly interesting is the demonstration of the 17th-century matchlock musket. The matchlock was a large shotgun that was the forerunner of the flintlock musket that would be used 150 years later during the French and Indian War and the American Revolution. Pulling the handle-like trigger on a matchlock releases a spring that brings a smoldering rope into contact with gunpowder in a small bowl. Once that powder is ignited, a spark flashes into the musket, setting off the charge inside the musket's barrel. That, in turn, sends a charge of lead balls toward the target, be it Indians or game. Visitors are encouraged to try on armor and helmets to get a sense of their feel and weight.

While the period depicted here is 1620, interpreters are also willing and capable of discussing Jamestown's complicated existence from its founding in 1607 through its eventual abandonment in 1698.

In 1622, 15 years after the settlement had been founded, the Indians finally realized that the Englishmen would never stop coming to the shores of America. On a single day, they attacked several settlements outside of Jamestown and killed more than 350 Englishmen, nearly a third of the population. The English colonists reacted by attacking the Indian villages.

In addition to worrying about Indians, the colonists also had to concern themselves with what was happening back in England. In 1649, King Charles I was overthrown and beheaded. The Jamestown colony was then threatened with abandonment by the new parliament. In 1660, England restricted the colony's active trading with the Dutch. In 1676, some outlying colonists under a settler named Nathaniel Bacon raided Jamestown and burned it to protest their belief that the colonial government was not doing enough to protect their outlying farms from Indian raids.

Jamestown Settlement interpreters make the point with visitors that the gentlemen who first settled Jamestown were not lazy (as they have sometimes been characterized in print). They were simply unprepared for the rigors of the American wilderness and untrained in survival skills. The planners of the expedition had always intended to keep the colony supplied with food from England rather than ensure that the settlers were trained how to hunt or grow their own food once the colony was firmly established.

At the waterfront are replicas of three ships that brought the Jamestown settlers across the Atlantic: the *Susan Constant, the Godspeed,* and the tiny *Discovery.* All three ships are seaworthy and occasionally set forth to visit coastal cities to promote Jamestown Settlement. Interpreters are on board to describe sailors' chores and skills, such as how the navigators found their way across the ocean. One simple device on board shows how navigators estimated their hourly speed—by using a board dragging behind and feeling knots of rope pass through the sailors' fingers. The term "knot" is still used by modern sailors to describe their average speed through the water. A new *Godspeed,* still based on 17th-century ship designs, is scheduled to be delivered mid-2006.

Outside the stockade is a recreated Powhatan village as might have existed when Powhatan and his daughter Pocahontas kept a friendly but wary eye on the colonists. The Indian huts are made of bark. During growing seasons, the interpreters demonstrate how food was grown and processed. These Indians coexisted with the settlers until 1622.

The galleries inside the modern buildings present the story of the first English colonies in well-done displays and panels. Colonization is viewed from both the English and the Indian sides.

Allow at least three hours to see the film and to visit the settlement and ships.

GETTING TO AND AROUND JAMESTOWN

Jamestown can be reached by air from two different airports that are equally distant from the site. To the north about 60 miles is Richmond International Airport, served by seven airlines and car rental companies. To the southeast is Norfolk International Airport, served by six airlines and seven rental car companies. There are no public transportation options to reach Jamestown. Richmond likely makes the most sense as a destination airport because it is on the south side of the city. Norfolk's airport is closer in to the city and more likely to be affected by heavy traffic. (However, visitors wanting to include Civil War tour sites as well as visits to the ocean may find Norfolk's airport more convenient to those attractions.) Private aircraft can land at the Williamsburg-Jamestown Airport, but there is no commercial airline service here.

Visitors heading from or through southern Virginia north toward Jamestown and Williamsburg might want to consider taking a ferry to those towns rather than taking the interstate loop around Richmond on I-195 to I-64 east. Jamestown is within a mile of the Jamestown-Scotland Ferry. During daylight hours, the ferry runs every 20 minutes across the James River. The trip itself takes about 20 minutes. At night, the trips drop back to every hour from each side with the Scotland side leaving on the hour and the Jamestown side leaving on the half hour. The trip may or may not save time considering Richmond's traffic, but the experience of the ferry ride across the wide, historic James is quite relaxing.

Jamestown is linked to both Williamsburg and Yorktown, 25 miles away, by means of the Colonial Parkway, a two-lane, limited-access road that runs from the James River to the York River. The speed limit is only 45 miles per hour. Visitors who want to bring their bikes can easily ride between Yorktown and Jamestown.

Left to right, top to bottom:

1. Yorktown Victory Monument, VA

2. Abatis at Fort Ticonderoga, NY

3. Statue of Gen. Nathaniel Greene
   Guilford C.H., Greensboro, NC

4. Benjamin Franklin's Grave,
   Philadelphia, PA

5. Lost Colony Theater on Roanoke
   Island, NC

Left to right, top to bottom:

1. British soldiers' grave in Concord, MA

2. Capitol of New Bern, NC

3. Captain John Smith at Jamestown, VA

4. Moores Creek Bridge, NC

5. Colonial Cemetery, Savannah, GA

GRAVE OF BRITISH SOLDIERS

"THEY CAME THREE THOUSAND MILES AND DIED,
TO KEEP THE PAST UPON ITS THRONE:
UNHEARD, BEYOND THE OCEAN TIDE,
THEIR ENGLISH MOTHER MADE HER MOAN."

APRIL 19, 1775

Left to right, top to bottom:

1. Bunker Hill monument outside Boston, MA

2. Cannon overlooking Hudson River at Saratoga, NY

3. George Rogers Clark statue, Vincennes, IN

4. Fort Stanwix, NY

5. Castillo de San Marcos, St. Augustine, FL

Left to right, top to bottom:

1. Minute Man statue in Concord, MA

2. Mural of Clark meeting Indians, Vincennes, IN

3. Cabins at Tannenbaum Historic Park, Greensboro, NC

4. Green River Road in Cowpens, SC

5. Colonial Army doctor's tools at Yorktown Victory Center, VA

Left to right, top to bottom:

1. Old State House, Boston, MA

2. Ferguson's cairn at Kings
   Mountain, SC

3. Castillo de San Marcos in
   St. Augustine, FL

4. Spinning flax, historic
   Brattonsville, SC

5. Front gate of Fort Stanwix, NY

Left to right, top to bottom:

1. Cold Stream Guards in Old
   Salem, NC

2. Governor's Palace,
   Williamsburg, VA

3. The *Godspeed* at
   Jamestown Settlement, VA

4. Crest held by Tories at Kings
   Mountain, SC

5. Interior of Plimoth Plantation
   house, Plymouth, MA

Left to right, top to bottom:

1. Cannon at Brandywine, PA

2. Main house at Mount Vernon, VA

3. Tavern, Camden, SC

4. The dungeon, Old Exchange, Charleston, SC

5. Plimoth Plantation, Plymouth, MA

Left to right, top to bottom:

1. Sentry at Old Barracks,
   Trenton, NJ

2. American artillery at
   Saratoga, NY

3. Cannons, Ft. Ticonderoga, NY

4. Washington's Headquarters in
   Morristown, NJ

5. Winter quarters, Valley Forge, PA

ACCOMMODATIONS

A Boxwood Inn of Williamsburg

708 Richmond Rd., Williamsburg
T: 888-798-4333 or 757-221-6607
boxwoodinn.com
$99–$195

This Dutch colonial was built in 1928 and is just a few blocks from the historic district. It is noted for its award-winning perennial gardens and its back porch.

A Williamsburg White House

718 Jamestown Rd., Williamsburg
T: 866-229-8580 or 757-229-8580
awilliamsburgwhitehouse.com
$115–$199

This home was built in 1904 and is the oldest home currently operating as a bed-and-breakfast in Historic Williamsburg.

Colonial Houses of Historic Williamsburg:
make reservations at history.org or call 800-447-8679

These restored colonial-era houses are on the property of Colonial Williamsburg and are ideal for people staying for several days who want to tour the town casually. The Colonial Houses offer accommodations in colonial style at 28 guest houses, some as small as one room within a tavern and others as large as 16 rooms. All are furnished with authentic period reproductions and antiques that makes one feel as if one is living in a period house.

Fife and Drum Inn

441 Prince George St., Williamsburg
T: 888-838-1783
fifeanddruminn.com
$155–$175

A. Webster Hitchens was a successful merchant in the 1920s and he built this house in 1933. The inn is still owned and operated by the Hitchens family.

Williamsburg Manor Bed & Breakfast

600 Richmond Rd., Williamsburg
T: 800-422-8011 or 757-220-8011
williamsburg-manor.com
$109–$179

This is a colonial-looking house built in 1927 and decorated in Colonial Williamsburg colors and period furniture. The Manor is conveniently located three blocks from the historic area and one block from the College of William and Mary.

Note:
Also see the accommodations on p.139.

Williamsburg &
Yorktown

Virginia

Bruton Parish is an original church building.

THE EARLY YEARS

The premier colonial history destination of the nation started humbly in 1633 as Middle Plantation, a small settlement midway between the York and James Rivers that acted as an early-warning station for the settlers at Jamestown in the event of an attack by Indians.

Jamestown was low and swampy and prone to flooding during heavy rains. Williamsburg was higher and drier with fresh streams surrounding it. When the courthouse at Jamestown burned to the ground in 1698, the settlers decided it was time to move the entire population inland to Middle Plantation.

The move precipitated a new sense among the settlers that Virginia had a bright future. Perhaps anticipating a move in the future, the leaders of the colony, including the settlers of Jamestown, had petitioned the king to bring a college to Virginia. Even in early discussions, the location of that school was always going to be Middle Plantation rather than Jamestown. In 1693, six years before the capital moved, King William and Queen Mary chartered and funded a college at Middle Plantation that would bear their names. The first building opened in 1700, one year after Middle Plantation changed its name to Williamsburg in honor of King William III.

As the 18th century dawned, Williamsburg and Virginia flourished with the exploding popularity of tobacco in Europe, guaranteeing the arrival of more colonists and the accompanying increased need for all sorts of merchants and craftsmen. The skill-less gentlemen of Jamestown who had struggled to survive during the first years of the colony were replaced by more ambitious men and growing numbers of women.

By the mid-18th century, Virginia was firmly established as one of the most successful of the English colonies. Its general assembly governed the people with a two-house system. The House of Burgesses was elected from the counties, and a 12-member upper-house governor's council was appointed by the king. The colony's government had been in place for more than 100 years before the first true visible rifts between Virginia and England appeared in 1765 with the king's imposition of the Stamp Act.

This first attempt to tax the colonies came as a shock to the Virginians. They believed that since Virginia had no representatives in England, there should be no taxation without representation. The House of Burgesses sent a formal protest of the Stamp Act to the king. Younger firebrands in the House of Burgesses, who had fewer ties to England, denounced the tax in speeches that some elders considered bordering on treasonous. Still, the resistance was so vehement that King George III repealed the tax in 1766.

Virginia's once-warm relationship with the king and his governors never recovered. Early in 1771, Patrick Henry and Thomas Jefferson, two of the legislators most angry with the king, organized a committee to begin coordinating protests with other colonies. Until now, most colonies had traded with each other but had seen no need to organize into any force that would lobby on their behalf before the king. In 1774, when Virginia's House of Burgesses voted for a day of fasting in support of the recent Boston Tea Party, the royal governor dissolved the body. That resulted in the same men deciding among themselves to form Virginia's delegation to the First Continental Congress in 1775.

In May 1776, members of the Virginia Convention voted to ask the Continental Congress to declare the colonies free of England, producing a document that Jefferson would use as a model for the Declaration of Independence. Patrick Henry was elected the first governor of the new commonwealth and moved into the home of the former royal governor.

Ironically, Williamsburg's lead in pushing for colonial independence would be its undoing. In 1780, the capital moved to Richmond because Williamsburg, located between the York and the James Rivers, was deemed too open to British attack (and the town did indeed experience a brief British occupation before Lord Cornwallis surrendered his forces in 1781). With the capital gone, Williamsburg reverted to being just another quiet Virginia town until the early part of the 20th century, when historical preservationists recognized the opportunity to turn it into a living-history town that would forever commemorate the early days of colonial America.

Nearby Yorktown, located on the western banks of the York River, was founded in 1691 as a port to ship tobacco back to England. It was an immediate success and a bustling place into the mid-18th century. It escaped the war until the summer of 1781 when it attracted the attention of British General Lord Cornwallis. After winning the bloody Battle of Guilford Courthouse, North Carolina, in March of that year, Cornwallis did not stay in either of the two Carolinas where results in defeating the Americans had been mixed. Instead, he moved north into Virginia, intending to decimate the scattered, small units of Patriots. Those units, under the young French nobleman Lafayette, fell back before him, luring the British further down onto the Virginia peninsula between the York and the James Rivers. Cornwallis had not considered that by moving onto a peninsula he would be limiting his own ability to escape.

Cornwallis finally stopped his march at Yorktown where he settled in to wait for reinforcements and supplies from his superior, Henry Clinton, then in New York City. Clinton's army was being harassed by French and American troops and was in no position to help Cornwallis, who had moved to Virginia without any direct orders.

When word reached American General George Washington and French General Comte de Rochambeau that a British force was camped at Yorktown, they embarked on a bold plan to capture it. In late August, the French and American armies began a secret 450-mile march south toward Yorktown, coordinating with a French fleet that would blockade the mouth of the York River to prevent any supplies from reaching Cornwallis.

By mid-September, the pieces were in place—the French fleet was cruising the Chesapeake Bay and the combined American and French armies were in Williamsburg, just 10 miles from Cornwallis. The French fleet fought and drove off a British fleet that intended to resupply Cornwallis, and the Allies began a siege of the British trenches.

For three weeks, the Americans and French shelled British positions. When the British fleet sailed away without breaking the French blockade, Cornwallis was trapped. On October 19, 1781, his army of 8,000 men surrendered. The British Parliament's will to continue fighting was broken. The treaty ending the war was signed two years later.

SITE
13

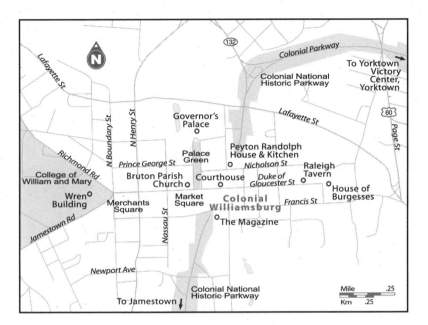

SOURCES & OTHER READING

Colonial Houses: The Historic Homes of Williamsburg, Hugh Howard, Henry Abrams, 2004

Guns of Independence: The Siege of Yorktown, 1781, Jerome Greene, Savas Beattie, 2005

The Majesty of Colonial Williamsburg, Peter Beney, Colonial Williamsburg Foundation, Pelican Publishing, 1997

Victory at Yorktown: The Campaign that Won the Revolution, Richard Ketchum, Henry Holt, 2004

Williamsburg Before and After: The Rebirth of Virginia's Colonial Capital, George Yetter, Colonial Williamsburg Foundation, 1988

Williamsburg, Virginia, A City before the State: An Illustrated History, Robert P. Maccubbin, University of Virginia Press, 2000

WILLIAMSBURG & YORKTOWN TODAY

Williamsburg is a thriving, small town of fewer than 12,000 people. It is the county seat of James City County. The town's central attractions are Colonial Williamsburg and the College of William and Mary, one of the oldest universities in the nation.

Few visitors go anywhere in Williamsburg other than Colonial Williamsburg, but there are some nice shops on the west end of the historic area that buffer Colonial Williamsburg from the College of William and Mary. The college itself is open to tourists who want to stroll the campus to see its oldest building, the Wren Building, which dates back to 1700.

The holidays in Williamsburg, particularly around Christmas, are crowded with tourists. That is because the Colonial Williamsburg-owned houses and buildings are decorated as they might have been in colonial times.

Yorktown remains small with fewer than 200 people. Yorktown retains a colonial look with several homes from that period. There is no longer a port of Yorktown, the reason for its founding, but it does have a thriving waterfront with shops, restaurants, and a museum that looks at the life of Virginia's watermen. Visitors should find a place to park on the waterfront in Yorktown then stroll the village, up one street and down the other. They will find a mix of private homes and shops.

POINTS OF INTEREST

Colonial Williamsburg ★★★★★
Exit 238 from I-64 (follow signs)
T: 757-229-1000
history.org
Daily 9am–5:30pm
Admission: There are a variety of ticket plans. The two most popular are $34 for a single day ticket or $59 for a year's pass. Seasonal nighttime programs such as singing, watching a period trial, etc. are extra, with most around $15 per person

By the early 1920s, Williamsburg, once the colonial capital of Virginia, had become just another Virginia town. Its colonial buildings were disappearing, and its ties to the history of the nation were being forgotten. The rector of Bruton Parish Episcopal Church on Duke of Gloucester Street went to philanthropist John D. Rockefeller with a bold idea: restore and recreate the historic downtown as it was during the American Revolution. Rockefeller jumped at the idea. The Colonial Williamsburg Foundation was created, and 80 different colonial-era buildings were saved and restored to their 18th-century appearance. The authenticity of the restoration and recreation is due to surviving insurance sketches made by adjusters of the 18th century.

Today, Colonial Williamsburg encompasses more than 300 acres with the buildings that are open for touring marked with a flag. All of the houses found in the historic district are owned by Colonial Williamsburg, some of which have been assigned as living quarters for employees. These are not open for touring, but during the Christmas season these homes become part of the historic area's attraction because their front doors are decorated with wreaths of greenery, fruits, and nuts. There are buildings where trades such as gunsmithing, silversmithing, millinery, cabinetry, and blacksmithing are all open to the public. Interpreters talk about their crafts and life in the 1700s. The following are just a few of the more popular buildings.

House of Burgesses ★★★★★ is where Virginians like Thomas Jefferson, George Washington, and Patrick Henry met to discuss the future of the colony. This was also where court was held. Programs conducted here include the trial of a suspected witch based on an actual case with the actors reading lines recorded from the trial's transcript. At Christmas, choirs sing period carols and religious songs.

Raleigh Tavern ★★★★★, established in 1717, was one of the centers of rebellion before the American Revolution. When the House of Burgesses was dissolved in 1769 by the royal governor of Virginia, the legislators walked down the block and met at the Raleigh Tavern.

The Magazine ★★★★★ was a central part of Williamsburg, meant to supply the citizen militia with gunpowder, shot, and muskets in the event of a military emergency. It proved to be a flash point of rebellion on April 20, 1775 (one day after the British and Patriot militia clashed in Lexington and Concord, Massachusetts), when the British royal governor tried to confiscate the gunpowder under cover of darkness. Alert citizens surrounded the

magazine and drove off the British soldiers. By June of that year, the governor had fled and the magazine fell into Patriot hands. Today's magazine displays a collection of original and reproduction Brown Bess muskets, the primary weapon of the British army.

Bruton Parish Church ★★★★★ is still an active Episcopal church, but visitors are welcome to tour it during the weekdays and attend church on Sunday. The building dates back to 1715 and features the colonial-style pulpit from which the rector stands high above the congregation. Thomas Jefferson, George Washington, Richard Henry Lee, George Wythe, Patrick Henry, and George Mason all worshiped here in these simple wooden pews.

Governor's Palace ★★★★★ is breathtaking. It was designed to impress, and it does. When visitors first walk into the foyer and look up, they see scores of muskets mounted on the ceiling. The display of firepower was meant to awe the governor's friends and intimidate his enemies, implying that any man who had access to so many muskets was not a man to be taken lightly.

The original palace took more than 16 years to build, finally opening to an awed public in 1722. The 10,000-square-foot house, acting as both the governor's mansion and his official office, was one of the largest buildings in the new nation. Nine different governors, including Patrick Henry and Thomas Jefferson, lived here before and after the Revolution. The original palace burned in 1781. It was rebuilt and opened to the public in 1934.

Near the Governor's Palace is the **Peyton Randolph House ★★★★★**. Randolph, the first president of the Continental Congress, is not well remembered as one of the leaders of the American Revolution. That is because he died on

October 23, 1775, barely six months after the shooting began at Lexington and Concord. Randolph was known as a cool and cautious man with a steady nature, just the sort of man to slowly but surely lead the discussion on beginning a rebellion. His house, dating back to 1715, was restored in the 1930s.

There are several operating taverns in the historic area with similar dining fare. All require reservations at night, but allow walk-up dining at lunch. During the evening, entertainment in the taverns might range from strolling musicians to a discussion of the politics of the day with a costumed character. Mr. Shields himself has been known to walk among the diners at Shields Tavern.

Wren Building ★★★★★, two blocks west of the historic area, is also open to tourists. The original building for the College of William and Mary named for Christopher Wren, the famed English architect, was destroyed by fire on three different occasions, but restored each time to its present look. Students still attend classes in the building.

Living history at Williamsburg does not end after most of the buildings close. There are a variety of nighttime programs including concerts, period dancing, trials based on actual transcripts, and even ghost walks within the historic area. Book these extra programs before leaving the visitor center.

Seeing Williamsburg properly will require at least two full days and maybe three if visitors would like to spend time talking to the interpreters.

YORKTOWN

Yorktown Battlefield ★★★★★

Colonial National Historical Park
Exit 242 or Exit 250 from I-64
(follow signs)
T: 757-898-2410
nps.gov/yonb/
Visitor Center: 8:30am–5pm; grounds open sunrise to sunset
Admission: $5 for Yorktown. Combine with Historic Jamestowne for $10 admission

Yorktown's National Park Service rangers do their best to dispel misconceptions about what happened at Yorktown. The two statements they most often hear from visitors are that "the British army was captured" and that "the American Revolution was won" at Yorktown. The truth is that "a" British army of 8,000 men surrendered here. More than 30,000 British soldiers were still in the colonies, and the British still held the major ports of New York City and Charleston. Cornwallis's surrender was embarrassing, but it was not militarily devastating.

As to the second misconception, the American Revolution did not end at Yorktown. There were numerous skirmishes, though no major battles, after Cornwallis's men left. The overall British commander in the colonies was still in place in New York City and he had not authorized any wholesale surrender of his forces. The war technically continued until the Treaty of Paris was signed on September 30, 1783. During those two years, both sides nervously eyed each other until the last British forces left New York City in November 1783, more than two years after the Siege of Yorktown.

What really happened after Yorktown was that the British Parliament finally acknowledged years of simmering frustration and the fact that their commanders had not won the war in America much earlier. When word of Cornwallis's surrender of 8,000 soldiers got back to England, Parliament grew more vocal about saying it was time to let the colonies leave the British empire. Even though it would take two years for the colonies and England to reach an agreement, all real support for continuing the war ended.

Yorktown's visitor center has two rare artifacts on display, a Hessian flag and Washington's campaign tent. The tent is displayed so that a visitor can walk inside it (the tent itself is protected by Plexiglas). A scale model of a British ship, complete with its original cannons, has been reconstructed inside the visitor center so that visitors can get a small taste of how confining life on an 18th-century ship must have been.

The visitor center is near the center of the British inner defensive line. Just to the south is a set of **reconstructed trenches** ★★ that were once occupied by the British. To the east of the visitor center is a collection of **period artillery** ★★★★. About 300 yards further south are **Redoubts Number 9** ★★★★★ and **10** ★★★★★. The capture of these two small forts from the British on the night of October 14, 1781, doomed the British interior line. From these forts, the Allies could wheel in heavier cannons and shell the British lines from an easy distance. Three days after the loss of these redoubts, Cornwallis sent word to the Allies that he wanted to surrender.

The Grand French Battery ★★★★★, noted as Stop B on the tour road map, marks the first siege line established on October 9 by the French. A heavy French cannon is found here. It was not until this line was established and the first French shells began to land within his lines that Cornwallis realized how truly dire his situation was.

The rest of the sites around Yorktown Battlefield must be seen either by bicycle or car. There are two tour roads—a seven-mile battlefield tour and a nine-mile Allied encampment tour. The most significant feature on the battlefield tour (aside from Redoubts 9 and 10 which can be reached by walking from the visitor center) is the **Moore House** ★★★★★, Stop E. This restored house is where both sides met on October 18, 1781, to discuss the terms of surrender. It is only open seasonally, but can be viewed from the outside even when it is closed.

Stop F ★★ is little more than an open field today, but it is important because it is where the British surrendered. From this field, the nine-mile American encampment tour begins.

Yorktown Battlefield can be seen in about two hours.

Yorktown Victory Monument ★★★

Corner of Main and DeGrasse Sts.

Though authorized for construction the same year of the battle, this ornate, 98-foot monument topped by Lady Liberty was not built until 1881, 100 years after the victory. If one monument in the nation can be considered symbolic of the victory of the Patriots over the British, it is this imposing marble shaft.

Nelson House ★★★★

Corner of Main and Nelson Sts.

The owner of this house, Thomas Nelson Jr., signed the Declaration of Independence, but during the siege of October 1781, he ordered the artillery under his command to target the house because Lord Cornwallis was using it as his headquarters. Two cannonballs were placed in the walls during the 20th century to illustrate Nelson's dedication to the cause of liberty for the colonies. The house is open during the summer.

Other colonial-era houses ★★

The map obtained from Yorktown Battlefield shows the locations of several other colonial-era houses that survived the siege. Most are in private hands and cannot be toured, but they can be viewed from the street.

Yorktown Victory Center ★★★★★

Rte. 1020, on northern edge of Yorktown, just off Colonial Pkwy.
T: 757-253-4838
historyisfun.org/yorktown/yorktown.cfm
Summer daily 9am–6pm; fall, winter, and spring daily 9am–5pm
Admission: $17 combination ticket with Jamestown Settlement; $8.25 if only visiting Yorktown Victory Center

This combination living-history village and museum is operated by the Jamestown-Yorktown Foundation, a division of the commonwealth of Virginia. Visitors enter the site by walking past a lengthy, but handy illustrated timeline that demonstrates the slow but sure march toward rebellion. The timeline leads visitors into a museum that is well stocked with period artifacts and weapons, as well as displays explaining the war.

Among the artifacts is a brace of dueling pistols given to Lafayette. The displays give interesting information, such as the one estimating that one third of the British army was populated by Germans (who were known collectively as Hessians though only two of the German provinces fit that description). Another display gives the surprising information that the average British soldier was 27 to 30 years old and an unemployed laborer who was forced to join the army to make a living.

Outside is a camp populated by colonial soldier interpreters who are able to answer questions about life in the army. One part of the camp that may surprise visitors is the camp kitchen, a 16-foot-diameter circle dug into the earth with the dirt gathered into a mound in the center. A series of eight cubbyholes is then carved into the resulting mound, giving each eight-man detachment a place to do their cooking. Other displays are set up to show the crude, but sometimes effective, medical treatment of the time period.

After leaving the soldiers' camp, visitors move to an 18th-century working farm, populated mostly by women interpreters who explain how the principal cash crop of the average farm was tobacco. Tobacco grown on the farm is drying in a nearby barn. During growing seasons, the women can be found cultivating food in a vegetable garden.

All of the interpreters speak as modern-day people even as they demonstrate 18th-century skills. Seeing Yorktown Victory Center requires a commitment of at least two hours.

Getting to and around Williamsburg

People have the option of flying into Richmond, 50 miles to the north, or Norfolk, 50 miles to the southeast. Both are off I-64. Both airports have at least six commercial airlines serving them and plenty of rental car companies from which to choose.

If seeing just Williamsburg, Yorktown, and Jamestown, Richmond is probably the better choice, as it is on the southeast side of the city. That means visitors to Williamsburg can be on their way quickly without getting into too much traffic.

Norfolk, to the southeast, is a good airport, but it is in a much more heavily populated area. If you are coming from Norfolk, consider taking a bus that runs from Newport News Transportation Center to Colonial Williamsburg for only $1.50 each way.

Once in Williamsburg or Yorktown, the traveling gets easier. The hardier tourist might even want to bring or rent a bicycle. The distance from Yorktown to Jamestown is just 25 miles on the Colonial Parkway, a two-lane highway with a speed limit of 45 miles per hour.

Visitors to Colonial Williamsburg will want to park at the visitor center and take one of the continuously running buses or walk. The walk is paved and accessible to wheelchairs. One attraction that is accessible only by walking is a colonial-era farm that is being developed just over the pedestrian bridge leading to the historic area from the visitor center.

Accommodations

Duke of York Motel

508 Water St., Yorktown
T: 757-898-3232
dukeofyorkmotel.com/contact.html
$80–$110

This is a family-owned waterfront motel right on the York River, one block from waterfront shops and less than a mile from Yorktown battlefield and a mile from the Colonial Parkway.

Marl Inn B&B

220 Church St., Yorktown
T: 800-799-6207 or 757-898-3859
marlinnbandb.com
$95–$140

This bed-and-breakfast in historic Yorktown is on a lot that was originally surveyed in 1691 and is where George Washington's army won the last battle of the American Revolution. Marl Inn is located a half-block from the restored Village of Yorktown and two blocks from Yorktown's beach and Riverwalk along the York River.

North River Inn

8777 Toddsbury Ln., Gloucester
T: 877-248-3030 or 804-693-1616
northriverinn.com
$85–$205

The inn is a Virginia Historic Landmark, located on the north side of the York River, across from Yorktown. A 17th-century Colonial built in 1650, and family owned, it is 10 miles from Yorktown.

Roanoke Island

North Carolina

Site of *The Lost Colony* play that is presented every summer

THE EARLY YEARS

Roanoke Island is home to the first English colony, the first white birth in that colony, a model of the first ship to carry the first English settlers to the New World, and it is near the nation's best beaches on the Outer Banks.

After the first of Christopher Columbus's voyages to the New World in 1492, Spain quickly capitalized on his findings. Within a few decades, Spain was sending home ships laden with gold its explorers had found in Mexico and Central America. By the 1580s, the other countries in Europe were debating what they could do to catch up.

As news of the treasure fleets docking in Spanish ports filtered back to her palace, Queen Elizabeth felt that England was losing ground to its old enemy. At first, the queen compensated by sending out privateers to attack the Spanish treasure ships. But members of England's upper crust, as well as the common folk, began to wonder if more riches might be had by setting up colonies in this new wilderness. They began to press the queen to find a place for England in the New World.

An adventurer named Humphrey Gilbert set out in 1572 to find a site to set up a colony. He died on his second voyage, and his mission to find riches in the New World was taken up by his half brother, Walter Raleigh. Raleigh, a soldier of fortune who had worked his way close to Elizabeth, suggested to the queen that he would be willing to set up some colonies far from the Spanish colonies. In 1585, a fleet of seven ships sailed for an area that had already been explored. On June 20th, the fleet reached what is now called the Outer Banks of North Carolina, low-lying barrier islands of sand that lie just off the mainland coast. In late August, a fort was built and occupied by 107 men on Roanoke Island, the island closest to the mainland and shielded from the ocean by the other islands. This marked the first real attempt to establish an English colony.

The local Indians, including two named Manteo and Wanchese, were friendly at first, showing the strange, pale-skinned men where to find fresh water and edible plants. The Englishmen were not much for farming, however. They let the summer slip into fall without planting any crops of their own. As winter came and food grew scarce, they began to steal from the Indians. The Indians began to have second thoughts about these men, particularly when members of the tribe began to die of diseases they had never before experienced. (Written descriptions describe what were likely measles and smallpox.)

The colonists grew increasingly hostile with the Indians, finally killing and beheading one of their chiefs. Not long after, England's famed privateer Sir Francis Drake visited the colony and offered one of his ships to return the men to England. The colonists, fearful that an already-overdue supply ship would never come, readily agreed. Manteo and Wanchese also left for England. Two days later, the supply ship arrived to find the fort abandoned. The two ships had missed each other in the open sea.

The commander of the relief expedition persuaded 15 men to stay behind to guard the fort and the houses for another colonization effort that would be coming along in a few weeks. These few men are considered the second attempted English colony.

On January 7, 1587, a third colonial mission left England, this time with 107 people, including 17 women and nine boys. Among the colonists was Manteo, who intended to try to negotiate between the new colony and his tribe. Heading the colony was a man named John White, who had sketched Indians, animals, and plants during the first colonial attempt. His art, still surviving today, was the first evidence delivered to England of what native life was like in the New World.

When this third group of colonists arrived, they found the site of the original colony, but Drake's crew, the men who had been left behind, were missing. The new colonists shrugged off the mystery and moved into the cabins. Drake's men were never found. While the first colony had been little more than a military outpost, Raleigh's goal was to create a real working community. Among the incentives promised the colonists were 50-acre tracts of land for each family.

On August 17, 1587, White's 19-year-old daughter gave birth to Virginia Dare, the first English Christian child born in Virginia (then the name of the colony, as the colony of North Carolina had not been formed).

Within a few months, during which conditions at the colony deteriorated, White headed back to England for supplies. While readying his return fleet, White was shocked when Queen Elizabeth ordered that no ships leave England because of the threat of imminent war with Spain. White could do nothing but wait for the queen to change her mind.

It took three years for a return mission to Roanoke from England. On August 17, 1590, White landed on Roanoke Island, anxious to see the granddaughter he had left. The relief party found that the houses had been pulled down and weeds were growing in the fort. The only thing they found was the word "Croatoan" carved into a piece of wood. The Croatoan were a friendly tribe of Indians living on the Outer Banks. White had instructed the colonists to carve a cross into wood if they had suffered any distress. No cross was found. The fear of storms (now known as hurricanes) kept the ships' crews from searching the nearby islands for surviving colonists. White returned to England without dropping off any supplies and without ever learning the fate of his family.

There are many theories about what became of the Lost Colony. The most plausible is that the colony was assimilated into the Croatoan tribe, as the carving would seem to indicate. Another is that the colonists moved north and were killed by less-friendly Indians. A third theory with a number of supporters is that they crossed Albemarle Sound and headed inland, since some Indian tribes in south-central North Carolina have white racial features.

The failure of the first colony and the disappearance of the second and third sealed Raleigh's fate. Upon the death of Queen Elizabeth in 1602, Raleigh was imprisoned by her successor, King James I, and beheaded in 1618 when he was suspected of treason. James finally gave in to pressures from entrepreneurs who insisted that the New World offered promises of riches for England. James granted a colony charter to a company that would land at Jamestown, Virginia, in 1607. The first successful English colony was established more than 23 years after those three unsuccessful colonies on Roanoke.

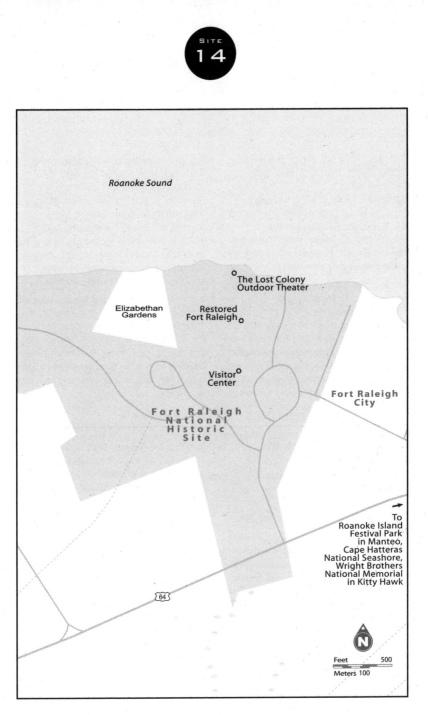

Roanoke Sound

The Lost Colony
Outdoor Theater

Elizabethan
Gardens

Restored
Fort Raleigh

Visitor
Center

Fort Raleigh
City

Fort Raleigh
National
Historic
Site

To
Roanoke Island
Festival Park
in Manteo,
Cape Hatteras
National Seashore,
Wright Brothers
National Memorial
in Kitty Hawk

64

N

Feet   500
Meters 100

ROANOKE ISLAND TODAY

With a full-time population of fewer than 3,000 people, the 12-by-three-mile Roanoke Island is the first of the barrier islands encountered when heading east from the North Carolina mainland on US 64. The island has only two towns, Manteo and Wanchese, named after the two Indians who helped the first English settlers when they arrived.

Much of the marshy island remains wooded compared to the heavily developed barrier islands across the bridge to the east. The string of islands to the east, host to towns like Nags Head and Kitty Hawk, are crowded and bustling with beach tourists moving in and out each week. The much quieter Roanoke Island is where most of the natives of the Outer Banks choose to live and where the beach tourists come when they want to stroll Manteo's downtown with its shops and a well-stocked bookstore at Manteo Booksellers. Manteo has several family-run motels, and a German restaurant, the Weeping Radish, which is a landmark for tourists looking for more than fast-food fare. Though small, Manteo has its own nationally known celebrity. Actor Andy Griffith lives here.

While Roanoke Island and Manteo have all of the amenities to make them year-round attractions, one of the main attractions, the outdoor drama *The Lost Colony*, plays only during the summer. Visitors who are traveling from some distance should plan accordingly and book accommodations far in advance.

POINTS OF INTEREST

Fort Raleigh National Historic Site
★★★★★

1401 National Park Dr., Manteo
T: 252-473-5772
nps.gov/fora/
Daily 9am–5pm; closed major holidays
Admission: Free

While it may seem odd to have a visitor center for a colony that disappeared and whose exact geographic location in this area is still unknown 400 years later, the Lost Colony may one day be found again. In recent years, funding has been obtained to begin archaeological digs on Roanoke Island to find the locations of the first huts and the palisade. It is known through written accounts that the colony was founded on the north end of the island, on land that the National Park Service owns. The search for the colony will begin in the waters north of the beach in anticipation of the possibility that coastal erosion over 400 years might have worn away evidence of the forts and houses.

Visitor Center ★★★★ has a good film explaining the fitful starts of the three English colonies attempted on Roanoke Island beginning in 1585. The attempts to colonize Roanoke came 23 years before the first successful colony at Jamestown in Virginia, and 36 years before Plymouth Colony in Massachusetts. There are a few artifacts on display that show what life was like in those days.

The visitor center also has an extensive display on the history of the outdoor play

The Lost Colony, which runs every summer from early June through late August. Costumes and photographs from various performances are on display.

A half-mile **nature walk** ★★★ starts at the visitor center and takes walkers to a replica dirt fort that is presumed to be what the first fortification on the island may have resembled. Nearby is a marker erected in 1896 commemorating the baptism into the Christian faith of both Virginia Dare and Manteo, the Croatoan Indian who tried to help the settlers establish their colony.

The Lost Colony Outdoor Drama ★★★★★

The Lost Colony Outdoor Theater, on site of Fort Raleigh
T: 252-473-3414
thelostcolony.org
Early-June–mid-August Mon–Sat 8:30pm
Admission: $16

The history and timeline of the three failed colonies on Roanoke Island can be confusing. The first in 1585, made up of adventurers who were looking for gold, quickly angered the local Indians. These colonists grew homesick and took advantage of a visit by English ships to abandon the colony. A second colony of only 15 men disappeared in 1586. It was the third colony that arrived in 1587 that acquired the unfortunate nickname of the Lost Colony. It is the story of these doomed men, women, and children brave enough to start a new life in a strange land that is dramatized during the summer months in an outdoor theater behind the National Park Service visitor center.

Written as an outdoor play by Pulitzer Prize–winner Paul Green in 1937, *The Lost Colony* tells the story of how Walter Raleigh first convinced Queen Elizabeth to back the creation of a colony in the new land of Virginia. He then had to convince dozens of English families to trust his word that the new land that awaited them would be lush and rewarding. Once the settlers arrived on Roanoke, they encountered people already living on the island, Indians who are wary but still friendly to these strangers. The play progresses through the birth of Virginia Dare, the first white child born in Virginia, who represents the spirit of hope for the future for the colonists. The play ends abruptly without speculation on what happened to the colonists, a fitting end to a mystery that remains unsolved 400 years later.

The most famous alumnus of the play is actor Andy Griffith, who starred as Sir Walter Raleigh in 1949 in the years before he became famous. Griffith never forgot his early success in the play. His retirement home lies less than a mile away from the theater. Eileen Fulton, a regular on the TV soap *As The World Turns*, was introduced to acting with her role in the play. A more recent alumnus is Chris Elliott, once a writer for TV talk show host David Letterman. Elliott is now a comedic movie actor.

Because the stage backs up to Albemarle Sound, visitors should bring plenty of mosquito repellent.

Elizabethan Gardens ★★

Adjacent to The Lost Colony Outdoor Theater
T: 252-473-3234
outerbanks.com/elizabethangardens
June–Labor Day daily 9am–8pm; Labor Day–May daily 9am–5pm; closed major holidays
Admission: $6

Run by the Elizabethan Garden Club of North Carolina, this 10-acre garden has been attracting nature lovers for more than 50 years. The garden changes with the seasons in riots of colors in the spring and summer, and subdued colors in the fall and winter.

Roanoke Island Festival Park ★★★

Manteo Waterfront
T: 252-475-1500
roanokeisland.com
Summer daily 10am–6pm; fall, winter,
and spring daily 10am–5pm; closed major
holidays
Admission: $8

Try on armor; watch men practice with the pole arm or spear, which was the most common weapon of the day; and learn the basics of firing a matchlock musket at the military camp hidden in the woods behind the visitor center. The camp is set up with canvas tents, much like the first camp of 1585 looked on Roanoke Island when all of the colonists were military men hoping to find gold. On some weekends, Elizabethan reenactor hobbyists are in attendance, giving insight into what the late 1500s was like for noblemen living in England. These hobbyists speak in Old English accents and play games of the period. They talk in first person, meaning that they speak and act as if tourists are also in the 16th century.

The ship in the water, the *Elizabeth II,* was built in the 1980s. While the original plans of the first *Elizabeth*, one of the seven ships that brought settlers to Roanoke, have never been found, the *Elizabeth II* was built based on the designs of common English trading vessels of the day. It was built on Roanoke Island by skilled wooden-ship builders. Interpreters are on board to describe sailing technology and skills of the period. On occasion, the *Elizabeth II* puts to sea for voyages along the eastern seaboard.

The Roanoke Adventure Museum at Festival Park covers the 400-year history of the island starting with the Algonquin and Croatoan Indians. The Battle of Roanoke Island in 1862, when the Union Army captured the island's four forts, is also covered, as is the Freedman's Colony. The Freedman's Colony was created by the Union Army for the slaves freed by the capture of the island. At one point, more than 3,000 blacks lived near the central part of the island. It was one of the first attempts of the federal government to set up a society of freed slaves in the South. In 1866, the Freedman's Colony was disbanded. Allow at least two hours to see this attraction.

SITES NEAR ROANOKE ISLAND

While the following sites are not from the colonial time period, they are well worth visiting if you are in the area.

Wright Brothers National Memorial
★★★★★

Kitty Hawk (15 miles northeast of Manteo on US 158)
T: 252-441-7430
nps.gov/wrbr/
Summer daily 9am–6pm; fall, winter, and spring daily 9am–5pm
Admission: $3

It seems only fitting that the first settlement of Englishmen in the New World, virtually signifying the birth of America, would be within 15 miles of the site where powered flight was first accomplished, thus making America responsible for the linking of the world through air travel. At Kitty Hawk, in December 1903, descendants of those first English settlers figured out how to fly. Barely 100 years later, the airplane has become the way most people travel the world. A trip across the Atlantic ocean that took two months in 1585 takes just six hours today.

Orville and Wilbur Wright came to Kitty Hawk from their bicycle shop in Dayton, Ohio, because they had learned that the wind nearly always blows a steady 13 miles per hour coming in from the north on this stretch of flat, treeless beach beside the Atlantic Ocean. That was important because the brothers needed a strong, steady wind to help them design their gliders. Once they had mastered the design of their wings, the Wright brothers intended to attach a motor to the wings and do what many inventors at the turn of the 20th century were also racing to accomplish—fly under their own power.

They flew on December 17, 1903. The museum here has a model of their glider and their first airplane. Outside are reproductions of the hangars in which they kept their aircrafts. Markers show the length of the flights they accomplished. On a small hill is a marble monument topped by an eternal flame that is dedicated to the determination of the two brothers. Rangers give regular talks throughout the day about the brothers' experiments in flight.

In December 2003, the difficulty of flying was reinforced in the mind of the public. After spending more than $1 million duplicating the original Wright flyer for the centennial celebration, a skilled pilot was poised to duplicate the flight. The airplane plopped down on the ground after being launched from a catapult similar to the one that sent the original Wright flyer into the air. The model never did fly.

Ironically, once the brothers proved that powered flight was possible, the steady wind of Kitty Hawk was not needed. The brothers wrote that they "packed our goods and returned home, knowing that the age of the flying machine had come at last." It would be nearly two years before they would develop an aircraft that could stay in the air more than a few minutes.

Cape Hatteras National Seashore
★★★★★

From the intersection of US 64/264 and Rte. 12 at Nags Head, 70 miles south

Always threatened by hurricanes but always popular with tourists, the barrier islands that make up the Hatteras National Seashore constitute one long beach protected from development by the National Park Service. In addition to the beaches, the national seashore is also host to a number of historic sites, including the Bodie Island Lighthouse and the more famous Hatteras Island Lighthouse.

Along that 70 miles of beach are small villages outside the protected areas that provide visitors with food, fuel, and lodging. There are two good museums along the drive south. One is a museum dedicated to the now-defunct US Lifesaving Service, a group of men who kept watch on the ocean for shipwreck survivors who had to be rescued from drowning. The other is a museum dedicated to the shipwrecks themselves. That museum is appropriately and grimly called the Graveyard of the Atlantic Museum. Here visitors can learn about the dangerously shallow water off the Outer Banks, how those waters were prowled by German U-boats in World War I and World War II, and how pirates such as Edward Teach (Blackbeard) hunted these same waters for shipping prey in the early 18th century.

GETTING TO AND AROUND ROANOKE ISLAND

Because this area is so remote from the mainland, check weather forecasts for any approaching hurricanes, and make motel reservations well in advance. The Hatteras National Seashore is extremely popular during the late spring through early fall months with vacationers and surf fishermen and there are only a limited number of motel rooms within easy driving distance of the National Seashore.

Getting to Roanoke Island, North Carolina, by commercial airline takes some patience. The closest major airport is Norfolk International Airport, 90 miles to the north in Virginia. Norfolk is served by six airlines and seven rental car agencies. However, residents on Roanoke Island generally choose to drive to Raleigh-Durham International, which is about 210 miles to the west. Flights are less expensive and can be reached in three hours of driving compared to the two hours it takes to reach traffic-choked Norfolk.

Reaching Roanoke by private airplane is easier. The Dare County Airport is just a few miles from the site of the Lost Colony.

It does not have any rental cars on-site but Enterprise Rental Car at Kill Devil Hills will deliver a car to the airport. There are also taxis that operate on the Outer Banks.

The best way to visit Roanoke Island and the Outer Banks is to arrive by private car, which offers the most flexibility. One thing to keep in mind is that the eastern North Carolina coastline in the summer is occasionally affected by hurricanes. Tourists are always asked to evacuate first, so having a car facilitates that if the need arises.

Once on Roanoke Island, it is possible to see all of the island's sights by bicycle touring. A paved bicycle path adjacent to the main road running across the island keeps bikers and motorists safely separated. Walkers staying at one of the motels or inns on the island could walk to the Lost Colony site, but it would be a hike of several miles.

For a quiet visit to the beach, come in the late fall or early winter when motels are available and their prices are reasonable. The traffic is also very light then.

SOURCES & OTHER READING

Roanoke Colony: America's First Mystery, Tracy Esplin, PublishAmerica 2004

Roanoke: Solving the Mystery of the Lost Colony, Lee Miller, Arcade Publishing, 2001

Roanoke Island: The Beginnings of English America, David Stick, University of North Carolina Press, 1983

Roanoke: The Abandoned Colony, Karen Kupperman, Rowman & Littlefield, 1984

The Virginia Adventure: Roanoke to James Towne: An Archaeological and Historical Odyssey, Ivor Hume, University Press of Virginia, 1997

Websites:

statelibrary.dcr.state.nc.us/nc/ncsites/english1.htm

ACCOMMODATIONS

Bald View Bed & Breakfast

3805 Elijah Baum, Kitty Hawk
T: 252-255-2829
baldview.com
$109–$186

Bald View is located in Historic Kitty Hawk. It is located on 11 acres of Maritime Forest on the sound front of Kitty Hawk Bay and only a five-minute walk from the ocean.

Cypress House Inn

500 N. Virginia Dare Tr., Kill Devil Hills
T: 800-554-2764, or 252-441-6127
cypresshouseinn.com
$80–$150

The Cypress House was built in the 1940s as a small hunting and fishing lodge. The interior is finished in cypress tongue-and-groove paneled walls. The ocean is just a one-minute walk to the east.

Island House of Wanchese

104 Old Wharf Rd., Wanchese
T: 866-473-5619 or 252-473-5619
islandhouse-bb.com
$70–$145

This house was built in 1902 for George B. Midgett, a US Coast guardsman who was stationed on Hatteras Island. Island House retains all the original wood flooring and walls.

The White Doe Inn

319 Sir Walter Raleigh St., Manteo
T: 800-473-6091 or 252-473-9851
whitedoeinn.com
$160–$260

The White Doe Inn was constructed in 1910 by local builders for Theodore S. Meekins and his family. Mr. Meekins was a member of one of the Outer Banks' oldest families whose ancestors had inhabited the area since before the American Revolution. The inn is a grand three-story late-Queen Anne–style house and is the largest residence on Roanoke Island.

New Bern

North Carolina

North Carolina's reconstructed royal palace

THE EARLY YEARS

W hen Charles II, king of England in 1663, was looking for a way to reward the men who supported his ascension to the throne, he had just the gift in mind: land. In 1663, he granted eight of his friends land in the New World that he generously described as stretching from the Atlantic Ocean to "the South Seas" (the Pacific Ocean), and from Albemarle Sound down to the Georgia-Florida border.

The new Carolina colony was below the Virginia colony, and often attracted colonists moving south in search of more productive land. In 1706, Bath was incorporated along the Pamlico River, the first town in Carolina. Four years later, a group in Germany and Switzerland seeking religious freedom began to explore their options for leaving Europe. They petitioned the Carolina government to allow them to lay out a town at the confluence of the Trent and Neuse Rivers, then the site of an abandoned Indian village. It would be called New Bern in honor of Bern, the capital of Switzerland.

The champion of these oppressed people was Baron Christoph von Graffenried of Switzerland, who bought 19,000 acres. Von Graffenried looked over his prospective colonists and chose "young people, healthy, laborious and of all kinds of avocations and handicrafts in number about 650." It was a rough trip across the Atlantic. About half died in the crossing, and a French pirate stole most of their possessions once they arrived. When they finally arrived at the town site, they had virtually nothing left with which to create a new town. When Graffenried arrived, he put everyone to work. Within a year and a half, New Bern was successful and growing. But the next two years, 1711–12, saw the town cowering in terror as the Tuscaroa raided and pillaged the area.

For several decades, the coastal counties of North Carolina vied with each other for economic and political dominance. In 1728, the town of Edenton, near the Virginia border, was named the colonial capital. The northern counties in the general assembly voted to have five representatives each in the general assembly, at the same time passing a law that southern counties would get only two representatives. In 1746, the rivalry culminated when only 15 members out of 54 met as the general assembly in Wilmington. At that meeting the group decided to make New Bern the colonial capital. The governor sent the report of the assembly on to London, never mentioning that the assembly did not have a quorum.

The king vetoed the bills, so the northern counties continued to feud with the southern. One of the major complaints of both sides was that the colony still did not have a capital. For the past 40 years, the capital had been wherever the royal governor lived, and where he lived was up to him. The general assembly also rotated between New Bern, Edenton, and Wilmington.

In 1766, the general assembly passed a law calling for the construction of a governor's palace in New Bern. Money was diverted from a school fund and a liquor tax was imposed to pay for it. Construction began in 1767, and it was completed by the winter of 1770. For the first time in 107 years, the colony of North Carolina finally had a permanent capital and a governor's palace.

The erection of a governor's palace came just in time for a crisis over taxation that would become the focus of future colonial unrest. The construction of the governor's mansion in New Bern did not sit well with the scattered settlements in the colony's westernmost towns. They complained that their taxes were paying for a building none of them would ever see. More important, they argued that the general assembly did not pay them any attention or send them any improvements in exchange for the tax dollars they sent to the capital. The numbers of irritated tax payers began to coalesce into a movement they called the Regulator movement. The term referred to the fact that the colonists on the frontier wanted to regulate their own lives rather than send their taxes to New Bern where they had no influence.

They had a point. In 1770, only 15 members of the 81-member general assembly came from the western counties, even though those counties contained more than a third of the colony's population. The government officials who collected the taxes were friends of the governor and general assembly, and the tax collectors often had little regard or respect for the people they were taxing.

Finally, in September 1770, the Regulators raided Hillsborough and accosted Edward Fanning, a local judge. Fanning, a Harvard and Yale graduate who had been appointed by the governor, Lord Tryon, had abused his position for years. The Regulators whipped him, an act of violence that they knew would demand attention from the governor.

When word of Fanning's thrashing reached New Bern, Tryon called out the militia and began marching into the interior looking for the Regulators. A brief battle ensued, during which Tryon killed and hanged a number of Regulators. Tryon pardoned the rest for their previous lawlessness.

Tryon's replacement, Josiah Martin, was the wrong man in the wrong place at the wrong time. Just when revolutionary talk was coming into the open in the northern colonies, Martin came along with a strong identification with the Crown and a disdain for the general assembly. Martin was unable to stop a growing movement that was leading toward rebellion. When Martin learned of a Patriot plot to capture the palace on May 31, 1775, he fled to the safety of a British ship. Martin tried to manage the colony's affairs from the ship, but North Carolina remained rebellious. Martin never returned to the palace at New Bern.

New Bern remained the capital of North Carolina for only a few more years. The capital was transferred to Raleigh in 1791 to appease tax payers who wanted a more central, balanced location for the capital. New Bern, once the center of attention of the colony, and the place where taxation anger started in the colonies, reverted to being the small town it is today.

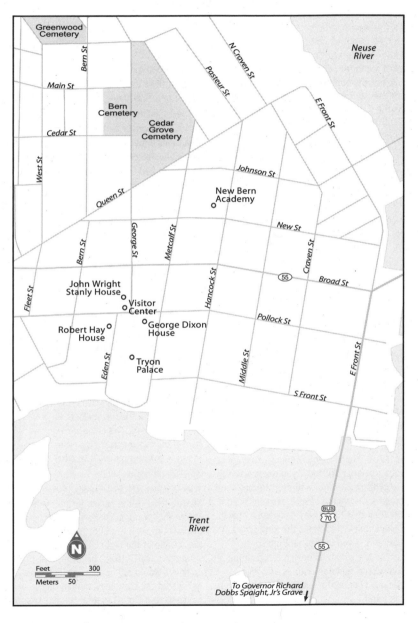

Greenwood
Cemetery

Bern St

Main St

Bern
Cemetery

Cedar St

Cedar
Grove
Cemetery

West St

Queen St

N Craven St

Pasteur St

E Front St

Neuse
River

Johnson St

New Bern
Academy
o

George St

Metcalf St

New St

Bern St

Craven St

55

Broad St

Fleet St

John Wright
Stanly House
o

Visitor
Center
o

Robert Hay
House

George Dixon
House
o

Hancock St

Pollock St

Eden St

Tryon
Palace
o

Middle St

E Front St

S Front St

N

Trent
River

BUS
70

55

Feet   300
Meters   50

To Governor Richard
Dobbs Spaight, Jr's Grave ↓

New Bern Today

With a current population of 24,000, this town at the confluence of the Trent and the Neuse Rivers may be destined to grow, as the surrounding county has more than 90,000 residents. The core of the town, however, will remain unchanged as the owners of houses in the historic area are restricted with regard to the kinds of changes they can make to their historic homes. Many of these homes date back to before the Civil War.

New Bern is a small town where it is easy for visitors to get out and stroll. The down-town shopping district is only two streets wide and two blocks long, but is filled with interesting shops. On one corner is a gift shop selling Pepsi and Pepsi gift items; appropriate because it was there that Caleb Brabham invented the drink in 1893. Two blocks in one direction is a waterfront park. Two blocks in another is a marina with a modern motel.

To properly enjoy New Bern, visitors should plan to spend at least two days and one night in town.

Points of Interest

All of the following sites except Governor Spaight's grave are administered by the Tryon Palace and have the same hours. Allow an hour in each.

Tryon Palace ★★★★★

610 Pollock St., New Bern
T: 252-514-4900
tryonpalace.org/
Mon–Sat 9am–5pm, Sun 1–5pm; closed Sun during the summer
Admission: $15

In 1765, North Carolina's newly appointed royal governor William Tryon made a tactical error in presenting himself to the colonists he would govern. He sent word to the king that the colony deserved a "royal" palace that would make the king proud. To that end, Tryon invited an English architect to the colony to design the building that would function both as an office of the governor, and a residence for him and his family.

The original North Carolina palace, enclosing more than 10,000 square feet including the basement, was built in just three years, a remarkable feat in colonial times. (By comparison, the governor's palace in Williamsburg took more than nine years to construct.) If Tryon ever thought the yeoman farmers who made up most of the population of his colony would be awed when they saw the new palace, he greatly misjudged them. The colonists who had paid taxes to support the construction of the new palace thought it was too big and too ostentatious.

Tryon's successor as governor, Josiah Martin, lived in the palace for four years before increasing tensions with rebellious colonists drove him out of New Bern in the middle of the night. (He fled to the safety of a British ship, believing that the colonists would either come to their senses, or that the combined military forces of Loyalists and British regular soldiers would subdue the talk of rebellion.) Four Patriot governors subsequently used the palace as the center for North Carolina government during the Revolution.

New Bern's palace burned to the ground in 1798. Over time, the building ruins in New Bern disappeared under newer development. At one time, a major highway was constructed through what had been the main hall of the building.

In the 1930s, historians began to discuss the idea of rebuilding the palace. Lobbying of the North Carolina general assembly finally convinced the delegates that the building would be a tourist attraction that would capture national attention. Archaeological digs uncovered the original building's foundations, and the architect's plans were found in an archive in England. Governor Tryon's inventories of the palace's original furnishings were located as well.

The reconstructed Tryon Palace opened to the public in 1959. Today, costumed guides lead visitors through the palace that is decorated as it was in 1770, the last full year Governor Tryon occupied it. None of the furniture is original to the house since Tryon took all of his possessions with him when he moved with his family to New York. However, all of the furniture is either original to the time period, or a reproduction of the period. The colors of the paint and wallpaper, the doors, mirrors, and other trimmings were all typical of the colonial period. The cantilevered staircase leading from the ground floor to the second is interesting in that it appears to be a heavy staircase with no columns supporting it.

On some days, the actor representing Governor Tryon is in his office on the ground floor. He can either address visitors as modern-day tourists, or greet visitors like out-of-town citizens of 1770–71 who have stopped in to pay their respects to the governor. Tourists who come into the meeting with Governor Tryon with a working knowledge of the Regulator movement will be rewarded with a lively discussion. It would be wise to side with the governor unless visitors want to find themselves in a noisy argument.

The time period interpreted by the palace's costumed guides is late 1770. The governor is concerned about the Regulator movement in the western counties. Tryon's dealings with the Regulators is coming at about the same time that other colonies are experiencing tax protests against the broad new taxes being imposed by King George III and the English Parliament. The governor is likely to be tense and irritable as he discusses the problem of these backwoods farmers who are letting themselves be riled up by their radical neighbors.

At the same time, visitors should not confuse localized protests against taxes with broader rebellious talk against the king. The Regulator Movement that Governor Tryon had to confront was different in that the taxes the backcountry farmers (about 200 miles west of New Bern) were protesting were local property taxes imposed by and collected by men employed by the governor of North Carolina. The farmers in the western counties had few quarrels with King George III imposing taxes on paper and tea. They were more concerned with local tax collectors confiscating horses to pay for property taxes imposed on homes. The Regulators came to see the tax collectors as dishonest men who enforced the tax collection laws on some, but not all. The Regulators believed that the courts that were set up to try their cases of tax evasion were stacked against them.

Chief among the Regulator leaders was a man named Herman Husband, a Quaker by faith, who is mentioned by Governor Tryon as the chief agitator among the Regulators. The actor playing Governor Tryon slanders Husband and mentions that the farmers in the backcountry counties need to be taught a lesson. If led in that direction, the governor may scoff at the trifling county seat of Mecklenburg County, which consisted then of hardly more than a few backwoods cabins. (What the 1770 Tryon does not know yet is that the county seat of Mecklenburg County will grow into Charlotte, the largest city in North Carolina.)

The guides will lead visitors to the second-floor bedrooms, through the basement kitchen area, and then out to the front yard. From there, visitors can wander around the extensive gardens located on the back side of the palace. During the spring and summer months, the gardens are in full bloom. Statuary that was popular in the 18th century is scattered around the grounds.

On occasion, when he is not in his office, the governor and Mrs. Tryon might be out on the front lawn. After greeting tourists, they might invite them to bowl. The game the governor plays is much like bocce ball and it takes about five minutes to engage in a game with him.

John Wright Stanly House ★★★★★

George St., New Bern
next to Tryon Palace Visitor Center
Tours on the half-hour (included in ticket price of Tryon Palace)

This is the house that privateering built. John Wright Stanly was a successful merchant-ship owner during the American Revolution when he secured permission for his ships to be turned into privateers. Privateers were a step above pirates, albeit a small step. Stanly's ship captains were granted official permission to raid British ships. In exchange for turning over the booty his ships captured, Stanly was given a cut of the proceeds from the sale of the captured goods.

Stanly became one of the richest men in the colonies. He built this house in the early 1780s, but lived in it only nine years before dying of yellow fever. The house was empty for nearly two years before it was opened in 1791 as a place for George Washington to sleep on his famed Southern Tour. The Stanlys' oldest son lived in the house until 1802.

George W. Dixon House ★★★★★

Pollock St., New Bern
in front of Tryon Palace
Tours on the half-hour (included in ticket price of Tryon Palace)

The Dixon house was built in the 1830s by a prosperous man who made money making clothes for other wealthy people in the town. His house is on the grounds of the palace because the state of North Carolina subdivided the land and sold it into lots after the palace burned in 1798. The house is furnished with pieces that were commonly found in wealthier homes from 1800–40 (as compared to the English-made pieces that were imported for use in the palace).

Robert Hay House ★★★★★

Eden St., New Bern,
next to the Tryon Palace Museum Shop.
Included in ticket price of Tryon Palace

This house is hosted by living-history interpreters who stay in first person while talking about what is happening around them in 1835, the time when the house was occupied by the Hay family. A kitchen is in the basement. People practicing crafts such as basket-making can be found on the other floors.

New Bern Academy ★★★★

Hancock and New Sts., New Bern
four blocks north of Tryon Palace
Self-guided tours (included in ticket price
of Tryon Palace)

The present building has been on this site
since 1809, on the original site of the first
public school building authorized by the
North Carolina legislative assembly in
1766. The school was groundbreaking in
its day because it was coeducational at a
time when most schools admitted only
young boys. The building today has four
major exhibits: one focusing on the history
of New Bern, one focusing on the architecture of New Bern, one focusing on the
Union occupation of New Bern, and one
room showing how the building was used
as a hospital by the Union during the
Civil War.

Governor Richard Dobbs Spaight Jr.'s grave ★★

Madam Moore Ln. (Take US 70 Business
south across river. After crossing the river,
turn right onto SR 1004. Follow the signs
for SR 1004 onto Madam Moore Lane.
Drive approximately 1.3 miles to a historic
marker on the right of the road.)

On September 5, 1802, two wealthy, powerful men angered each other. One killed
the other. The incident was so shocking
that it led to a North Carolina law that
banned dueling in the state forever.

Richard Dobbs Spaight had served three
terms as governor and had lived in the
palace before it was burned. Before being
elected to Congress, he had been instrumental in having the state capital moved
to Raleigh so that it would be closer to the
rest of the population. Spaight's successor
to the congressional seat was John Stanly,
son of the man who built the Stanly
house. Stanly was apparently afraid that
Spaight would once again run for the congressional seat.

Stanly began writing insulting letters to
Spaight. The two men traded insults for a
while, and the affair apparently died
down. Then Spaight gave the local newspaper copies of the letters, which were
reprinted. Handbills were made of the letters, and these were passed around town.
Both men's sense of honor was now being
challenged in public.

Spaight challenged Stanly to the duel. The
men exchanged shots three times before
Stanly finally hit Spaight in the heart. The
North Carolina legislature passed a law
two months later outlawing dueling. The
law read in part that anyone participating
in a duel would not be able to hold public
office. The fear of not being able to run
for office was more frightening than the
fear of getting shot. Dueling stopped
immediately in the state.

During the Civil War, Union soldiers dug
up the cast-iron coffin holding Spaight
and dumped his body on the ground. They
then impaled his skull on a stake. Once
officers learned of the incident, they
retrieved the coffin and returned the former governor to the spot where he still
rests today.

GETTING TO AND AROUND NEW BERN

Craven Regional Airport serves New Bern with one airline, US Airways, providing eight flights per day to Charlotte, a major hub that is accessible to all other airlines. Rental cars are available at the airport. Visitors who enjoy sailing or motorboating on the Intercoastal Waterway will find it easy to chart a course for the town as it is on the confluence of two rivers, the Trent and the Neuse, and a well-appointed marina is on the river. (Visitors arriving by boat will not need a car if visiting only New Bern, as all the sites are within walking distance of each other.)

Even though New Bern is small, with a population of only 25,000, it does have a tourist trolley tour that caters to the considerable numbers of tourists who visit each year. The 90-minute tours run $12 per person and travel through the historic residential district as well as to the museums and Tryon Palace. The tours generally run once a day at 2pm. Call 252-637-7316 for information on exact times as they vary during winter months.

All of the museums and restaurants are within easy reach of all of the accommodations downtown and along the waterfront. The only time a car is necessary is if visitors want to venture out of town.

ACCOMMODATIONS

Harmony House Inn

215 Pollock St., New Bern
T: 800-636-3113 or 252-636-3810
harmonyhouseinn.com
$89–$160

This 1850 four-room house was built for Benjamin and Eliza Ellis. Several additions were made to the house as the Ellis family grew. Another change was made in 1900 when the house was sawed in half, separated nine feet, and a separate entrance and stairway were installed to construct two dwellings.

Howard House Victorian Bed & Breakfast

207 Pollock St., New Bern
T: 800-705-5261 or 252-514-6709
howardhousebnb.com
$89–$129

The James M. Howard House, built between 1888 and 1892, is an example of Queen Anne–influenced architecture in New Bern. Howard engaged in mercantile and business pursuits and was a partner with Elijah Hester in the Farmer's Tobacco Warehouse Company. The B&B opened after restoration in 1997.

Meadows Inn

212 Pollock St., New Bern
T: 877-551-1776 or 252-634-1776
meadowsinn-nc.com
$86–$126

The house was built in 1847 by John Alexander Meadows and enlarged to its three-story size in 1900. This home is rich in history. It became New Bern's first bed-and-breakfast in 1980.

Sources & Other Reading

Breaking Loose Together: The Regulator Rebellion in Pre-Revolutionary North Carolina, Marjoleine Kars, University of North Carolina Press, 2002

Colonial North Carolina: A history (A History of the American Colonies), Hugh Letter, Scribner, 1973

Historic Tryon Palace: First Permanent Capital of North Carolina, New Bern, N.C., James D. Henry, Americraft, 1960

Loyal Revolt: The Regulator Movement in the North Carolina Backcountry, Colleen Walsh, self-published, 1995

North Carolina through Four Centuries, William S. Powell, University of North Carolina Press, 1989

Websites:

studyworld.com/regulators_of_north_carolina.htm

tamu.edu/ccbn/dewitt/mckstmerreg1.htm

16

Moores
Creek Bridge

North Carolina

The Patriot victory here boosted the Revolution.

THE WAR YEARS

After the humiliation of having its army shot at from behind trees and fences the previous April 1775 in Massachusetts, the British Crown was anxious to bring the colonies quickly back under its control. Though the Regulators had given the royal governor fits as early as 1771 in North Carolina, that colony was considered more loyal than any of the New England outposts. During the previous 40 years, Highlanders from Scotland had virtually flooded North Carolina, and now King George III was going to call on them to show their support for him.

That the Scots answered that call at all has always surprised historians. Just 30 years earlier at the Battle of Culloden in Scotland in 1746, the English had massacred wounded Highlanders. But after that battle, the Scots, who had fought English domination of Scotland for hundreds of years, seemed to submit completely to English rule. Instead of continuing the fighting, the remaining Highlanders began joining the British army. The Scottish regiments were sent to the far-flung reaches of the British Empire, and helped fight the French and Indian War in Canada and the American colonies.

Historians speculate that the English subjugation of the Highlanders was so complete and the war against the clan system so effective that the Scots finally submissively accepted the English as their rulers. Other historians see the sudden turnaround from fierce rebels of the British to fierce defenders of the British to be a practical choice of survival. The Highlanders had been given two choices: fight for the English overseas or endure further subjugation at home. Even the Scots living in the eastern United States became loyal to the Crown. Again, historians speculate that the immigrant Loyalist Scots remained loyal out of fear that their families back in Scotland might be harmed if word got back that the American Scots were siding with the Patriots.

In January 1776, Josiah Martin, the British governor of North Carolina, fled his palace at New Bern out of fear that the Patriots would capture him. Safely on board a British warship, Martin issued a call to all Loyalists then living in North Carolina to rally to his side to defend King George III's rule. Among the first to respond were the Highland Scots. Curiously, leading them was a British officer named Donald MacDonald who had fought at Culloden for the English. A man who had slaughtered wounded Highlanders in Scotland was now leading them in North Carolina.

MacDonald planned a march from Cross Creek (modern day Fayetteville) to capture the Patriot stronghold of Wilmington. From there, the combined force would march through North Carolina suppressing any Patriot resistance they came across.

When the Patriot militia started marching northwestward from New Bern to protect Wilmington, both sides knew an important battle was about to be fought. Only one real battle had taken place since the small skirmish at Lexington and Concord in Massachusetts (the Battle of Bunker Hill, Massachusetts). Since that fight eight months earlier, neither side had been anxious to move against the other.

All that changed on February 26, 1776. Loyalist scouts found about 1,500 Patriot militiamen camped on the west side of Moores Creek, about 17 miles north of their goal of Wilmington. That information was both interesting and troubling. It was interesting because military common sense said that no force should ever camp on the same side of the creek as an approaching attacking force. If overwhelmed, the defending force would have nowhere to go other than in the creek. The Loyalist commander MacDonald thought the militiamen might be creating a ruse as a trap.

That same night, MacDonald fell ill and command was transferred to his second in command, Donald McLeod. McLeod was determined to catch the Patriots before dawn, so he pushed his men forward. When the Loyalists arrived at Moores Creek, they found that the camp had been abandoned. Campfires still burned, but there were no men. The Patriots had disappeared in the darkness.

McLeod, a young, inexperienced officer, believed that the 1,600-man force under his command had so frightened the Patriots that they had simply abandoned the field to him. McLeod and another officer walked up to the bridge and noticed that the planking had been pulled up. He believed the Patriots had not had time to burn the bridge.

McLeod and the other officer began to step gingerly across the 30-foot-wide creek using the stringers or long pieces of wood on which the planking normally rested. They were not armed with pistols, but with claymores, the ancient, huge swords that the Highland Scots had used for centuries against invading English armies. (Of the 1,600 Loyalists in the army, only a few hundred were equipped with muskets. The rest had only swords or were totally unarmed.) The two officers had to use their swords to balance themselves because the wily Patriots had greased the stringers with pig fat. As they made their way across the creek, the officers waved for their men to follow them. Neither man looked at the eastern bank of the creek before waving their men from cover into the open.

Just as the two officers stepped on the bank and the bridge stringers became loaded with tiptoeing Loyalists, the Patriot militia opened up with hunting rifles from earthworks they had dug on the east side of the creek. Most of the militia were men who hunted for food, and they could put a lead ball into the head of a deer at 300 yards. Hitting a man at 30 yards was no contest.

McLeod and the other officer were dead before they hit the ground. The men who were crossing the bridge shared their fate. In a battle that participants said lasted no more than three minutes, more than 30 Loyalists were shot dead and another 50 were wounded. Many of the Loyalists drowned. Only one Patriot was killed.

Within minutes of the battle, the Patriots organized a chase of the survivors. MacDonald himself was captured. The Loyalists were permitted to go home on the promise that they would take no further part in the American Revolution.

This tiny, early battle ensured North Carolina's loyalty to the Patriot side for the rest of the war. When Loyalists in other colonies heard of the defeat, many began to reevaluate their loyalty to King George III.

SITE
16

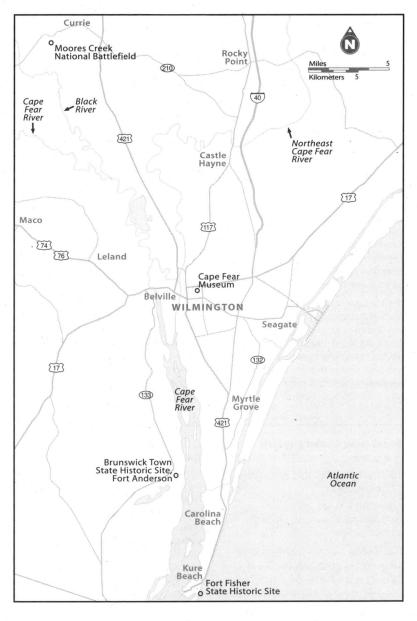

Currie

Moores Creek
National Battlefield

Rocky
Point

210

Cape
Fear
River

Black
River

40

421

Castle
Hayne

Northeast
Cape Fear
River

17

Maco

74

76

Leland

117

Cape Fear
Museum

Belville

WILMINGTON

Seagate

132

17

133

Cape
Fear
River

Myrtle
Grove

421

Brunswick Town
State Historic Site,
Fort Anderson

Atlantic
Ocean

Carolina
Beach

Kure
Beach

Fort Fisher
State Historic Site

Miles   5
Kilometers   5

N

MOORES CREEK TODAY

The Moores Creek Bridge National Battlefield remains as isolated today as it was in 1776 when the battle was fought. The city of Wilmington, which was occupied by the British during the war, is just 20 miles to the south, but development has not touched the sandy plains around the park.

The bridge itself was not of major tactical importance during the war. The creek it bridges is only a few yards wide, though the water is deep enough to drown someone with a broadsword on his back. Had the bridge not existed, the advancing Loyalists could have easily felled a few trees growing close to the creek and created their own bridge.

But the Loyalists took the easy way out to reach Wilmington. They continued along a well-known route heading into Wilmington called the Negro Head Point Road. Patriot militia commander Richard Caswell, who had been unable to catch up to the Loyalists up until this point, decided to wait for them here at the bridge. Caswell guessed correctly that the Loyalists would make for Wilmington in the most direct route possible once they got close.

The visitor center at Moores Creek Battlefield is a small unit with only a few artifacts on display, but it does have an excellent movie explaining the battle in detail. (The movie actually lasts longer than the three-minute battle.) The asphalt trail to the battle site is one mile long, making it accessible for most visitors.

Wilmington, a city of 78,000, makes an excellent base from which to visit Moores Creek. Wilmington has a fine history museum downtown, the USS *North Carolina* (a World War II battleship), an interesting riverfront walk, and a pleasant downtown. About 20 miles to the southeast beside the Atlantic Ocean is Fort Fisher, a feared Confederate dirt fort that protected the Cape Fear River from blockading ships.

POINTS OF INTEREST

Moores Creek National Battlefield
★★★★★

40 Patriots Hall Dr. (Rte. 210), Currie
T: 910-283-5591
nps.gov/mocr
Daily 9am–5pm
Admission: Free

This 87-acre national battlefield in the middle of the woods was the site of a battle that could be more correctly called a slaughter. It pitted Americans who wanted to be free of English domination against Americans who remained loyal to King George III. Here, frontier rifles, military muskets, and a two-pound cannon devastated the ranks of men mostly carrying broadswords, weapons their ancestors had once used to great effect, but which were useless against the modern firearm. It was here that the fate of North Carolina for the next eight years would be decided. And it was here that the colonists, who had been badly bloodied at their first major battle at

Bunker Hill, Massachusetts, the previous year, would get a victory that they could point to with pride.

The trail to Moores Creek begins just behind the visitor center. At one point, it parallels the still visible trace of Negro Head Point Road, the main route to Wilmington in the 1770s. The trail becomes a boardwalk over the creek's swamp and then makes a sharp turn back toward the visitor center through what was the Patriots' west-bank camp, which was set up precisely to lure the Loyalists into attacking. The trail then crosses the wooden bridge. (The planking of the bridge had been removed before the battle, but now that the bridge is part of the trail, it is complete.)

The Battle of Moores Creek Bridge was not one of large armies maneuvering back and forth, trying to draw the other side into a disadvantage, and can be easily understood by tourists unfamiliar with military tactics. All it took to win this battle was a clever ruse on the part of the Patriots.

On February 20, 1776, the Scots under General Donald MacDonald began marching toward the coast to meet up with the supply ships expected from England with muskets and regular soldiers. Trying to stay in front of them in order to slow them down was a force of American Patriot militia that was stalling to give other militia forces time to gather.

It became clear to the Patriots under Colonel James Moore that the Loyalists were heading for Wilmington along Negro Head Point Road, which crossed Moores Creek. If the Patriots did not stop the Loyalists here, they would not be stopped before occupying the city.

Colonel Alexander Lillington of the Patriot militia arrived first at the bridge on February 25. He dug a set of earthworks on the east side of the bridge. Another force arrived and dug a set of earthworks on the west side. The Loyalists were camped less than six miles away.

Aware of the fact that the Patriots blocked the way, MacDonald sent a scout who told him that the Patriots were camped on the west side of Moores Creek. No sign of that camp remains today on the west side of the bridge, but the flat ground here indicates that it would have been a natural campsite (but for the militarily unwise idea to camp with one's back to a natural obstacle to retreat such as the creek.)

Tourists today can walk across the bridge to the east side to an area the scout could not see. Once across the bridge, visitors can see the reproduced earthworks that sheltered the Patriot riflemen. In the hours before dawn, these earthworks would have been virtually invisible to anyone approaching from the west. There are some reports indicating that it was also a foggy morning, which would have further helped to hide the Patriot position.

It is somewhat unsettling walking the path from the bridge through the earthworks to continue the walking tour. More than 30 Scotsmen died in the creek and in these few sandy yards between the creek and the earthworks. Dozens more were wounded. Not a single one of them was able to wield his fabled claymore to attack his unseen foe. The bridge and all of the men who had crossed it were well within range of Patriot muskets and rifles. Muskets had a range of 100 yards.

Four monuments are found along the rest of the walk looping back toward the visitor center: one to the single Patriot who was killed, one to the Loyalists who fought for what they believed, one honoring a man who helped preserve the battlefield, and a rare monument to the women of the Cape Fear region who did their part in the Revolution, including one woman who rode a horse to the battlefield to nurse both wounded Patriots and Loyalists alike.

The three-minute battle at Moores Creek Bridge could hardly be called a battle since it pitted Patriot muskets against Loyalist swords. However, the political implications of the outcome of the battle were much more important than the actual victory itself.

The effect of the Patriots so decisively crushing Loyalist sentiment in the coastal counties of North Carolina was measurable in the rest of the colonies. When word of the victory filtered to the rebelling colonists in the northern colonies, it gave hope to the still-forming Patriot armies that they too would be able to defeat a British-backed force.

Plan to allow an hour for you visit here.

SITES NEAR MOORES CREEK BRIDGE

Brunswick Town/Fort Anderson ★★★★★
8884 St. Philip's Rd. SE (Off Rte. 133 southwest of Wilmington)
T: 910-371-6613
ah.dcr.state.nc.us/sections/hs/brunswic/
    brunswic.htm
Tue–Sat 10am–5pm
Admission: Free

This North Carolina state park encompasses two features and two time periods: the ruins of Brunswick Town, the North Carolina capital before New Bern, and Fort Anderson, a well-preserved Confederate fort designed to protect Wilmington from invasion by Union ships.

Brunswick Town was founded in 1726, just 14 years after the colony was established, by entrepreneurs who saw the need to develop a pine pitch industry for the British navy. The pitch was used to seal cracks in ship hulls. With the British navy then ruling the world's oceans, developing "naval stores" from the state's abundant pine trees would prove profitable. The port thrived and was named the colonial capital. The colonists were not always pleased with their king. In 1765 a number of merchants in Brunswick protested so vehemently the king's right to collect taxes that the practice was halted. The more

famous Boston Tea Party was still eight years in the future.

Brunswick Town began to lose its status with the growth of nearby Wilmington and the move of the colonial capital to New Bern in 1770. By 1776, it was hardly more than a village when British troops burned it to the ground in retaliation for the Battle of Moores Creek Bridge, 20 miles to the north.

In 1861, Confederate forces built Fort Anderson, a dirt fort similar in design to the much larger Fort Fisher at the mouth of the Cape Fear River. Fort Anderson came under fire in March 1865 after Union troops had captured Fort Fisher. Because it is on a river rather than the ocean, much more of Fort Anderson is left than of Fort Fisher. Today, Fort Anderson remains one of the largest, most intact dirt forts ever constructed.

The state park museum here is excellent. It uses a historical timeline to trace the history of the region starting from precolonial times through the end of the Civil War. There are a number of artifacts on display that archaeologists discovered at the site in the 1950s and 1960s. The pride of the site is the Confederate garrison flag that flew over the fort in 1865. It was captured by Federal forces when it accidentally fell off of a wagon. Until recently, it had been in private hands.

The original brick foundations of many of the Brunswick Town houses are found to the south of Fort Anderson. Among them are the ruins of the first colonial capital of the colony. The only structure that has walls remaining is the St. Phillips Anglican Church, which dates back to 1754. The rest of the church was burned by the British in 1776. The church is right outside the visitor center.

Allow at least an hour to see Brunswick Town and Fort Anderson.

Cape Fear Museum ★★★

814 Market St., Wilmington
T: 910-341-4350
capefearmuseum.com
Memorial Day–Labor Day Mon–Sat
9am–5pm, Sun 1–5pm; rest of the year
Tue–Sat 9am–5pm
Admission: $5

This museum traces the city's history, with some bypasses into special subjects such as the history of former professional basketball player Michael Jordan, who was famously cut by his first high school coach because he was not good enough to make the team.

Fort Fisher ★★★★★

US 421 in Kure Beach, 20 miles southeast of Wilmington
T: 910-458-5538
ah.dcr.state.nc.us/sections/hs/fisher/
    fisher.htm
Tue–Sat 10am–4pm
Admission: Free

Only about 10 percent of Fort Fisher remains. It once was shaped like a capital "L" with a long side facing the ocean that stretched more than a mile long. The Atlantic Ocean has claimed all of that sea face. Only part of the perpendicular section of the sand walls remain.

During the Civil War, Fort Fisher was the most feared of the Confederate forts because of its large guns and accurate crews. Most Union ship captains preferred to stay far at sea rather than risk getting close to Fort Fisher, which protected the mouth of the Cape Fear River so that blockade runners could have access to the port of Wilmington. It was shelled twice, once in late December 1864 and then again in January 1865. It was taken in heavy, bloody, hand-to-hand fighting.

The visitor center features good displays on the construction of the fort, including a model of a Whitworth cannon, a rare breech-loading artillery piece that was deadly accurate. Also on display is a model of an Armstrong gun, an English-made cannon that threw 100-pound shells. It was the most feared of the heavy cannons used by the Confederates.

GETTING TO AND AROUND
MOORES CREEK BRIDGE

Getting to the site of the Battle of Moores Creek, North Carolina, takes some work. The national battlefield is not far from Wilmington, but it is located in the woods a good distance from nearby towns and major highways and there are few signs directing travelers to it.

The nearest airport is Wilmington Airport, about 20 miles to the southeast. The airport is served by two airlines and several rental car companies. The only way to reach Moores Creek is by private car; there are no public transportation options.

To reach the national park, take US 117 south from the airport. Take US 421 north from its intersection with US 117. Drive 16 miles north to the intersection with Rte. 210. Drive west approximately five miles. Watch for the entrance to the park. If arriving from I-40, take Exit 408 onto Rte. 210 and drive west until you reach the park. Be aware that signs along these roads are sometimes missing.

Once at the park, visitors will find it easy to see the significant parts of the battlefield. The path is easily negotiable and the ground mostly flat. The park service has even replanked the reproduction of the Moores Creek Bridge.

SOURCES & OTHER READING

The Highland Scots of North Carolina, 1732–1776, Duane Meyer, University of North Carolina Press, 1957

North Carolina through Four Centuries, William S. Powell, University of North Carolina Press, 1989

Southern Campaigns of the American Revolution, Dan Morrill, The Nautical & Aviation Publishing Company of America

Touring North Carolina's Revolutionary War Sites, Daniel Barefoot, John F. Blair Publisher, 1998

Websites:

ah.dcr.state.nc.us/sections/hp/colonial/Bookshelf/Monographs/Scots/scots4.htm

cr.nps.gov/history/online_books/mocr/adhi_1.htm

statelibrary.dcr.state.nc.us/nc/ncsites/moores.htm

Accommodations

C.W. Worth House

412 South Third St., Wilmington
T: 800-340-8559 or 910-762-8562
worthhouse.com
$130–$160

Charles W. Worth began construction of the Queen Anne–style home in 1889. It was completed in 1893, and the family resided in the home until 1930. Worth was a wholesale grocery merchant and a commission merchant in cotton and naval stores at the turn of the 20th century. His father, David Gaston Worth, was the only son of North Carolina Governor Jonathan Worth of Asheboro.

Rosehill Inn Bed & Breakfast

114 South Third St., Wilmington
T: 800-815-0250 or 910-815-0250
rosehill.com
$99–$199

Henry Russell Savage, a prominent Wilmington businessman and banker, built this house in 1848. It was also the home of Henry Bacon Jr., architect of the Lincoln Memorial in Washington, D.C. It was restored and opened as an inn in 1995.

The Verandas

202 Nun St., Wilmington
T: 910-251-2212
verandas.com
$150–$225

Built in 1853 by Benjamin Beery, this Victorian Italianate mansion suffered from fire and water damage in 1992. Its present owners purchased the boarded-up mansion in 1995 and renovated it.

Guilford
Courthouse

North Carolina

A rare British monument on the battlefield

THE WAR YEARS

he Battle of Guilford Courthouse did not have the feel of the last major battle of the American Revolution. Indeed, Guilford Courthouse was a British victory, but one so dear that England began to think of ending the war.

When he soundly defeated British Lt. Col. Banastre Tarleton at Cowpens, South Carolina, on January 17, 1781, Patriot General Daniel Morgan knew there would be hell to pay. He was right. British General Cornwallis immediately sent his army into North Carolina in pursuit of Morgan's force.

Southern Theater commander Patriot General Nathaniel Greene was also racing back into North Carolina. Greene had proven himself to be a good desk general by keeping the army supplied, but he had not won many battles when Washington sent him down to command the southern colonies. Now he found himself retreating over one river after another just ahead of Cornwallis. Finally, Greene crossed the Dan River into Virginia and took up all of the boats with him while Cornwallis could only watch and seethe on the south bank.

Although Cornwallis had successfully chased Greene and Morgan out of North Carolina, he had left behind or burned all of his heavy supplies so that his army would not be encumbered on its attempt to overtake Morgan. The army almost out of food, Cornwallis detoured to Hillsborough in hopes of acquiring supplies.

Cornwallis then issued a hopeful call for North Carolina Tories to rally to him. Few came, as the remaining Loyalists in North Carolina sensed that there were too many Patriots in the colony for them to safely help the king.

Greene recrossed the Dan into North Carolina to lure Cornwallis into chasing him once again, this time to the southwest. Greene stopped at Guilford Courthouse. Greene had an army of 4,300, but 2,600 of them were militiamen who might run at the first volley from the British. Cornwallis had fewer than half the men that Greene had, but almost all of them were regular soldiers.

While considering how to fight Cornwallis, Greene remembered how Morgan had beaten the British at Cowpens with militia and put the same strategy into action. Greene put the most experienced militia in the front line and then rode among them with one request, "Three rounds, my boys, and then you can fall back." He backed them up with some more experienced militia. The final line were Continentals, the most experienced, hardened soldiers.

One man penned a letter to his expectant wife while waiting for the first signs of the British, "The day seems at hand that will render North Carolina perfectly happy or perfectly miserable. This is the very day that I hope will be given me a creature [his new child] capable of enjoying what its father hopes to deserve and earn—the sweets of Liberty and Grace."

That man likely fled with the rest of the North Carolina militia who fired two volleys rather than the requested three, but then some of the first line of North Carolinians decided to hide in the woods after firing their volleys. From their treed cover, they were able to deliver a flanking fire into the redcoats, who were then advancing on the Patriot second line.

Cornwallis lost control of his men as clusters of them broke off from their regiments and plunged into the woods after the Patriot militia. The key to British domination of any battlefield had always been solid lines of men charging with bayonets. When those lines were broken, it was easier for small groups of Patriots to fight them. The British attacked the Continentals in a piecemeal fashion, but they got within the American lines. When Cornwallis himself viewed the scene, he could not tell where his line ended and the American line began. He then issued a controversial order. He told his artillery-men to load their cannons with grape shot and fire into the fighting before him. British redcoats and Continental bluecoats fell side by side, but the shelling had the effect Cornwallis had hoped for: The two sides separated.

As the astonished Greene took in what he had just seen, he also saw the rest of the British army coming into sight. With his third line bloodied by British artillery and his first two lines collapsed, Greene ordered a general retreat. Cornwallis, with fewer than half the number of men under Greene's command, had won the battle. It had been a horrendous victory for the British. Of the 1,924 men Cornwallis had sent into battle, more than 500 were killed or wounded. Still without food or tents, he started limping his way toward Cross Creek (modern-day Fayetteville) in hopes that he could find supplies from one of the few towns that harbored Tories.

Greene understood that even with the loss at Guilford Courthouse, he had won the campaign. Cornwallis had burned all of his supplies in South Carolina in order to catch and destroy Morgan and Greene. But, Greene had forced a British army to leave the region in search of friendly territory before it starved to death. When word of Cornwallis's march toward Cross Creek and Wilmington filtered through both Carolinas, it was a clear sign to the Patriots that they could assault the Tories with impunity. The British losses at Kings Mountain and Camden and the bloody, hard-won victory at Guilford Courthouse were clear evidence that the redcoats were being whittled away.

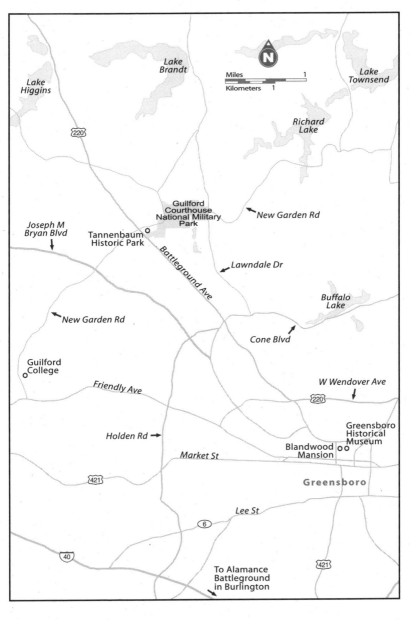

Lake Brandt

Lake Townsend

Lake Higgins

Miles 1
Kilometers 1

Richard Lake

220

Guilford Courthouse National Military Park

New Garden Rd

Joseph M Bryan Blvd

Tannenbaum Historic Park

Battleground Ave

Lawndale Dr

Buffalo Lake

New Garden Rd

Cone Blvd

Guilford College

Friendly Ave

W Wendover Ave

220

Holden Rd

Greensboro Historical Museum

Blandwood Mansion

Market St

421

Greensboro

Lee St

6

40

421

To Alamance Battleground in Burlington

Guilford Courthouse no longer exists. Only the Guilford Courthouse National Battlefield protects the area that has otherwise been swallowed up by housing developments serving the central business district of Greensboro to the south.

During the Revolution, this part of North Carolina was sparsely settled. There was barely a need for a courthouse, but because Guilford County existed, provisions had to be made for one. The judge for the court only came by when necessary. No one knows what the courthouse looked like, but we do know that it was located on a hill that is today within the national park.

The city of Greensboro, one of the state's largest with around 225,000 residents, was not founded until nearly 30 years after the Battle of Guilford Courthouse was fought. The battle site is about eight miles north of the city's central business district. The only true connection today's city has to the battle is that it was named after Patriot General Nathaniel Greene, who was in command of the army on that day.

POINTS OF INTEREST

Guilford College area ★

New Garden Rd. in front of the College, Exit 213 from I-40 west of Greensboro

Guilford College was founded in 1837 by Quakers as the New Garden Boarding School. A skirmish that led to the Battle of Guilford Courthouse was fought here in front of the boarding school on New Garden Road when British cavalry officer Lt. Col. Banastre Tarleton attacked an American outpost here. The Americans rode back up New Garden Road to alert General Greene that the British were coming. The Quakers in this area took in the wounded of both sides and nursed them back to health. There are some dead of both sides buried in unmarked graves throughout this area. Follow the brown signs east on New Garden Road toward the main battlefield.

Tannenbaum Historic Park ★★★★

2200 New Garden Rd., Greensboro
T: 336-545-5315
greensboro-nc.gov/Departments/Parks/
    facilities/tannenbaum/
Tue–Sat 9am–5pm; call ahead for seasonal hours
Admission: Free

This very fine city-owned park is on the same ground where Cornwallis opened the Battle of Guilford Courthouse by setting up his artillery on the farm of Joseph Hoskins. The 7.5 acres are occupied by period log cabins, kitchens, and barns. During the warm seasons, vegetables are grown in a family garden. Cornwallis set up his cannons on New Garden Road (the same road on which the park is accessed) pointing east toward the entrance of the national park.

Inside the museum is a detailed diorama of the battle. On the walls are maps showing North Carolina during colonial times. The museum has a separate exhibit room detailing the frontier life of men, women, and slaves. Some objects can be handled, which makes the museum popular as a school fieldtrip destination.

Guilford Courthouse National Military Park
★★★★★

2332 New Garden Rd., Greensboro
T: 336-288-1776
nps.gov/guco/
Daily 8:30am–5pm
Admission: Free

Legend says that Betsy Ross of Philadelphia made the first flag of the United States. That story is likely a fable. What is definitely known is that a copy of the first United States flag ever carried on a battlefield can be seen in the museum at Guilford Courthouse.

The flag at the visitor center, the original of which is in the North Carolina Museum of History in Raleigh, looks much like the familiar United States flag, but with all of the colors mixed up. In the upper left is the expected canton, but it is white and much larger in proportion to the rest of the flag. The 13 stars are blue instead of white. The thirteen stripes are red and blue instead of red and white. Who designed or made the original flag is unknown. As far as any historians can determine, this was the only battle in which the flag flew. All that is known about it are written reports that the red, white, and blue flag was carried by the North Carolina militia in the battle.

This interesting artifact is only one reason to visit this national park. The other reason is that it was here, in what was then rural North Carolina backcountry, that the war finally tilted in favor of the Patriots. After Cornwallis won this battle, a fight where he had to fire artillery into his own men to win the day, he limped away, com-

plaining that he could not afford to win too many more such victories. Cornwallis's army never regained its strength, and he surrendered his 8,000-man army a few months later at Yorktown, Virginia.

The visitor center, behind where the American first line was formed, offers a movie about the battle and a valuable electronic map display. Visitors should view the map before going onto the battlefield to understand the battle.

Elsewhere in the museum are several mannequins displaying uniforms. Before leaving the museum, ask rangers for directions to the memorial to Kerrenhappuch Turner. She is known to have ridden hundreds of miles to nurse her wounded son.

Visitors have two options to see the battlefield—a two-and-a-half-mile driving and biking tour, or two miles of walking trails—that both stop at all the same points of interest. Stopping at each location on the driving trail takes about a half hour. Taking the walking trail takes at least an hour. While it is longer, walkers will also get a feel for the land that the soldiers had to negotiate, particularly a ravine that the British had to march through to try to reach the third line.

Stop 3 ★★★★ is the location of the American second line. The left flank of this line now extends into a cemetery, but the bulk of it is preserved inside the national park. **Stop 6 ★★★★** is the location of Guilford Courthouse and where the third and final line of the Americans was located. It was into this line that Cornwallis fired his cannons, hitting Patriots and British alike. There is no evidence of the courthouse itself.

Driving visitors will want to get out and walk the trails starting at **Stop 7 ★★★★** where there is a display on the British soldier. There are monuments on the trails honoring soldiers from Delaware and

Maryland and for the Continental Regulars. There is also one monument to a British officer who was killed assaulting the third line.

Another important stop is **Stop 8** ★★★★★. Here is the huge statue of General Nathaniel Greene erected in 1815 by Francis Packer, who was a student of famed bronze artist Augustus Saint-Gaudens. Here too is a statue dedicated to the men from North Carolina who signed the Declaration of Independence. (Note that this statue is not linked to the battle, as none of the men honored by it were present that day.)

SITES NEAR GUILFORD COURTHOUSE

Greensboro Historical Museum ★★★

130 Summit Ave., Greensboro (downtown)
T: 336-373-2043
greensborohistory.org
Tue–Sat 10am–5pm, Sun 2–5pm
Admission: Free

This modern museum traces the history of the area dating back to colonial times with special attention paid to local residents such as Dolley Madison, the wife of fourth president James Madison. Among its collections is a fine display of Confederate firearms, artifacts belonging to World War II fighter ace George Preddy, and pioneering TV newsman Edward R. Murrow. Both Preddy and Morrow were born in Greensboro.

Blandwood Mansion ★★

447 West Washington St., Greensboro
(downtown west of the historical museum)
T: 336-272-5003
blandwood.org
Tue–Sat 11am–2pm, Sun 2–5pm
Admission: $5

Blandwood, built in 1846, was the home of Governor John Motley Moorehead, one of the state's governors before the Civil War. The house is believed to be the oldest example of Italianate villa architecture in the nation. It was in this house that Confederate General Joseph E. Johnston watched his surrendered troops march past on their way home to an uncertain future in late April 1865.

Alamance Battleground ★★★★★

5803 South Rte. 625, Burlington
(Alamance County 40 miles east of Greensboro)
T: 336-227-4785
ah.dcr.state.nc.us/sections/hs/alamance/alamanc.htm
Mon–Sat 9am–5pm, Sun 1–5pm
Admission: Free

In 1771, some of North Carolina's colonists were growing angry about paying taxes, but it was not King George III and his taxes on paper and tea that most frustrated these settlers who lived in the backcountry of the colony. Few of these settlers thought about the king on a regular basis. He, and even the coastal merchants, were too far away to have that much influence.

North Carolina's yeoman farmers were more frustrated with the tax collectors in the backcountry who worked for the colony's Royal governor, who was at that time William Tryon. While the governor had been appointed by the king, the farmers thought of the governor's tax collectors as local officials. Some of these tax collectors had been in power in the colony for more than 30 years and had grown corrupt and abusive. They often confiscated important property such as plow horses or the plows themselves to settle debts.

Finally in late 1770 and early 1771, a handful of farmers in the central part of North Carolina known as the Piedmont took action. They formed a loose organization called the Regulators, meaning that they intended to regulate the abuse of power that the tax collectors had over them. The Regulators vowed that if the governor was not going to rein in the abuses of his collectors, they would.

The Regulators started small by refusing to pay taxes. Their disobedience grew. Some tax collectors were captured and tarred and feathered. Royal courts were disrupted by Regulators coming to the defense of their members. Finally, a personal friend of Tryon, Edward Fanning of Hillsborough, was beaten by the Regulators and his house set afire.

Tryon had had enough of these men disputing his authority to gather taxes. In March 1771, he moved out from New Bern on the coast with a militia made up of men mostly from the eastern and coastal parts of the colony. By March 11, Tryon was on the banks of Alamance Creek with a force of about 1,000 men. A group of Regulators, numbering about 2,000, was five miles away. Though he was outnumbered, Tryon pressed forward, demanding that the Regulators break up and return to their homes.

On March 16, the two sides met at Alamance Battleground. The Regulators, who had been bold when attacking individual tax collectors, were less brave when facing the muskets of a drilled militia. Many of them ran at the sight of the ranks in their front so the numerical advantage the Regulators had started with was quickly lost. According to one story, Tryon himself initiated the battle when he grabbed a musket and shot a Regulator leader in the back after the man had demanded that Tryon and his men leave the field.

The two sides opened up on each other. At the end of the battle, Tryon reported that nine members of his militia had been killed and at least 60 were wounded. The numbers of killed and wounded on the Regulators' side have never been confirmed, but are believed to have been many more. Tryon took 15 prisoners, later hanging seven of them in Hillsborough as an example to other would-be rebels.

Tryon warned the Regulators who had escaped that he could discover their names. He offered amnesty if they would come in and sign an oath of loyalty to the king. Those who refused moved on to the frontier lands in Kentucky and beyond.

The Alamance Battleground site today is marked by a granite monument erected in 1880 as well as by blue flags showing the lines of the Regulators and red flags showing the lines of the governor's militia. The park office has a movie about the background of the battle that focuses on the Regulator leader Herman Husband, who may or may not have been at the battle itself. Also here is a cabin constructed around 1780 that was once owned by a member of the Regulators.

Technically, the Regulator War, if one engagement can be called that, was not a precursor to the American Revolution, as the Regulators were not protesting the abuses of King George III. They were protesting local corruption of the king's tax collectors. But the Regulator War does show how early the colonists began to grow angry with laws and taxes that they did not think were being applied fairly.

While the Boston Massacre predated the Battle of Alamance, this was the first armed engagement between colonists and militia representing the king of England. It would be another four years before the same type of anger would boil over at the battles of Lexington and Concord. It can be said that the Revolution's roots may be traced back to this now-quiet field in the Piedmont of North Carolina.

GETTING TO AND AROUND GUILFORD COURTHOUSE

Both Greensboro and Winston-Salem are served by the Piedmont Triad International Airport, which is located about 20 miles from each city with Winston-Salem to the west and Greensboro to the east. A variety of airlines fly into PTIA so it is well served by connections and rental car agencies. There are airport shuttles to both cities as well as taxi services. Amtrak also makes a stop in Greensboro. The train station offers connections for public transportation, and taxis, available here. There are several downtown motels.

Two interstates cross in Greensboro—I-40, which links the California to the coast of North Carolina, and I-85, which runs from Petersburg, Virginia—into Alabama.

A car is the best way to see Guilford Courthouse Battlefield, though a public bus does run to the national park. Call the visitor center to get the bus schedule. If walking, be aware that the ground can be hilly. The walking trails within the park are dirt, but walkers and bikers can also follow the paved road for vehicles.

Greensboro as a city does not have a colonial downtown, as it was founded after the battle of Guilford Courthouse. The battle took place several miles to the north of the central business district. If visitors are starting from downtown, look for brown historic signs heading north along Battleground Road. If visitors are looking only for the battlefield and have no interest in seeing downtown Greensboro, watch for those brown signs west of Greensboro on I-40 at the exit for New Garden Road.

SOURCES & OTHER READING

The Cowpens–Guilford Courthouse Campaign, Burke Davis, University of Pennsylvania Press, 2002

Guilford Courthouse, John Hairr, DeCapo Press, 2002

The Road to Guilford Courthouse: The American Revolution in the Carolinas, John Buchanan, Wiley, 1999

Southern Campaigns of the American Revolution, Dan Morrill, Nautical and Aviation Publishing Company of America, 1993

Touring North Carolina's Revolutionary War Sites, Daniel W. Barefoot, John F. Blair Publisher, 1998

Washington's General: Nathaniel Greene and the Triumph of the American Revolution, Terry Golway, Henry Holt & Company, 2005

ACCOMMODATIONS

Andrea's Troy-Bumpas Inn Bed and Breakfast

114 S. Mendenhall St., Greensboro
T: 800-370-9070 or 336-370-1660
troy-bumpasinn.com
$95–$150

The inn was built by the Reverend Bumpas in 1847 and occupied by his family until 1976. Bumpas chose a Greek Revival design for the house and set it on a knoll overlooking what is now Greensboro College.

Burke Manor Inn

303 Burke St., Gibsonville
T: 888-287-5311 or 336-449-6266
burkemanor.com
$125–$169

The home has been restored to its original 1909 Victorian grandeur. Cone was a textile magnet who founded Cone Mills, still in operation today. It was restored in 1999 and opened as an inn in 2000.

Old Salem

North Carolina

The Coldstream Guards picketing Old Salem's Tavern

THE EARLY YEARS

Freedom to practice various religions was a dominant reason many people left the Old World of Europe for the New World of America in the 1600s and 1700s. Old Salem portrays daily life in a Moravian town just before the Revolution.

The 15th century was not a good time to introduce new religions anywhere in Europe. Catholic priest John Huss learned that the hard way in 1415 when he was burned at the stake for heresy. His crime was questioning the pope on the issue of why only priests were allowed to drink communal wine rather than the parishioners.

Huss's persecuted followers did not give up on their religion. They kept moving from place to place in Europe until the early 1700s when they encountered a friend in Count Ludwig von Zinzendorph, who offered them refuge on his estate in what is now the Czech Republic. Able to practice their religion without fear of abuse, they began to think of missionary work.

In the early 1730s, Huss's followers, by then called Moravians, began to send missionaries to the New World in America. They first landed in Georgia, but found it too inhospitable. They moved on to Pennsylvania, where they founded the towns of Bethlehem and Nazareth.

Anxious to claim new lands for themselves so that they could expand their religion, several settlers set out from Bethlehem in 1752 in search of a tract of land in unsettled North Carolina. After traveling for weeks with a surveyor, they finally settled on 98,000 acres in the western part of the colony. They dubbed the land Wachovia, which had been a place name in their Czech homeland. The land had everything settlers would need to carve out a new life—productive land, fresh drinking water, forests, and game.

In November 1753, the first settlers from Bethlehem arrived at an abandoned cabin they found on their land. They dubbed their new community Bethabara, a word meaning house of passage, indicating that they only intended this humble little house to be the first of many to come. As more Moravian settlers arrived, other communities were built nearby. The Moravian communities lay along the Great Wagon Road, a major road that settlers in the northeastern colonies used on their way south. Thousands of settlers bound for other colonies passed through Wachovia on their way to build new lives.

On January 6, 1766, two work parties from Bethania and Bethabara, the first two Moravian towns in Wachovia, gathered at the planned site of another community to begin felling trees. The name chosen for the new community was Salem, meaning peace in Czech. The town's plans had been created in Europe and sent over by boat. (The Moravians did not leave much to chance when it came to planning their communities.)

The idea for creating more Moravian villages was as much for economic reasons as for any concern about outgrowing resources. The creation of new villages gave newly released apprentices locations where they could open shop. It was Moravian custom that the former apprentice did not set up shop near enough to his former trade teacher that they would be in competition with each other.

As the Moravian communities grew, they stuck to a philosophy of hard work (in contrast to the colonists in Jamestown founded by noblemen who had never worked with their hands, nor at Roanoke Island, where soldiers were more interested in finding gold than in planting crops.) Remembering how European governments had targeted them for persecution, the Moravians tried to remain as isolated as possible from colonial government. They even petitioned the governor to exempt them from militia duty during the French and Indian Wars. The 1770 governor of North Carolina, William Tryon, allowed them leeway because the settlers of Wachovia paid their taxes without complaint—something the English-descended settlers were less prone to do.

In 1771, when the Regulator Movement of tax protests was raging in surrounding communities, the Moravians ignored it. They wanted to stay in good standing with the governor. Four years later, as talk of revolution stirred, the Moravians still tried to maintain their neutrality. They saw no reason to fight England. In fact, many Moravians began to suspect that some of their neighbors were pushing for war in order to acquire some of their property.

When war broke out between England and the colonies, the Moravians continued to remain neutral. When questioned as to their loyalties, they replied that it was their nature to affirm their allegiance "to those in authority over us," an encompassing doctrine that they believed would apply equally if the British were in charge or a new rebel government won over North Carolina.

The communities were visited several times by both British and Patriot militia forces. The Moravians tried to remain neutral but their patience was tried most by the Patriot militia, which they considered lawless. Even the Moravian women reported having weapons drawn on them by the militia. Each time the militia would come through, the Moravians, who had not enlisted, were accused of being Tories. Their homes were searched for proof that the peaceful Moravians had ties to the British. They fared just as poorly when British General Cornwallis and his army marched through Salem on their way to Guilford Courthouse in March 1781.

Any suspicion as to the loyalty of the Moravians was quickly dispelled in the post-war peace. The governor and the state's new general assembly met twice in Salem and left with a new appreciation of the Moravians. When North Carolina's governor issued a request of the state that there be a planned observance in celebration of North Carolina's independence, apparently only the Moravians responded.

On July 4, 1783, there were prayers, hymn singing, and a love feast celebrated with coffee and rolls shared by the townspeople. That was followed by a parade around Salem's square. Records indicate that this was the first celebration of the Fourth of July in the new nation. The other communities in Wachovia had other celebrations, all of which revolved around offering up prayers for peace. The Moravians of Salem, who had longed for centuries to be left alone, had finally joined the new United States and were the first to celebrate its formation.

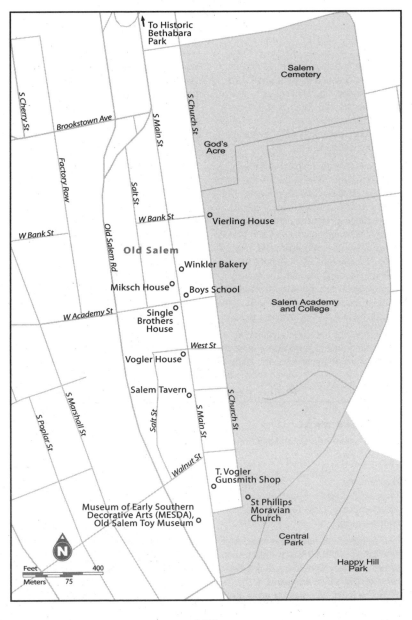

To Historic
Bethabara
Park

Salem
Cemetery

S Cherry St

Brookstown Ave

S Main St

S Church St

God's
Acre

Factory Row

Salt St

W Bank St

Vierling House

W Bank St

Old Salem Rd

Old Salem

Winkler Bakery

Miksch House

Boys School

W Academy St

Single
Brothers
House

Salem Academy
and College

West St

Vogler House

Salem Tavern

Salt St

S Main St

S Church St

S Marshall St

S Poplar St

Walnut St

T. Vogler
Gunsmith Shop

Museum of Early Southern
Decorative Arts (MESDA),
Old Salem Toy Museum

St Phillips
Moravian
Church

Central
Park

Happy Hill
Park

Feet   400

N

Meters   75

OLD SALEM TODAY

Old Salem is both a distinct neighborhood of Winston-Salem and a historical attraction within the city. Encompassing several square blocks, Old Salem is still centered around the same square that was planned as a public space in 1766, the year the community was founded.

Historians love the efficiency of the Moravians, who came to this part of North Carolina along the Old Wagon Road. The Road was the super highway of colonial times, running from the northern colonies through the southern colonies and then on to the far reaches of settlements, like Kentucky. Travelers often stopped in Salem to rest and resupply themselves, and the Moravians dutifully recorded the comings and goings of the travelers. Those records are now in the Moravian archives.

Moravians kept track of everything. In 1989 when a tornado ripped up most of the trees on Old Salem's square, historians went back to the Moravian records, found the species and location of each tree that had been originally planted, and replaced them with the same trees that had been planted in the 1760s.

Winston-Salem became a hyphenated city in 1913 when Salem, a Moravian town of artisans, merged with the nearby factory town of Winston, which had grown up around the tobacco-processing plant built there by Richard Joshua Reynolds. (That was not long after the R.J. Reynolds Tobacco Company had invented the cigarette rolling machine, which would revolutionize the tobacco industry and turn it into the cigarette industry.)

Today, Winston-Salem is a city of 185,000 people with an increasing emphasis on medicine and biotechnology, in addition to the manufacturing that once made it the largest city in North Carolina.

POINTS OF INTEREST

Old Salem ★★★★★
900 Old Salem Rd. (South Main Street)
Winston-Salem
T: 336-721-7350
oldsalem.org/
Tues–Sat 8:30am–5:30pm, Sun 12:30–5:30pm; closed major holidays.
Admission: $21

Like Williamsburg, which was saved from destruction in the 1930s by citizens concerned that they were losing their colonial heritage, Old Salem was saved in the 1950s. A foundation was set up to preserve the homes and shops that had formed the heart of the community. Old Salem then opened as a historic attraction with a special focus on explaining the lives of the Moravians who had come to the region in 1753 from Bethlehem, Pennsylvania.

Moravians are a group of Christian denomination dedicated to missionary work to reach nonbelievers. In colonial days, they professed allegiance to no power other than God. They interpreted that belief to mean that they would follow the government dictates of whatever government won the American Revolution. The Moravians were advanced compared to many other communities of the period in that they believed in the equal education of men and women. Salem College for women was established in 1772, making it the oldest women's college in the nation.

Moravians followed a choir system in their faiths. Boys and girls were educated separately. That separation of the sexes in public continued even into death. For instance, married men were buried in the cemetery in a section along with the other married men. All of the tombstones in a Moravian cemetery are the same size and placed on their backs in an expression of humbleness before God.

Any tour of Old Salem begins in the visitor center, where tickets are purchased. Visitors can read displays explaining the history of the religion and Old Salem. Visitors then walk over a wooden bridge into Old Salem to tour the homes and buildings that belong to the foundation. Many homes in Old Salem remain in private hands and have signs identifying them as private residences.

One museum directly across from the visitor center is the **Museum of Early Southern Decorative Arts (MESDA)** ★★★★. This museum is divided into 24 period rooms and six galleries, with each room set up to display furnishings that were common to the era in different parts of the South through the early 1800s.

MESDA is ideal for visitors who are interested in antiques. Visitors can see how a frontier cabin might have looked, then move into a room that shows how a room in a wealthy person's home might have been assembled during the same period. All of the rooms were taken from actual homes in the Carolinas, Virginia, and Maryland that were built during the period. All of the furnishings are original.

Old Salem Toy Museum ★★★★, in the same building as MESDA, features toy displays dating from 225 AD to 1925 AD Most were in a private collection donated to Old Salem. The museum displays show how toys for wealthy children through the ages often used the latest technology while toys for children of average or poor families were often cleverly designed but cheaper to create. Among the toys are elaborate doll houses, circus animal displays, wooden toys, and dolls.

At the north end of Old Salem is the building of most interest to those who want to learn about the Moravians. The **Single Brothers House** ★★★★★ housed the single men in Salem. It is half-brick and half-timber construction. The timber section was built in 1769 and the brick expansion was built in 1786. As a boy progressed into manhood after age 14, he left his parents' house and moved into this large dormitory-like building. The boy then lived here until he had learned a trade and was ready to make his own way in the world. He saw his parents and any girls in whom he might be interested only at church on Sundays.

Many of the skills the tradesmen of Salem practiced are demonstrated in the Single Brothers House. One room is set up for a tinsmith. Another is set up for a joiner or a person who made furniture. Another room shows how dyeing of thread was performed. The Single Brothers House kitchen is also preserved in the basement. One of the things that fascinated visiting George Washington in this basement was the wooden pipe and faucet that constituted the only place in Salem that had running water. The water was piped from a nearby spring.

During Christmas season, love feasts are held in the kitchen. Love feasts are a Moravian tradition in which coffee and sugar cake are shared in memory of Jesus' last supper with his disciples. The coffee usually has milk and sugar already blended into the coffee, which is then boiled. "Strangers," people who are not Moravian, are invited to participate. In the sub-basement below the Single Brothers House kitchen is a putz, or display of Old Salem in the 1800s, that is put out each year at Christmas.

The Boys' School ★★★★★, erected in 1794, is across the street from the Single Brothers House. It is now a museum housing a number of artifacts of the early Moravians. It is a good place to find a deeper understanding of the religion, which now has 50,000 members in the United States.

God's Acre ★★★, on the north side of Old Salem, remains an active cemetery, though its earliest burials date back to colonial times. Each Easter Sunday, Moravians from around the country return to Winston-Salem to form brass bands to play hymns for sunrise services in God's Acre. The service attracts thousands of participants from all religions. The service officially begins when the pastor of Home Moravian Church on the square emerges on the balcony to announce "Christ is risen" to the crowd waiting in the streets. The crowd then marches quietly down to God's Acre to hear the bands echoing each other's hymns from different places in the cemetery. Slowly, the bands form in one spot to play together.

Winkler Bakery ★★★, at 529 South Main Street, still bakes bread, sugar cakes, cookies, and other goods the old-fashioned way—in a brick oven that first saw service in 1800. Visitors can buy the baked goods in an adjacent sales center where the cash registers are hidden in deep wooden boxes to preserve the illusion that the bakery is still in the 19th century.

Miksch House ★★★ across the street from Winkler Bakery, is typical of the types of houses built by the Moravians in Salem in the 18th century. Built in 1771, its simple construction consists of logs covered in clapboards. It was also the first house that was lived in by a single family. (The other early houses in the new settlement were shared by several people until other houses could be constructed.) Though small, the Miksch house has the rounded Moravian arch over its entrance that visitors to Old Salem will see on virtually all Moravian dwellings.

Vierling House ★★★★, on Church Street near God's Acre, demonstrates (when compared to the small Miksch House) that while equal in death, Moravians were free to show off wealth through their dwellings. Dr. Samuel Vierling arrived in Salem in 1790 as the town's doctor. Displays of physicians' tools and supplies are shown on the second floor.

Vogler House ★★★★, on Main Street, has been restored to what it looked like in 1840, which allows visitors to compare what the early Moravian settlers experienced compared to those in later, more prosperous times. One room of the house is set up to display Vogler's trade as a silversmith and watchmaker.

Salem Tavern ★★★★ is really two Salem Taverns. The original, built in 1781, was designed to be a moneymaker for the town, as it usually hosted "strangers" (out-of-town visitors who were not Moravians). This tavern is set up as a museum to demonstrate what a tavern was like in colonial times. It was a combination restaurant and motel with food served on the ground floor and bed space that could be rented on the top floors. (Bed space, not entire rooms, was rented.) The tavern is also missing windows on the ground floor. That was to keep younger Moravians from observing too many of the strangers' activities. George Washington spent two nights here on his 1791 tour of the colonies.

The second tavern is a real tavern restaurant where visitors can sample colonial-era fare such as Moravian chicken pot pie. Reservations are generally not required except during holiday seasons.

T. Vogler Gunsmith shop ★★★★, on South Main beyond the Tavern, may surprise visitors since the Moravians repeatedly professed that they were neutral observers during the Revolution. But the Moravians were hunters and sportsmen who liked the competitive nature of shooting. By 1831, Salem willingly complied with a new North Carolina law that each town should have a trained militia force. Mr. Vogler likely worked on the militia muskets, as well as repaired the rifles of local people. While the Indians in this part of North Carolina never attacked the settlers, game animals and predators were frequently hunted, so most families in outlying regions kept firearms. The gunsmith shop is the newest building in Old Salem and is staffed by two skilled gunsmiths.

One block to the east of the gunsmith shop are **two churches ★★★** that were used by black Moravians, both slave and free. One is reconstructed of logs and is used as an interpretive center and museum focusing on the lives of black people in colonial Salem. The original log church was razed in 1823. The brick church is St. Phillips Moravian church. The current building replaced the original log church. It dates back to 1861 and is believed to be the oldest standing black church in North Carolina.

Old Salem can be seen in a day, but seeing all of the sites associated with Winston-Salem will likely require an overnight stay.

Historic Bethabara Park ★★★★★
2147 Bethabara Rd., Winston-Salem
T: 336-924-8191
bethabarapark.org/maphome.htm
Tue–Fri 10:30am–4:30pm,
Sat–Sun 1:30–4:30pm
Admission: $2

This city-owned historic park is on the site of the original Moravian settlement of 1753. Once this and the nearby village of Bethania were established, the expansive-minded Moravians set about starting the planned town of Salem more than a decade later. The museum and visitor center include displays explaining the founding of the settlement.

The reconstructed palisade fort, built on the original site and of the same size, was originally constructed in 1756 in response to fear of Indian attacks. The colonists feared that the French would encourage the tribes to attack any outposts of the English colonists during the French and Indian War. Those attacks were more common in the northern colonies, but there were some incidents of roving bands of Cherokees attacking settlers near Bethabara. Settlers from miles around rushed into the fort when they felt threatened. The fort never came under attack. (But Cherokees once heard a brass horn blowing right before they were ready to make their attack. The Indians interpreted the horn blowing to mean that they had been discovered. In reality, it was the Moravian watchman blowing his horn to call people to prayer.)

On site are two gardens, one for vegetables and one for herbs that were used for medicines. Nearby are log cabins that are much more rudimentary than the houses that would be built at Salem in the following decade. The first settlers of Bethabara were true pioneers and did not have the time to build fine houses. Their goal was simply to put up a fort, then cabins, then create gardens. It took time to develop the idea of creating the city of artisans that would become Salem.

Other buildings open for touring include a church built in 1788 and several houses dating back to the early 19th century. God's Acre Cemetery dates back to 1757, making it the oldest Moravian cemetery in North Carolina. The first sunrise service was held here the following year in 1758.

American Revolution reenactors camp at Bethabara several times a year. Call 336-924-8191 for details and directions.

GETTING TO AND AROUND OLD SALEM

Winston-Salem is served by Piedmont Triad International Airport, 20 miles to the east along I-40. The airport hosts several airlines and rental car companies. There is a regular airport shuttle operating between downtown Winston-Salem and the airport. If visiting only Old Salem, it is possible to take the shuttle from the airport to a downtown hotel or bed-and-breakfast, and then walk to the historic area. Old Salem is about six blocks south of the central business district, and the visitor center is located at the south end of Main Street.

Winston-Salem also has an executive airport, Smith Reynolds Airport, located just three miles north of downtown. It does not have commercial airline service, but is served by two rental car companies and taxi service.

Old Salem is not as large as Colonial Williamsburg, but is similar in concept. Tourists walk the sidewalks to view restored shops and houses that have been preserved or restored to the way they were in colonial times. All access is paved, but most of the colonial structures do require people to climb stairs. One difference between the two attractions is that Old Salem is restored while Williamsburg's buildings were mostly built to colonial specifications.

While Old Salem is within walking distance of downtown, the first Moravian settlement, Bethabara, now a city-owned historical park, is not. Visitors will need to take a taxi or their own car to see this well-preserved piece of city and Moravian history that is now on the north side of Winston-Salem.

Winston-Salem is part of the Piedmont Triad with Greensboro to the east and High Point to the southeast. All of these cities are easily accessible except during the spring and fall furniture markets when thousands of furniture buyers come to High Point to see the latest styles offered by furniture manufacturers. Tourists should check with the visitor bureaus in these three cities before booking a stay to make sure their dates do not conflict with the market.

ACCOMMODATIONS

Augustus T. Zevely Inn

803 S. Main St., Winston-Salem
T: 800-928-9299 or 336-748-9299
winston-salem-inn.com
$90–$235

This historic inn is in the center of Old Salem. Originally built in 1844, it was restored in 1994. Rooms are furnished with Old Salem collection furnishings, based on originals found in local museums and private homes. Augustus T. Zevely was a doctor. His office is now used as a breakfast room where a continental-plus breakfast is served.

Summit Street Bed & Breakfast Inns

420 & 434 Summit St. at West Fifth, Winston-Salem
T: 800-301-1887 or 336-777-1887
bbinn.com
$79–$179

The inn consists of two large adjacent Victorian homes listed on the National Register of Historic Places: the 1887 Jacob Lott Ludlow House and the 1895 Benjamin Joseph Sheppard House.

SOURCES & OTHER READING

A Separate Canaan: The Making of an Afro-Moravian World in North Carolina, 1763–1840, John Sensbach, University of North Carolina Press, 1998

A Walk through Old Salem, Walker Stone, John F. Blair Publisher, 2000

The Moravian Community in Colonial North Carolina: Pluralism on the Southern Frontier, Daniel Thorp, University of Tennessee Press, 1989

The Moravians in North Carolina, Levin Reichel, Clearfield Company, 2002

The Quiet People of the Land: A Story of the North Carolina Moravians in Revolutionary Times, Hunter James, University of North Carolina Press, 1976

Serving Two Masters: Moravian Brethren in Germany and North Carolina, 1727–1801, Elizabeth Sommer, University of Kentucky, 2000

Charleston

South Carolina

The dungeon under the Old Exchange

THE EARLY YEARS

Charleston, the most famous and important, as well as the largest, of the English colonial cities in the South, could have been founded even earlier than St. Augustine and by the Spanish or French had those explorers been a little luckier. The Spanish landed in 1526 just north of Charleston and the French landed in 1562 just south of it. However, both of those colonies failed to establish any kind of permanent settlement in the area.

It wasn't until 1670 that Charles Town was founded up the Ashley River by English colonists. By 1680, the colony had diversified with the arrival of some French Huguenots who had left Europe to pursue religious freedom. In 1690, the settlers decided that the peninsula between the two rivers would actually be a better site for their town, so they moved.

Charleston grew quickly thanks to its port, from which it exported indigo and rice and imported slaves. By 1775, the city had 11,000 residents, making it the fourth-largest city in the colonies behind New York, Philadelphia, and Boston.

During the early debates about seeking independence, Charleston's merchants were reluctant to cut ties with Britain, a position that struck the ousted Southern Royal governor as indicative of an undercurrent of Loyalist sentiment. After being driven out of Boston in the summer of 1775, the British were looking for an easy victory. Based partially on the governor's hopeful remarks, British General Henry Clinton set sail for Charleston in May 1776.

When the nine British ships mounting 300 cannons arrived on June 28 outside Charleston's harbor, the only thing standing between them and the city was a low, unimpressive, half-finished fort made of sand and palmetto logs. All day, the British pounded the fort, located on Sullivan's Island, but their cannon balls bounced off the palmetto logs or burrowed into the sand. The Patriot gunners did serious damage to two of the ships, and one of them had to be abandoned. The humiliated British, who had come south in order to save face after being humiliated in Boston one year earlier, sailed away. The citizens were so happy with the gallantry of the fort's garrison and its unassuming palmetto logs that they added the palmetto tree to their colonial flag, where it remains today as an integral part of South Carolina's state flag. The fort was named Fort Moultrie in honor of its commander, William Moultrie, who would later serve as one of the state's early governors.

In the spring of 1780, the British returned. They were feeling more confident after beating off an allied siege at Savannah in October 1779. By April 10, 1780, the British had landed a land force on James Island, southeast of Charleston, that marched north then swung back south toward the city to cut off any escape routes. The British fleet then sailed past the now-dilapidated Fort Moultrie into Charleston's harbor. Charleston was virtually surrounded, though a few reinforcements did manage to enter the city. Some historians believe British General Clinton allowed those troops in so that he could capture them, making his almost-certain victory even more important.

The siege ended on May 12, 1780, with the surrender of more than 5,500 Americans to a British force nearly three times that size. Judged by the numbers of men captured, this was the worst defeat suffered by the Patriots during the war.

The Americans had some measure of revenge when the British collected all of their muskets and tossed them into a small magazine. A few of the captured Patriots raised their hands to say, "Those are still loaded," but the victorious British ignored them. No one knows exactly what happened, but the gunpowder-filled magazine with the loaded and apparently primed muskets exploded. At least 50 people were wounded and a fire burned down a number of buildings. While the Patriots laughed, the loss of the muskets was actually a disaster for the British. A supply ship loaded with 4,000 muskets had already gone down, and now another 3,000 muskets had been destroyed by fire. Those 7,000 muskets would have normally gone to arm Loyalist Tories who were known to quietly exist in the South Carolina back country. Now the Tories would have to wait several months before another British supply ship could outfit them.

Charleston remained in British hands for the rest of the war, and the Patriots made no attempt to free it. It became home base for the British campaign to take the South Carolina backcountry, which ultimately failed due to the British losses at Cowpens and Kings Mountain.

When word reached Charleston that Cornwallis had surrendered at Yorktown, the distressing news actually meant little to the commanders in Charleston. They still held that city and they had received no orders telling them to relinquish it. They were firmly entrenched and would remain so for more than a year after Cornwallis's surrender. It was a strange time of watching and waiting. The colonials believed that the defeat of Cornwallis meant the end of the war, but the final decision would have to be made by Parliament in London. It would take time for news of the disaster to reach there and then more time for the king and Parliament to debate and still more time for them to accept the inevitable knowledge that England and its soldiers were tired of fighting.

The British occupation force in Charleston finally started sailing away in October, but did not fully leave the city until December 14, 1782. A Continental Army marched symbolically into the city the following morning. Charlestonians did not seem to have suffered much under the two years of occupation. Patriot homes had not been touched and little destruction had been visited upon the common populace. In fact, the presence of the British had been so strong that the colonials had wisely made the decision not to attack. In effect, the strong British presence in Charleston saved it from further warfare.

The Treaty of Paris, a document officially ending the war, was finally signed nine months later on September 3, 1783. Charleston began to recover its status as the center of Southern culture.

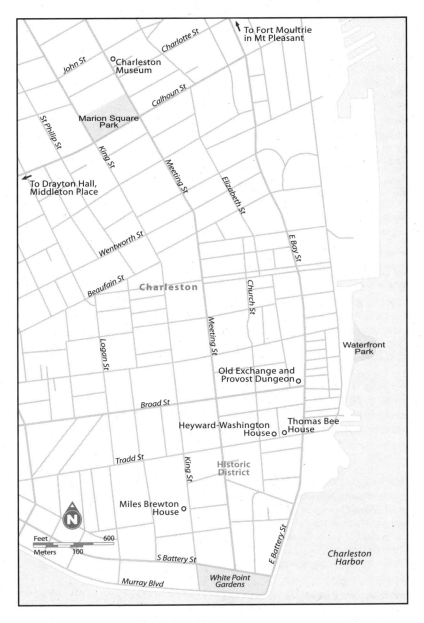

CHARLESTON TODAY

Charleston used to be one of the most important cities in the United States. It was once ranked the nation's fourth-largest city and the largest city in the South. That status could be attributed to its naturally deep harbor and role as the social and political center of the colonial Southern culture.

Today, Charleston is only the 76th-largest city in the nation with an area population of around 550,000, but it remains one of the top tourist destinations in the South.

Its harbor is still one of the finest on the East Coast, so visitors are able to see container ships making their way to the city's port facilities.

Charleston's compact nature makes it naturally tourist friendly. The historic center holds a number of important historic attractions, fine colonial architecture, restaurants and cafes, and numerous amenities for the visitor. Visitors should plan on spending at least two nights and three days.

POINTS OF INTEREST

Old Exchange and Provost Dungeon
★★★★★

122 East Bay St., Charleston
T: 843-727-2165
oldexchange.com/
Daily 9am–5pm
Admission: $7

The Old Exchange and Provost Dungeon at the corner of East Bay and Broad Street should be the first stop for anyone interested in the colonial period. As more ships began to dock at Charleston in the early 1700s, it became clear to the city's tax collectors that there was a need for a central point for the imports and exports to pass through so that they could be bought, sold, and taxed. Approved for construction in 1767 and finished in 1772, the exchange became the center of commercial and social life in Charleston, as it filled each day with ship captains, merchants, traders, and speculators.

Built at the edge of the city's seawall where the ships docked, the exchange was designed and constructed by master builders who had recently immigrated from Germany. The building may be one of the first examples of urban planning in the United States, as the site was carefully placed to be visible along the waterfront to encourage ship captains to frequent it.

The exchange was one of the best-known and most important buildings in all of the colonies. In 1773, two weeks before the famous Boston Tea Party, a meeting of citizens of Charleston demanded that a shipment of tea be refused in protest of the British-imposed tax on imported tea. To calm the citizens, the tea was unloaded but kept under lock and key rather than being sold. While the citizens' protest was not as dramatic as throwing the tea into the harbor, it was just as pointed. Just like their neighbors up north, Charlestonians did not want to pay taxes on tea.

In May 1788, delegates gathered at the exchange to ratify the United States Constitution, making South Carolina the eighth state to give its approval. In May 1791, President George Washington arrived in Charleston and reviewed a parade from the exchange. Later that day he attended a grand ball there.

Today, the exchange has excellent exhibits on the role of South Carolina in the American Revolution. There are displays focusing on the Declaration of Independence, the Constitution, Washington's Southern Tour, a discussion of Isaac Hayne, a Patriot who was executed in Charleston by the British, and a very detailed exhibit on the Confederate postal system. (The building served as Charleston's post office from 1815 to 1896.) There is also a display on Mrs. Daniel Horry, the first woman planter in the colonies, and Rebecca Motte, considered a heroine of the Revolution. Visitors interested in clothing can examine original silk dresses for ladies and men's waistcoats. Silkworms were an early crop of the colonies, though the silk industry was never firmly established there. In the basement are displays on how the basement was used as a dungeon by the British during their occupation.

Historic District ★★★★★

Private homes

Most houses in the historic area have plaques attached to them describing their age. Many in the district date back to before the Revolution. Although almost all are private residences, walking the sidewalks of Charleston's historic district to view the outsides of the homes is a worthwhile activity.

Heyward-Washington House ★★★★★

87 Church St., Charleston
T: 843-722-2996
charlestonmuseum.org/topic.asp?id=21
Mon–Sat 10am–5pm, Sun 1–5pm
Admission: $9

Billed as Charleston's Revolutionary War House, the Heyward-Washington House is one of two homes owned and operated by the Charleston Museum. The house was built in 1771 by Daniel Heyward as a gift for his son Thomas, who occupied it only when he left his plantation to visit the city. Thomas Heyward signed the Declaration of Independence and was an officer with the South Carolina militia until he was captured by the British in 1780. He survived his imprisonment and was exchanged the following year. Heyward also signed the Articles of Confederation, the forerunner of the Constitution.

In 1791, the city rented the house from Heyward as a place for George Washington to stay during his visit to the city. Heyward sold the house in 1794, and it passed through a number of hands before being acquired for the final time in 1929 by the museum. Since it was occupied by both a signer of the Declaration and the first president, it may be the most historic house in Charleston that can be visited by the general public.

Visitors to the house will be struck by the size and quality of the furniture on display. Charleston was home to more than 250 furniture craftsmen between 1720 and 1825 and much of their handiwork survives. After exiting the house, visitors should visit the backyard gardens and the kitchen house to gain a fuller appreciation of what it would have been like to live in the house during colonial times. Allow one hour for a complete tour.

Thomas Bee House ★★

94 Church St., Charleston
Private residence—view only from sidewalk

This house is both historic and tragically romantic. It was owned by Governor Joseph Alston, whose wife was Theodosia Burr Alston, the daughter of Aaron Burr, the vice-president of the United States, who killed Treasury Secretary Alexander Hamilton in a duel. Theodosia and all of the crew of the ship on which she was sailing disappeared in 1815. While no trace was ever found of the people or the ship, they were probably attacked and murdered by pirates. Poet Robert Frost made Theodosia famous in one of his early works.

In the 1830s, this house served as the meeting place for John C. Calhoun and other political leaders to talk about nullification (the idea that a state could refuse to obey the laws of the United States government if they believed it harmed their individual state). This was the basis for the idea of secession, which would flare up 30 years later.

As noted earlier, this is a private house and not open for touring, but it is one of scores of houses with major historical significance that can be seen from the sidewalk.

Miles Brewton House ★★★★

27 King St., Charleston
Private residence—view only from sidewalk

Built in 1769, this house is often described by architectural historians as one of the finest homes in Charleston. The British certainly thought it was. They appropriated it for their military headquarters in 1780. One of the striking things about the house is the ironwork, particularly the iron spikes topping the fence that were designed to prevent anyone from climbing it. These were added in 1822 after the planned slave revolt that was to be led by Denmark Vessey, a free black man, was uncovered by a slave who confessed to his owner what was about to happen. Vessey and 36 other ringleaders were tried and executed. These spikes can be found on homes scattered around the city.

Charleston Museum ★★★★

360 Meeting St.
T: 843-722-2996
charlestonmuseum.org/topic.asp?id=1
Mon–Sat 9am–5pm, Sun 1–5pm
Admission: $10. Combined ticket prices available for visiting one or more historic houses.

Founded in 1773, the Charleston Museum is the oldest museum in the nation. Its permanent exhibits trace the history of the city from its first founding on the Ashley River to today. Numerous artifacts are displayed from the colonial and Civil War eras, including the chair used by the chairman of the secession committee that withdrew South Carolina from the Union in December 1860, the prelude to the Civil War. Also on display are photographs of the 1886 earthquake which devastated the city. Earthquake bolts added to surviving houses can still be seen today.

Allow at least two hours here to enjoy the permanent exhibits and the rotating ones. The museum is known for unusual displays such as the one in 2006 that looked at two centuries of undergarments and beauty aids.

Drayton Hall ★★★★

3380 Ashley River Rd.
T: 843-769-2600
draytonhall.org
March–October daily 9:30am–4pm;
November–February daily 9:30am–3pm
Admission: $12

Construction began on Drayton Hall in 1738. Completed four years later by European and black craftsmen, it is considered the oldest surviving example of Georgian-Palladian architecture. The house has never been modernized with electricity, indoor plumbing, or even new paint. The house, both inside and outside, looks exactly as it did on the day it was finished, and docents call the house "preserved" rather than restored. The house survived foraging bands of both British redcoats and Union soldiers attached to William T. Sherman. It was the only plantation along the Ashley River to survive both wars unscathed.

The house is unfurnished, but a visit here offers a rare look at what a plantation home looked like at the time.

Middleton Place ★★★

4300 Ashley River Rd.
T: 843-556-6020
middletonplace.org
Daily 9am–5pm
Admission: $35 for house, gardens and stable yards

Begun in 1741, Middleton Place has been home to a succession of influential South Carolinians. Henry Middleton, the first owner, was president of the First Continental Congress in 1775. His son Arthur signed the Declaration of Independence. Arthur's grandson signed the Ordnance of Secession that took South Carolina out of the Union.

The full grandeur of the estate will never be known, as more than two-thirds of the estate was burned to the ground by Union forces. Only the gentlemen's guest wing, completed in 1755, remains.

The grounds of the estate can be toured, including a portion where rice, a staple crop of the plantation, was grown.

Fort Moultrie National Monument ★

Rte. 703 in Sullivan's Island (follow sign)
T: 843-883-3123
nps.gov/fomo
Daily 9am–5pm
Admission: $3

The current fort is more closely associated with the Civil War time period than the Revolution, but the fort that defended Charleston at the beginning of the war was built on this site. Visitors can get a sense of how Fort Moultrie protected Charleston Harbor. The original fort was made from palmetto trees and dirt. The British cannon balls were absorbed by the spongy trees, thus saving the fort from destruction. Carolinians were so impressed that they added the image of the tree to their state flag.

GETTING TO AND AROUND CHARLESTON

Charleston is served by Charleston International Airport, which hosts six airlines, two rental car companies, and several charter and limousine services. It is at the eastern terminus of I-26, which connects to major north-south artery I-95 so the city is easily reached by air or road.

Visitors might consider taking a shuttle or taxi in from the airport if they only want to see the historic downtown. Charleston is a walker's delight, with the historic area concentrated at the lower end of the peninsula between the Ashley and the Cooper Rivers.

However, if visitors want to visit the two plantation homes Middleton Place and Drayton Hall, they will likely need a rental car to reach them.

Charleston is well known for its carriage tours of the historic area. There are four carriage companies operating in town, all leaving from the outdoor market. To avoid crowding, carriages tour different areas of town. Ask the driver if he or she is headed for the Battery. Still, even if your carriage heads away from the historic area, the tours are well worth the investment in time, as they are a great opportunity to hear the stories about the houses and their owners through the years.

Gray Line operates three different bus tours of the city, a 90-minute $19-tour of historic Charleston, a two-hour $25-tour adding the historic homes, and a $27-tour of Charleston combined with a harbor tour or a run to Fort Sumter.

Several locally owned bus tour companies, including some that offer free pickup at downtown hotels, make runs out to Middleton Place. These all-day tours average $55. Some tours stop at Magnolia Gardens, but a better choice for those interested in Revolutionary War history is Middleton Place.

There are also a variety of walking tours that average around $20 for two hours. Most companies offer either Civil War or Revolutionary War tours.

ACCOMMODATIONS

Ashley Inn Bed & Breakfast

201 Ashley Ave., Charleston
T: 800-581-6658 or 843-723-1848
charleston-sc-inns.com/ashley
$95–$175

Built in 1832 by Alexander Black, an inventor of rice and cotton-processing equipment, this federal-style home was remodeled in 1993. This inn is known for its gourmet breakfasts.

John Rutledge House Inn

116 Broad St., Charleston
T: 866-720-2609 or 843-723-7999
johnrutledgehouseinn.com
$190–$385 seasonal

John Rutledge, one of fifty-five signers of the US Constitution, built his home in 1763. Now restored, it is one of only fifteen homes belonging to those signers to survive and the only one to provide overnight accommodations. Antique and historically accurate reproductions furnish each room. Each afternoon, tea is served in the ballroom where presidents and Patriots have dined. It opened as an inn in 1989 and is listed on the National Register of Historic Places.

King George IV Inn

32 George St., Charleston
T: 888-723-1667 or 843-723-9339
kinggeorgeiv.com
$89–$185

The King George IV Inn, built in 1790, is located in the heart of the historic district. All rooms have decorative fireplaces, high ceilings, original wide-planked hardwood floors, original oak doors, and architectural moldings and details.

The Thomas Lamboll House

19 King St., Charleston
T: 888-874-0793 or 843-723-3212
lambollhouse.com
$125–$185

In 1722, Thomas Lamboll purchased the land for his house and finished building it in 1739. The Lamboll House is a notable example of pre-Revolutionary architecture, which also shows evidence of later attempts of change. Many architectural periods are represented, ranging from the early Georgian to the Victorian period.

Sources & Other Reading

A Gallant Defense: The Siege of Charleston, 1780, Carl Borick, University of South Carolina Press, 2003

American Colonies: The Settling of North America (The Penguin History of the United States, Volume 1), Alan Taylor, Penguin Press, 2002

Charleston! Charleston!: The History of a Southern City, Walter Fraser, University of South Carolina Press, 1991

Patriots Pistols and Petticoats: "Poor Sinful Charles Town" During the American Revolution, Walter Fraser, University of South Carolina Press, 1993

South Carolina and the American Revolution: A Battlefield History, John W. Gordon, University of South Carolina Press, 2003

Websites:

patriotresource.com/battles/charleston.html (1780 Siege of Charleston)

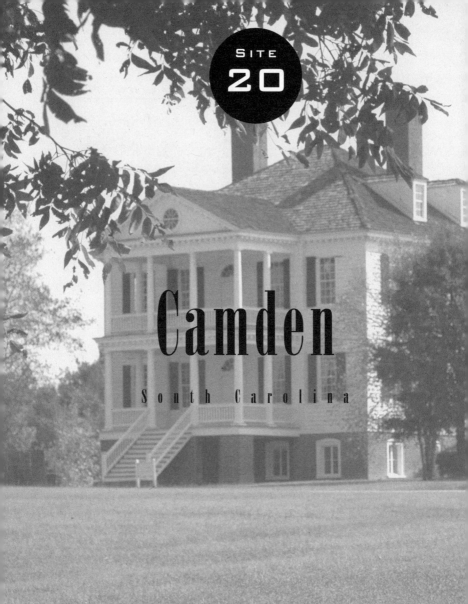

Camden

South Carolina

The Cornwallis-Kershaw House is a reproduced colonial-era home

THE WAR YEARS

I t was here that General Horatio Gates, a man who once thought he should be in George Washington's place as commander in chief, suffered one of the worst defeats the Americans experienced during the war. A reconstructed village gives visitors an idea of what it looked like at the time.

No historian has ever had anything good to say about the performance of General Horatio Gates at Camden on August 16, 1780. In fact, few historians have found anything good to say about the man at all. One historian labeled Gates "such a repellent personality that he still awaits his biographer."

A veteran of the French and Indian War, Gates was recommended for appointment to general by the Continental Congress in 1775. Early on, Gates lobbied for increasing responsibility, which he finally won when assigned to stop British General John Burgoyne's movement south from Canada. Gates won a stunning victory at Saratoga in 1777, forcing the British to surrender virtually their entire army. Gates's victory ended the British threat to cut the northern colonies off from the rest of the rebelling colonies.

Congress was impressed with this surprise victory over the British. So when the war began to go badly for the Americans in the South, Congress, without consulting Washington, gave Gates command of the entire Southern Department in July 1780. Gates considered it a giant step in his dream of supplanting Washington as commander.

Gates wasted no time in his quest for fame. He took command of an exhausted force of soldiers in Hillsborough, North Carolina, and started immediately for Camden, South Carolina, which was an important British storehouse. Without taking time to properly refit, scout, introduce himself to his officers and men, or even count the number of men he commanded (which he should have because he actually commanded about half the number he thought), Gates marched off looking for a fight.

The other problem with Gates's plan was that he intended to fight only the British already in Camden, having no idea that Lord Cornwallis had left Charleston with 2,000 men and was on his way to Camden with the express purpose of meeting Gates and his force. Gates made no provisions for scouting the way from Charleston or gathering any intelligence to see if the British force at Camden was going to be reinforced.

Gates made one more grave error on the march. Just before making the last march toward Camden, he fed his men a meal of "quick-baked" bread, fresh beef, and molasses, which upset the stomachs of virtually the entire army. Rather than wait for his men to recover, Gates ordered them into a forced march that began at 10pm that night.

Lord Cornwallis was also putting his men through a night march in order to reach Camden first. Camden was at that time a large British hospital with more than 800 sick soldiers. Cornwallis would not allow them to be captured without firing a shot. Cornwallis reached Camden first and began a march north of town to intercept Gates.

The two armies accidentally clashed in the middle of the night, one of the few times in the Revolution when there was night fighting. After firing blindly into the dark, both sides backed off to wait for dawn. Gates was reported to be "astonished" to learn that the man he was facing was Cornwallis. When the sun came up, Gates felt better when he realized that he outnumbered the British more than two to one. He smelled victory.

But the battle was far from won. The battlefield that they had stumbled onto was a broad plain with widely spaced trees. On either side were swamps. That meant the British could form their standard three ranks of muskets while Gates could not split his command and send them to either flank. It was a battlefield that lent itself to the Napoleonic stand-and-fire-in-ranks style of fighting favored by the British, and not to the hit-and-run style that the Americans wished to employ.

Gates made another mistake. In organizing his troops, he had put his least trained militia on his left flank in front of the British regulars. After the first round of yelling from the British troops and the first volley, the militia fled to the rear. Gates's numerical superiority had vanished in the time it took the men to run 100 yards.

The only bright spot for the Americans was the presence of the experienced Continentals, who were fighting under a professional soldier, 58-year-old Baron Johann de Kalb, a Bavarian in the French army who had volunteered to help the American cause. Just before the battle, de Kalb did something odd, but which may have been in reaction to a premonition of what would happen to him in the battle. He donned an old metal helmet, something that must have looked medieval to his men in their felt hats.

As the British soldiers grew close, they targeted de Kalb, recognizing him as an officer because of his extravagant uniform. De Kalb was wounded 11 times, mostly by British bayonets. Lord Cornwallis himself came to the scene and expressed regret that his men had purposely mortally wounded a man such as de Kalb, who was well known to the British officer corps. He died three days later of blood loss and infection.

With the wounding of de Kalb, the rest of the colonial line gave way to the British cavalry. What should have been a general retreat became a rout because General Gates was not around to give orders. He was riding his horse as fast as he could, making 60 miles in one day and spending the night in Charlotte, North Carolina. Two days later he was in Hillsborough, the town from which he had started his march on July 1. It had taken his army five weeks to walk from Hillsborough to Camden, but only four days for Gates's panicked ride back. "Was there ever such an instance of a general running away . . . from his whole army?" said Alexander Hamilton when he heard the reports.

As time passed, the disaster looked even worse. Gates had left Hillsborough with 4,000 troops. Only 700 returned and most of them had thrown away their muskets in disgust at the actions of their general. At least 1,000 soldiers had been killed by the British. British casualties had been light, with fewer than 90 killed and around 250 wounded. It was one of the most lopsided victories the British enjoyed during the war.

An embarrassed Congress, which had given Gates the job over Washington's objections, refused to lay any blame on him. Still, he was replaced as commander of the Southern Department and never again commanded any troops.

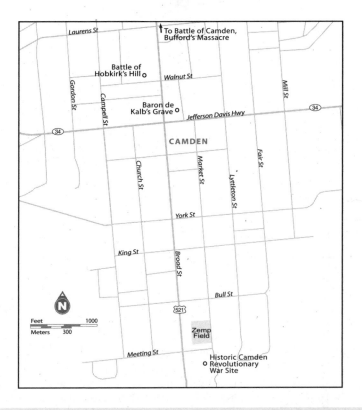

SOURCES & OTHER READING

Encyclopedia of the American Revolution, Mark Boatner III, Stackpole Books, 1966

The Glorious Cause, Robert Middlekauff, Oxford University Press, 1957

Horatio Gates and the Battle of Camden—"that unhappy affair," August 16, 1780, John Maass, Kershaw County Historical Society, 2001

Rebels & Redcoats, George Scheer and Hugh Rankin, DeCapo Press, 1957

Southern Campaigns of the American Revolution, Dan L. Morrill, The Nautical and Aviation Publishing Company, 1993

Touring South Carolina's Revolutionary War Sites, Daniel W. Barefoot, John F. Blair Publisher, 1999

Websites:

http://battleofcamden.org

CAMDEN TODAY

With a population of around 7,000, Camden is a small town where visitors will find side streets of attractive homes dating back more than 100 years, some public buildings designed by famous men, and cemeteries containing the graves of historically significant people.

Camden does not actively promote its status as an important colonial city. Visitors arriving in the town from I-77 have to search hard for a sign directing them to the town's main attraction, Historic Camden Revolutionary War Site.

Camden is a stop worthy of several hours for most travelers unless they are looking for ancestral information in the well-appointed Camden Archives and Museum at 1314 Broad Street. If so, plan on staying at least a day to sort through the archives' files.

POINTS OF INTEREST

Historic Camden Revolutionary War Site
★★★★★

US 521 (Broad St.) south of downtown Camden
T: 803-432-9841
historic-camden.net
Mon–Sat 10am–5pm, Sun 1–5pm
Admission: Free. Guided tours and admission to Kershaw-Cornwallis House is $5

Visitors to Camden should note that there were actually two battles of Camden, but neither of them actually took place in what is Camden today or at the Historic Camden Revolutionary War Site. The town of Camden, just north of the park, was an important outpost for the British after their capture of Charleston in 1780 because it lay along the road to Charleston. Virtually any attack coming from the Patriots would have to move through the town.

This 98-acre park of reconstructed and relocated buildings from the Revolutionary War period is maintained by the Historic Camden Foundation. The park, worth a stay of several hours at least, gives visitors a good sense of what the architecture of a village was like in the late 1770s. Dirt fortifications on the same locations where the original British forts were built are scattered around the site. These forts were built after the battles with the colonials.

Two log cabins on the property date back to the early 1800s and are typical of the backcountry houses of the era. One is set up as a museum of British occupation of the area. The gift shop carries souvenirs, including copies of both the Declaration of Independence and the United States Constitution.

The dominant building on the property is a replica of the Kershaw-Cornwallis House, which was burned to the ground by Union forces in 1865. In the spring of 1781, the house was nearly complete when it was captured by the British. General Cornwallis used it as his headquarters when he was in town. The house is fully furnished with pieces from that period.

Historic Camden holds Revolutionary War–related activities nearly every month. Check the website for a schedule.

Baron de Kalb's grave ★★★

Front lawn of Bethesda Presbyterian Church, corner of De Kalb and Little Sts., one block east of Broad St.

Here lies the grave of Baron de Kalb, the Bavarian-born soldier of fortune who gave his life in battle at the Battle of Camden while his commanding general fled to safety. The monument under which de Kalb rests was designed and carved by Robert Mills, the same man who designed the Washington Monument. De Kalb's body was placed under the monument in 1825. The inscription identifies de Kalb as "a citizen of the world."

Battle of Hobkirk's Hill ★

200 block of Broad St., Camden

Although a battle did take place here, there is little to see now other than the historic markers; a drive-by is all that is possible or necessary.

The Battle of Hobkirk's Hill took place on April 25, 1781, one month after the British army in the South had been left in a shambles after their tactical victory at the Battle of Guilford Courthouse in North Carolina. After Cornwallis had left the field, Patriot General Nathaniel Greene headed toward Camden, intent on disrupting Cornwallis's supply lines. On April 20, Greene made camp on this hill, hoping that the nearby British garrison at Camden would attack him. Greene was in a strong position to take the town if Lord Francis Rowdan attacked him, as Greene had almost twice as many men as the British garrison. Greene's plan worked. Rowdan left the safety of his trenches at what is now Historic Camden, and moved north in search of the American lines.

On April 25, the attack began. It was an unusual battle in that both sides were battle-hardened veterans. In this case, Greene had Continental soldiers from Maryland, Delaware, and Virginia and Rowdan had regular British troops. To the surprise of both sides, the British outflanked the Americans and drove Greene back, even though he had nearly twice the number of troops. Greene had 266 men killed and wounded, while the British suffered 358 killed and wounded. Even with the higher losses and smaller force, the British managed to remain in charge of the field at the end of the battle. Once again, Nathaniel Greene, considered one of the best generals in the Continental Army, had lost a battle.

Battle of Camden ★★

Six miles northeast of Camden
Take US 521 north to Rte. 28-58. Turn left; drive 2.3 miles to roadside marker.

Here, six miles from the center of downtown Camden today, almost a half-day's march from the Revolutionary War village, is where the Battle of Camden took place on August 16, 1780. On this ground, now a pine flat beside the road with a monument describing the battle, the British won one of their greatest victories of the war. The rout of American forces here convinced the British high command that the war in the colonies could be won if the British concentrated on capturing the South first.

With the capture of Charleston, the British believed they held the key to opening up and stripping any further resistance in the South. They imagined they would create a supply line deep into the South Carolina backcountry from which they would be able to attack into North Carolina. The village of Camden would serve as the major supply depot.

The Americans recognized the danger and Congress appointed General Horatio Gates, the man who had won the Battle of Saratoga, New York, to take command in the South to repel the British. Historians have had a hard time figuring out Gates's performance at Camden. Taking over his army in Hillsborough, North Carolina, Gates pushed his men south hard and fast in an effort to reach the British at Camden before they had time to dig in and create a fortress that would be too strong to attack. Gates pushed his men so much that they were exhausted and nearly starving by the time they reached the area.

On August 13, the two sides were 13 miles apart, about a short day's march. Gates had more than 4,000 men, but half of them were inexperienced militiamen whose battlefield performance often left much to be desired. Lord Cornwallis had around 2,000 men, all of them battle-tested British regulars.

When both sides met, the battle went poorly for the Americans after the militia ran from the field. Baron de Kalb stood his ground until he was shot down. A marker is placed on the site where he supposedly fell. Once de Kalb fell, American resistance ended and the men were routed from the field.

Gates then reacted in a manner still considered to be one of the most shameful incidents of the Revolution. He fled the field as fast as his horse would take him. It was reported that he briefly stopped in Charlotte before moving on to Hillsborough. Gates was replaced by Nathaniel Greene and Gates never again received a command.

Other than the marker, there is little else here to see, but visitors should bear in mind that it is estimated that more than 1,000 Patriot soldiers died in these piney woods compared to just 68 British soldiers. The American strategy of blunting the British assault into the South was in shambles. Only the Battle of Kings Mountain would put it back on track.

Buford's Massacre ★★★★

Junction of Rte. 9 and Rte. 522, east of Lancaster and 20 miles north of Camden.

Buford's Massacre is the best known of the surprisingly large number of atrocities committed by both sides during the war. It was at this crossroads on May 29, 1780, that the Americans gained a rallying cry that they would use for more than a year, "Remember Tarleton's Quarter!"

On May 12, 1780, the British took the port city of Charleston in a surprisingly short time. This left American armies who had been on their way to reinforce the Patriot force trying to hold on to the city out in the field. One American force numbered about 350 Virginians under the command of Colonel Abraham Buford. When Buford learned that Charleston had fallen, he reversed his course and started back for North Carolina, mindful that British troops had now landed and would be pushing inland searching for any pockets of Patriot resistance.

What Buford did not know was that some 300 British cavalrymen under Lt. Col. Banastre Tarleton had already heard of Buford's infantry column and were already trailing them.

On May 29, Buford was resting his men in this area when a British courier rode up with the demand that he surrender his entire command. Buford refused, telling the British that they would fight. For reasons that are still unclear, Buford did not go into a defensive mode and start digging entrenchments, nor did he seek any high or wooded ground that would have made a cavalry attack more difficult. Instead, he started marching his men north, apparently hoping that he could put some distance between his column and Tarleton.

The truth of what happened may never be known. The Americans claimed that when

Tarleton's cavalry came upon them, Buford ordered his men to surrender. The British claimed that they moved forward under a flag of truce and were fired upon. Regardless, what happened next is not in dispute. Tarleton's cavalrymen began hacking at the Americans with their sabers. Virtually the entire force of more than 200 men were killed or mortally wounded. Only 53 prisoners were taken.

Look for the marker and the mass grave on US 522 on the southwest side of the intersection. More than 80 bodies are buried under the rocks behind the iron fence. The original marker describing the action was erected in 1860. A more recent one with a more readable inscription was erected several years ago.

"Remember Tarleton's Quarter!" (meaning that Tarleton did not give quarter or mercy to the surrendering Americans) was heard that fall at the Battle of Kings Mountain when the Overmountain Men took out their revenge on the Tories they had captured. Many Tories were bayoneted and otherwise tortured in retaliation for what happened to the Virginians at this site.

GETTING TO AND AROUND CAMDEN

Camden can be reached by air by flying into the Columbia Metropolitan Airport, about 30 miles to the west. The airport is served by six airlines and has five rental car agencies. If arriving by car, Camden is reached from the south by east-west I-20 and from the west by north-south I-77. Camden is somewhat removed from major highways, it is well worth the time to spend several hours here.

A vehicle is necessary for seeing all of the sites around Camden, though Historic Camden is designed to be a walking tour.

For maps and directions to other historic sites around the town, stop by the visitor center at 607 South Broad Street, which is located in an old courthouse that was designed by Robert Mills, who designed the Washington Monument in Washington, D.C. Mills is widely regarded as the nation's first professional architect.

There is one carriage tour company operating in the town, Camden Carriage Company, that picks up along Broad Street. Call 803-425-5737 for details.

ACCOMMODATIONS

Greenleaf Inn

1308 Broad St., Camden
T: 800-437-5874 or 803-425-1806
greenleafinnofcamden.com
$99–$139

The Greenleaf Inn is a complex of two historically significant houses: The Victorian-style house built in 1890 and the Joshua Reynolds House, originally built as a general store in 1805. The first floor is also home to the Greenleaf Restaurant.

Kilburnie, the Inn at Craig Farm

1824 Craig Farm Rd., Lancaster
T: 803-416-8420
kilburnie.com
$125–$175

Kilburnie was built in 1827 and is believed to be Lancaster's oldest surviving residence. Kilburnie began as a federal-style cottage. It was restored in 1999 and opened as an inn in 2000. It is 29 miles from Camden.

Kings Mountain

South Carolina

Under this Scottish cairn rests the body of Lt. Col. Patrick Ferguson.

THE WAR YEARS

One of the military's greatest challenges was simply finding the enemy. Even though few roads or even maps of the roads were available, the opposing sides always came together. The battle at Kings Mountain shows the military's remarkable ability to find its way in the woods despite these challenges.

With the smashing victory over the rebels at Camden on August 16, 1780, the British were anxious to follow up with a major campaign. The commanders in Charleston hoped that a show of force would finally convince the recalcitrant Tories hidden deep in the backwoods of the Carolinas to openly choose sides.

The man Lord Cornwallis chose to open such a campaign was a native of Scotland, Lt. Col. Patrick Ferguson. Ferguson decided to try some psychological warfare by sending a letter by prisoner to the settlers in the Blue Ridge Mountains of North Carolina and Tennessee who were known to have Patriotic sympathies. Ferguson warned them that they either had to proclaim loyalty to the Crown or he would "lay waste their country." It was an idle bluff. Ferguson had no intention of climbing 3,000-foot-high mountains looking for small pockets of Patriots in tiny villages.

Although a bluff, it turned out to be the wrong thing to say. The Scots-Irish who had settled the mountains were descendants of the same people who had fought the English for centuries on the home islands. They did not like one of their own threatening them in the name of some distant king whose royal predecessors had drawn and quartered William Wallace (Braveheart) some 450 years earlier.

"It required no further taunt to rouse the patriotic indignation of Colonel Shelby. He determined to make an effort to raise a force, in connection with other officers which should surprise and defeat Ferguson," wrote Isaac Shelby, a Patriot militia leader.

On September 25, 1780, the first gathering of irate Patriot militia, who would forever be known as the Overmountain Men, took place at a crossing of the Wautauga River in North Carolina. Others gathered at other familiar fords and fields in Virginia, Tennessee, and South Carolina. All brought the rifles that they used for hunting deer and boar. Most had not a single day of military training, but all were deadly shots at 300 yards.

On September 30, Ferguson learned about the approaching threat and wrote a proclamation that he thought would bring more Tories to his side. He was not a man who believed in gentle persuasion: "If you choose to be pissed upon forever and ever by a set of mongrels, say so at once and let your women turn their backs upon you and look out for real men to protect them." The Tories did not respond positively to this message. The Overmountain Men were incensed when they learned that Ferguson was calling them "mongrels."

Ferguson, now in the open and hostile territory of the woods, started marching his 1,100-man army toward Charlotte, North Carolina, then occupied by Cornwallis. Fearful that he might be attacked in the open, Ferguson marched his soldiers to the top of Kings Mountain, actually a rocky hill rising just 600 feet above rolling terrain. Ferguson figured that holding the high ground would give him an advantage.

While that might normally have been true, Ferguson was overconfident and did little to prepare his men for the attack he hoped would come. His men were trained soldiers of the Crown and he thought they would be facing simple "backwater barbarians." In reality, just over 100 of his men were full-time soldiers dressed in red coats. The rest were Tories, American-born militiamen who had professed loyalty to King George III.

In the afternoon of October 7, 1780, the Overmountain Men (reinforced with some South Carolina militia) began their assault by surrounding the base of the mountain, then slowly starting up all the sides at once.

Ferguson was mounted on a white horse and used a silver whistle to blow commands. He wore a red-checkered battle shirt rather than a red coat with epaulets, likely so he would not be easily identified as an officer. Ferguson had done nothing to train his men how to shoot downhill. The optical illusion of falling ground made the Tories fire too high, over the heads of the attacking Overmountain Men. In addition, the attackers hid behind trees before shooting at the standing ranks of the Tories. One of Ferguson's two female camp followers rode her horse downhill, stopping only to tell the Patriots what Ferguson was wearing.

Before nightfall, Ferguson sensed the Overmountain Men were about to take the crest of Kings Mountain. He tried to escape, but at least seven rifle balls pierced his body.

The angry Patriots shouted "Tarleton's Quarter," referring to how British Lt. Col. Banastre Tarleton had slain scores of surrendering and wounded Patriots at Buford's Massacre in South Carolina, less than 100 miles from Kings Mountain. They fired on the Tories, who begged for their lives.

The Overmountain Men suffered only 28 killed and 62 wounded. They had killed 157 Tories and wounded 163 so badly that they were left on the field to die. They captured nearly 700 prisoners. Nine were hanged for crimes against civilians. Once the Overmountain Men had delivered the prisoners, they returned to the mountains. They were not militia and had no intention of becoming full-time Patriot soldiers. They just wanted to be left alone to hunt and fish like they had before being insulted by Ferguson.

The loss at Kings Mountain was shocking to Lord Cornwallis, who must have felt a little nervous, as his headquarters at Charlotte lay just 30 miles, barely more than a day's march, from Kings Mountain. He retreated back into South Carolina so he could be closer to the British stronghold at Charleston.

Sir Henry Clinton, commander in chief of all British forces in the colonies, declared that the loss "was the first link of a chain of evils that followed each other in regular succession until they at last ended in the total loss of America." Any Tories who had been thinking about joining the British now knew better than to declare their loyalties. The Carolina backcountry, which had been vaguely Loyalist, or at least noncommittal, had acquired a distinct Patriot loyalty.

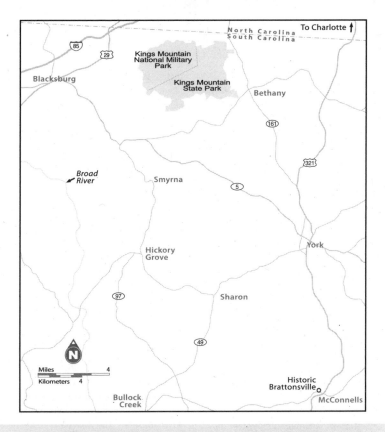

SOURCES & OTHER READING

Battle of Kings Mountain and Its Heroes, Lyman Draper, Overmountain Press, 1996

Kings Mountain—The Defeat of the Loyalists, Oct. 7, 1780, J. David Dameron, DeCapo Press, 2003

Overmountain Men, Pat Alderman, Overmountain Press, 1986

Partisans and Redcoats—The Southern Conflict that Turned the Tide of the American Revolution, Walter Edgar, Harper Collins, 2001

The Road to Guilford Courthouse—The American Revolution in the Carolinas, John Buchanan, Wiley, 1999

With Fire and Sword—Battle of Kings Mountain, 1780, Wilma Dykeman, National Park Service, 1991

KINGS MOUNTAIN TODAY

Visitors to Kings Mountain National Military Park should not take the I-85 exit for Kings Mountain, the town. The battlefield is actually a few miles away across the South Carolina state line.

With the exception of small stone markers placed at the spots where several Patriots were mortally wounded or killed, the Kings Mountain battlefield likely looks much the same as it did before the battle. There are two large monuments on top of the ridge where the Tories were camped. But until visitors reach the ridge and see the monu-ments, they can easily imagine what it was like to be climbing the steep, wooded hillsides of the 600-foot-tall mountain.

The exhibits at the visitor center's museum are among the best displayed in the park system. The movie detailing the battle is first rate, even down to the details of showing the actor portraying Lt. Col. Ferguson loading the breech-loading rifle he invented. Visitors not interested in the battle details will like the walk through the woods to reach the top of the mountain.

POINTS OF INTEREST

Kings Mountain National Military Park
★★★★★

2625 Park Rd., Blacksburg
(Exit 2 off I-85)
T: 864-936-7921
nps.gov/kimo
Summer daily 9am–6pm; fall, winter, and spring 9am–5pm
Admission: Free

Calling Kings Mountain a mountain may be charitable, but walking the 1.5-mile-trail to the top and back down again will make a believer out of most visitors. The trail is paved, but the crest is more than 600 feet from the base, so visitors should plan accordingly. Allow at least an hour to take a leisurely walk to the summit and back down again, and allow an hour at the visitor center.

It is a pleasant wooded walk to the top of Kings Mountain, but be careful. Ravines fall away from the pavement so stay on the trail. There are more than 16 miles of hiking trails in the park, but hikers on these trails must register with the rangers. A primitive camping site is available with a free permit. The adjoining Kings Mountain State Park has 116 camping sites for tents and RVs, as well as facilities for picnicking and swimming.

Start at the visitor center by watching the movie and viewing the exhibits in the small museum. The trail starts immediately outside the visitor center. Make sure to climb the mountain in a counterclockwise direction, as all of the informational plaques are in chronological order starting from where the main American militia attack began. There are a number of small monuments along the trail dedicated to the Patriot officers who were killed at those spots.

Normally, holding the high ground is an advantage for the defenders, but the Tories had not had time to clear a field of fire downslope. The ground was covered with trees, rocks, and crevices, giving the attackers plenty of places to hide. One Patriot reported that he stood behind a tree so long that sniping Loyalists shot the bark from it. Kings Mountain's slopes made the perfect fighting ground for the local men, who were used to blending into the background to surprise game.

The Tories' major disadvantages were gravity and equipment. Reports indicate that the Tories were equipped with Brown Bess muskets, smooth-bore muskets that were effective only for about 100 yards. Beyond that range, the .69 caliber lead ball lost its power and simply dropped to the ground. The Overmountain Men and the militia were equipped mostly with smaller-caliber rifles. They took longer to load because the lead balls had to be wrapped in a patch before being rammed down the barrel, but the rifle was accurate up to 300 yards. The Patriots had the advantage of being able to fire and hit their targets from a distance of more than 200 yards

further than the Tories. The final disadvantage facing the Tories was the optical illusion of shooting downslope, causing them to fire over the heads of their attackers.

The top of Kings Mountain is a spine-like ridge that runs for several hundred yards. Two obelisks dedicated to the men who took the mountain are here. The National Park Service created the Kings Mountain Battlefield Park in 1930.

On the downslope is an emotionally moving monument, the cairn of Major Patrick Ferguson, the commander of the Tories and the only British officer on the field that day. When Ferguson was shot from his horse, his boot hooked in his stirrup and he was dragged down to this spot before his body hit a tree and he was dislodged from the stirrup. After desecrating his body, the Patriot militia left him in the open. Someone buried him and started a stone cairn over the grave (a Scottish traditional burial) that remains today.

SITES NEAR KINGS MOUNTAIN

Overmountain Victory National Historic Trail ★★

Commemorative Motor Route
T: 864-936-3477
nps.gov/ovvi/

A brochure outlining a driving trail from western Virginia through eastern Tennessee, South Carolina, and North Carolina that roughly follows the routes of the Overmountain Men and the militias who came together to fight Ferguson at Kings Mountain is available at the Kings Mountain Visitor Center. There are several historic sites scattered along the 220-mile driving route, but no national park sites. Most of the 12 sites marked on the map show where the Patriots camped.

This is a tour that will interest only hardcore historical drivers who want to see the rugged terrain the Overmountain Men crossed in order to reach the Tories. These frontier settlers thought nothing of walking 20 or more miles a day over the mountains. Perhaps the most remarkable aspect of their assembling and attacking Ferguson at Kings Mountain is that they bothered to take action at all, as they were not immediately at risk in their homes.

Charlotte, North Carolina ★

It may be hard to find among the bank buildings built on the rubble of the buildings that were there more than 250 years ago, but Charlotte, the largest city in North Carolina, does have some colonial history that's worth seeking out. The oddest is at the intersection of Tryon and Trade Streets, the center of downtown. There, in the middle of the intersection, is a brass plaque inserted into the street commemorating the Battle of Charlotte, a small engagement that took place on September 26, 1780. The fight was small with only about 15 killed and wounded on the British side and a slightly larger number on the American side.

Charlotte only had 20 houses and the Mecklenburg County courthouse in those days, but after the battle, Cornwallis described the village as a "nest of hornets." After the battle, Cornwallis occupied the city. While there, the British general complained about Patriot militia harassing his men. There were so many militiamen operating in the area that it took Cornwallis a full week to learn of the massive defeat of Ferguson at Kings Mountain, even though that battlefield was only a two-day march away.

Hezekiah Alexander House ★★★

3500 Shamrock Dr., Charlotte
T: 704-568-1774
Tue–Sat 10am–5pm and Sun 1–5pm
Admission: $6

The museum is about three miles from downtown Charlotte. Call and ask for directions from I-77 or I-85, the two interstates passing through Charlotte.

The oldest house still standing in Charlotte is the Hezekiah Alexander House, now part of the Charlotte Museum of History. Built in 1774, it was standing when Cornwallis came through the area, but it was far removed from the fighting. Today, docents dressed in 18th-century clothes interpret the life of the time. Inside the building is a diorama showing what Charlotte looked like at the time of the Revolution. Alexander himself was a Patriot and was one of the signers of the Mecklenburg Declaration of Independence

in May 1775, a document calling for the colony of North Carolina to declare itself free of England.

Historic Brattonsville ★★★★★

1444 Brattonsville Rd., McConnells
(38 miles southeast of Charlotte. Take exit 32-B on I-77 and drive west through Fort Mill on Rte. 322 to Brattonsville in 20 miles. Watch for signs on rural road.)
T: 803-329-2121
chmuseums.org/Brattonsville.htm
Mon–Sat 10am–5pm, Sun 1–5pm
Admission: $6

Historic Brattonsville is a 775-acre living-history estate that includes the site of Huck's Defeat, a battle fought on July 12, 1780. There are more than 29 historic buildings on the property (some of which were used in the filming of Mel Gibson's 2000 movie about the American Revolution, *The Patriot*). A wall poster in the visitor center describes the scenes that were filmed at the historic site. Many of these buildings date back to the Revolution when this was the estate of William Bratton, a South Carolina militia leader. Bratton's modest wooden home is preserved here, as is an example of the type of cabins that were homes to the typical backcountry farmer who made up the bulk of the militia. Also found on the site are examples of typical upcountry log cabins and barns.

The battle began when Col. Bratton learned that a small force of Tories were on the adjoining property, Williamson's plantation, looking for him. Bratton's men arrived on the evening of July 11 and started their attack at dawn. Only one Patriot was killed, but scores of Tories were killed or wounded. The small battle served to bolster once-wavering Patriot and militia confidence that they could win the Revolution in the South.

The large white house that most would consider a plantation-era home was moved here from another location. It contains an interesting display of medical tools that were commonly used during the Revolution and well into modern times

On many weekends, Historic Brattonsville hosts living histories. Visitors will find militiamen willing to discuss the various types of rifles they carry; women carding cotton or spinning cotton and flax into thread; musicians playing period instruments such as mandolins and dulcimers; even a period surveyor using the same instruments and carrying metal chains that were used to divide the land into tracts. These volunteers are eager to talk to visitors about their skills. Call or check the website for upcoming events.

In addition to walking the battlefield site and visiting the historic houses, visitors with interests in animal husbandry will want to ask about Historic Brattonsville's Heritage Breed and Farm Program. Among the animals being raised here are Devon cattle, Cotswold sheep, and Ossabaw Island hogs, among the rarest breeds in the United States. All of these animals were around during the Revolution. The hogs are thought to be descended from animals left by the Spanish explorers in the 1500s.

GETTING TO AND AROUND KINGS MOUNTAIN

Visitors should fly into Charlotte Douglas International Airport, which is served by several airlines and rental car agencies. Charlotte is 30 miles from Kings Mountain.

Note that Kings Mountain is only about 30 miles from the site of the Battle of Cowpens, and it would be easy to see both areas with an overnight stay. Additional sites are found within reasonable driving distance, but adding them to a trip to see these two major sites will add at least a day. Plan on spending at least one night in the area if trying to see all of the suggested sites described in both chapters.

Both of these battlefields are in rural areas so visitors have no choice but to arrive by car. Bus service is unavailable and taxi service prohibitively expensive.

The path at Kings Mountain is entirely paved, though it can be a steep climb in some places.

Visitors will want to eat before or after making their way to the park because there are no concessions or nearby restaurants.

ACCOMMODATIONS

Walnut Lane Inn

110 Ridge Rd., Lyman
T: 800-949-4686 or 864-949-7230
greenville-bed-breakfast.com
$110–$125

Walnut Lane Inn is convenient to both Kings Mountain and Cowpens Battlefields. It rests on eight landscaped acres in the foothills of the Blue Ridge Mountains.

The White House Inn

607 W. Pine St., Blacksburg
T: 888-279-9687 or 864-839-0005
whitehouse-inn.com
$85–$120

This inn is built in a Greek Revival style with majestic columns topped with Ionic capitals. It is conveniently located near Kings Mountain and Cowpens battlefields.

SITE

22

Cowpens

South Carolina

Patriot and British Cavalry fought on this road.

THE WAR YEARS

The wily colonial generals and soldiers had one military advantage that the staid, stiff British generals and soldiers did not have. They cleverly knew how to use their shortcomings to their advantage. The Battle of Cowpens, demonstrating that cleverness, is a great site for understanding basic Revolutionary War tactics.

Though the bloody defeat at Kings Mountain on October 7, 1780, had embarrassed the British, they had not been cowed into admitting defeat altogether in the wilderness of the Carolinas. In late December of that year, Lord Cornwallis, holed up in Winnsboro, South Carolina, learned that the new American commander in the South, General Nathaniel Greene, had split his meager forces and put half under the command of General Daniel Morgan. Morgan was a self-taught military commander who had helped win Saratoga, New York, for the Patriots, and Morgan was then operating in western South Carolina.

Cornwallis saw a chance to do what every professional military commander dreams of— to defeat his enemy in pieces. He sent Lt. Col. Banastre Tarleton rushing after Morgan.

Morgan learned of Tarleton's approach so he stopped at the Cowpens, a plain where frontier farmers traditionally gathered their livestock for grazing and trade. With Morgan were 600 regular Continental troops, whom he trusted would fight well, and 300 militiamen, whom he doubted would stand at all when faced with British Brown Bess muskets and the deadly bayonets attached to them.

Morgan's selection of Cowpens as a site for battle was startling to his subordinates. It was a wide open plain. In other words, it was perfect ground for the British to form their ranks of muskets and bayonets, but poor ground for Patriots to shoot from trees. But Morgan really had no choice. Tarleton's cavalry was riding hard in his direction and he did not want to be caught in a marching column when they arrived. To counter the disadvantages of Cowpens as a battlefield, Morgan began to think of a plan.

The night before the expected battle, Morgan walked among the militia and told them that he did not expect them to stand up and fight. In fact, he did not want them to fight much at all. All he asked of them was that they each fire two volleys and then retreat. He slyly challenged the Georgia militia to compete with the North Carolina militia to see who were the better shots at picking off the British officers.

The next morning, Morgan arranged his lines with sharpshooters to the front, followed by the lines of the militia, and then his battle-hardened Continentals in the rear, where they would be well out of sight of Tarleton's men. Tarleton arrived at dawn on January 17, 1781, and immediately attacked. That was a mistake. His men had been riding and marching for several hours already, while Morgan's men had had a good night's sleep and a hearty breakfast.

In the first volley of the riflemen, 15 British officers—easily distinguished by the colorful epaulets on their shoulders—dropped dead. The riflemen melted away, knowing their marksman skills would be needed in later battles. Tarleton then pressed the militia, who fired their two volleys before fleeing to the rear.

Tarleton's men saw the fleeing militia and some British regiments broke their solid lines to charge after them. Morgan saw his chance. When the charging British reached the Continentals, Morgan ordered his regulars to deliver a withering volley. Morgan then rallied the militiamen and convinced them to turn around and fire into the advancing British left flank. At the same time, Morgan's cavalry, which had been held in reserve, attacked the advanced British line's right flank. A good number of Tarleton's men were now being fired upon from three directions at once.

Tarleton, watching his line being enveloped, ordered his reserve cavalry into the fray. They looked at him for a moment, then turned their horses and started heading for Charleston. More than 200 of the best cavalrymen that England could put into the field ignored their commander's orders and rode away. Only 40 men and 14 officers came to Tarleton's side as he tried to protect British cannons from being captured. Tarleton himself then began a retreat. William Washington, a cousin of George, chased Tarleton down and briefly fought a sword duel with him before Tarleton shot Washington's horse. Tarleton fired the last shot of Cowpens before running.

With their commander in rout, the remaining British soldiers in the field had no choice but to surrender. A few cries of "Tarleton's Quarters!" filled the air, no doubt sending shivers down the spines of the British, but the Continentals shushed the militia who were calling for the execution of the surrendered British. The regular Continentals would not stand for the killing of surrendered men as had happened at Kings Mountain.

A count of casualties showed that Morgan had lost only 12 killed and 60 wounded, but Tarleton had lost more than 100 killed and 229 wounded. The aim of the American sharpshooters who opened the battle was proven when 39 British officers were counted among the dead. More than 600 British soldiers and 27 officers had been captured.

In recent years, questions have arisen about the number of troops Morgan had at his disposal. He always said around 1,000, among them 600 seasoned Continentals. Modern historians looking at other written accounts speculate that as many as 1,000 more militiamen came to the battlefield at the last minute, which would have meant that Morgan had twice as many men as Tarleton had on the field.

It was the leadership of Daniel Morgan that explains the victory at Cowpens. While generals like Washington and Gates and virtually all of the colonial leaders came from landed gentry and considered themselves several cuts above the soldiers they commanded, Morgan considered himself one of the men. He sat around the campfires of his men and showed them the whipping scars he still bore from a run-in with a British officer during the French and Indian War. He used his scars to explain to his men why he was fighting the British at the advanced age of 45.

Morgan never again led troops. After serving as the winning general behind two major battles: Saratoga, New York, and Cowpens, South Carolina, he retired to his home in the Shenandoah Valley of Virginia.

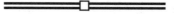

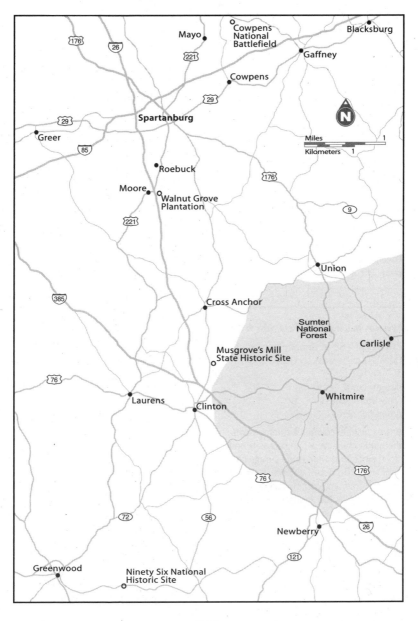

COWPENS TODAY

Cowpens today probably looks similar to Cowpens in the 1780s, with the exception that there are probably more trees than there were at the time of the battle. The farmers and cattlemen, in those days surrounding the area, had cut down many of the trees to build cabins. That would explain why it was described as a broader plain than it appears today.

People visiting Cowpens may want to take the time to visit an unusual nearby attraction that has nothing to do with the American Revolution. The BMW factory is located on I-85 between Spartanburg and Greenville, about 30 miles from the battlefield. The Z4 roadster sports car and the X5 SUV are both manufactured here, the only BMW manufacturing facility in the United States. Guided tours are offered daily for $5. Call 888-868-7269 to schedule a tour. A museum of BMW's history is also on the site and can be visited at no charge. The opening of this factory more than a decade ago started a rush to build other automotive factories in the Deep South.

Cowpens has no amenities such as restaurants or gas stations. It is a battlefield and a national park. Gaffney is about ten miles from the park. The closest other war sites are about 30 miles from Cowpens.

POINTS OF INTEREST

Cowpens National Battlefield ★★★★★

Exit 92 off I-85 in Gaffney.
Drive 10 miles west on US 11
T: 864-461-2828
nps.gov/cowp
Daily 9am–5pm
Admission: Free

At this historic colonial battlefield park, the battle maneuvers can be easily understood since they were quite simple on both sides. Because Cowpens is far removed from any commercial center, this quiet park sees few tourists. This means that visitors can spend a lot of time with the park rangers learning about the battle.

The visitor center at Cowpens has a theater showing a movie about the battle and a few artifacts, including a Brown Bess musket, Charleville musket (used by French and American troops), a Pennsylvania rifle (used by American militia), and a brass three-pounder cannon known as a grasshopper because of its tendency to jump in the air upon firing.

In the lecture room is a painting of British Lt. Col. Banastre Tarleton, who was nicknamed "Bloody" Tarleton after the war by American historians because of his ruthless treatment of the American troops he encountered at some battles. In front of Tarleton is a mannequin dressed as a British cavalryman, the type of troops that Tarleton commanded.

There is a pleasant one-and-a-half-mile paved walk across the battlefield with interpretive signs along the militia lines describing the actions of both the British and the Americans. This may be a hard battlefield to imagine, as there are no walls, no trenches, no cannon emplacements to explain what happened. The battle was quite simple: The American militia was formed in two lines. Once they fired two volleys, they ran to the rear, where they reformed with the more experienced Continentals. The British chased the militia, not expecting to run into the Continental line. With the help of American cavalry, the British lines were broken.

One battlefield feature that remains is Green River Road, now a lightly graveled flat road (easily negotiated by wheelchairs). One thing to keep in mind while taking the walking tour is that the visitor center is built near the final American line. This means the markers are not in chronological order; visitors are actually seeing the battle in reverse order of how it opened and ended.

Allow at least an hour and a half to visit Cowpens.

SITES NEAR COWPENS

Musgrove's Mill State Historic Site ★★
398 State Park Rd. (Hwy. 56, six miles northeast of Exit 52 from I-26), Clinton
T: 864-983-0100
southcarolinaparks.com/park-finder/
    state-park/3888.aspx
Thu–Mon 9am–6pm
Admission: $2

Guile could win battles in the American Revolution. On August 18, 1780, a body of 200 Patriot militiamen rode to this spot on the Enoree River to wrest control of the ford from what they thought was an equal number of Tory militia. When they arrived, they found that the ford was actually defended by better trained Tories who had full military equipment. The Patriots were outnumbered two to one.

To compensate, the Patriots sent their main body to a higher hill, then sent a smaller body into the sight of the British forces. Once the engagement was underway, the smaller Patriot force began retreating toward their main force, which had by then dug entrenchments. The Tories fell for the plan and were caught in the open when the main body of Americans hidden on the hill fired from a distance of only 40 yards. The smaller Patriot force won the battle, perhaps the only time that Patriot militia was able to defeat regular British forces. The Americans lost only a handful of men, but the Tories lost at least 60 killed and another 90 wounded. More important, it gave Patriot morale a boost, as American forces under Horatio Gates had been routed at the Battle of Camden, South Carolina, just two days earlier.

Walnut Grove Plantation ★★★
1200 Otts Shoals Rd., Roebuck
T: 864-576-6546
walnutgrove@mindspring.com
April–October Tue–Sat 11am–5pm,
Sun 2–5pm; November–March Sat–Sun
2–5pm only
Admission: $5.50

Walnut Grove is situated on land that was granted to its owner Charles Moore in 1763 by King George III. Far from being a palatial estate as might be seen in Charleston, Walnut Grove was and is a house that is quite typical of the homes found in the South Carolina backcountry. It is a complete plantation estate common to the period with main house, kitchen house, smoke house, barn, and a school.

There are two interesting stories associated with the house. One is that Kate Moore, 28, volunteered to scout for General Daniel Morgan in the days prior to the Battle of Cowpens. Another, more tragic, story is that three Patriot soldiers were visiting the house when it was raided by Tories. One officer, a sick man who was being nursed by one of the Moore daughters to whom he was engaged, was killed in his sick bed. The other two were shot down in the yard by the Tories as they tried to flee. The three bodies are buried somewhere on the grounds.

Ninety Six National Historic Site ★★★★

Two miles south of the town of Ninety Six on Hwy. 248
T: 864-543-4068
nps.gov/nisi
Daily 8am–5pm
Admission: Free

There are few surviving examples of colonial forts. The star fort in Ninety Six is one of the best. The background for the unusual name is uncertain, but may refer to how the crossroads appeared to be 96 miles south of a certain Cherokee town.

In October 1780, the Overmountain Men had overwhelmed the Tories at Kings Mountain. In January 1781, the British regulars under Lt. Col. Tarleton had been sent packing after the Battle of Cowpens. In March of that same year, Cornwallis had won the Battle of Guilford Courthouse in North Carolina, but the victory had come at a terrible cost. His supplies were running so low that he had to leave the battlefield and head back into South Carolina to refit before another Patriot Army brought him to combat.

Instead of chasing down Cornwallis, General Nathaniel Greene, the commander at Guilford Courthouse, pursued another strategy. He decided to mop up British resistance in the backcountry of South Carolina. The primary target was the village of Ninety Six, which was garrisoned by more than 500 Tories. Knowing that if he was attacked at Ninety Six he could expect slow reinforcement because his

outpost was so far from Charleston, British Lt. Col. John Cruger built a fort from dirt in the shape of a star as a defensive work just outside the village.

When Greene arrived on May 21, 1781, he marveled at the British earthworks in front of him. If he tried to attack any of the fort's dirt walls by frontal assault, his men would come under fire from three directions. Instead of attacking, Greene decided to put the star fort under siege. With a Polish civil engineer named Thaddeus Kosciuszko directing the work, Greene's men started building a series of trenches that would get them closer to the fort without exposing them to musket fire.

The men worked for nearly a month before a scout reported that a British column was on its way to reinforce the fort. On June 18, Greene attacked. The Americans succeeded in getting close enough to the fort to wreck some of its outer defenses, but their cannons could not knock down its dirt walls. Greene lost 185 killed and wounded with the Tories losing 85 killed and wounded. Greene withdrew less than a day before the British relief column of more than 2,000 men arrived.

There is an interesting story about how the Tories knew to hold out for the British column. A young woman who had been frequenting the fort and selling them produce had fallen in love with one of the British officers. When the British column neared, she met them then volunteered to take a message into the fort. She approached the American lines surrounding the fort and joked around with the men. As she flirted, she continued to ride her horse nearer to the fort. Before the Americans grew too suspicious, she spurred her horse over a barricade and made for the fort. She made it inside with her message without being shot.

Getting to and around Cowpens

Visitors to Cowpens should plan to fly into Greenville/Spartanburg Airport, which is served by a variety of airlines and rental car agencies. Spartanburg is about 20 miles from Cowpens.

Note that Kings Mountain is only about 30 miles from the site of the Battle of Cowpens, and it would be easy to see both areas with an overnight stay. Additional sites are found within reasonable driving distance, but adding them to a trip to see these two major sites will add at least a day. Plan on spending at least one night in the area if trying to see all of the suggested sites described in both chapters.

Both of these battlefields are in rural areas so visitors have no choice but to arrive by car. Bus service is unavailable and taxi service would be prohibitively expensive.

Both parks are walking parks, though Cowpens does have a driving loop with stops where visitors can get out and walk to read the historic markers.

The walkway at Cowpens is mostly paved, except for the gravel road leading back to the visitor center. It is easily negotiable by wheelchairs and is entirely flat.

Visitors will want to eat before or after seeing these parks because there are no concessions or restaurants in the vicinity.

Accommodations

Walnut Lane Inn

110 Ridge Rd., Lyman
T: 800-949-4686 or 864-949-7230
greenville-bed-breakfast.com
$110–$125

Walnut Lane Inn rests on eight landscaped acres in the foothills of the Blue Ridge Mountains.

The White House Inn

607 W. Pine St., Blacksburg
T: 888-279-968 or 864-839-0005
whitehouse-inn.com
$85–$120

This inn is built in a Greek Revival style with majestic columns topped with Ionic capitals. E. R. Cash, a wealthy textile magnate, built the inn in 1912.

Sources & Other Reading

A Devil of a Whipping: The Battle of Cowpens, Lawrence Babits, University of North Carolina Press, 2001

The Cowpens-Guilford Courthouse Campaign, Burke Davis, University of Pennsylvania Press, 2002

Daniel Morgan: Revolutionary Rifleman, Don Higginbotham, University of North Carolina Press, 1961

Downright Fighting: The Story of Cowpens, Robert Fleming, National Park Service, 1988

Partisans and Redcoats: The Southern Conflict that Turned the Tide of the American Revolution, Walter Edgar, HarperCollins, 2003

Website: nps.gov/cowp/dmorgan.htm

Savannah

Georgia

James Oglethorpe surveys his new colony from a Savannah square.

THE EARLY YEARS

T he City of Savannah realized early on that historical tourism would be an important economic engine. The public squares designed by the first governor of the colony remain an integral part of the city.

What can be said about a colony that specifically banned rum, slavery, and lawyers in its original charter? Call Georgia progressive. Founded in 1733 when James Oglethorpe landed at what is now Savannah on some bluffs some 20 miles up a river that emptied into the Atlantic, Georgia was the last colony settled by England. It was an immediate success because its founders had more than 100 years of colonial mistakes to learn from—from the failures of putting colonies in the wrong places to putting the wrong types of men in charge of the settlements.

Georgia, and its first city, Savannah, had several purposes. Its primary objective was to act as a buffer between South Carolina to the north and the hostile Spanish colony of Florida and its principal settlement of St. Augustine to the south. Secondly, it would provide work for the poor in England whom the Crown considered to be a burden on society. Third, it would provide yet another profitable colony sending goods such as naval stores and lumber back to England.

Savannah had few problems in its early development as the capital city of Georgia. The Indians were friendly, even pointing out the best location for the town to be built. The water flowing down what would be christened the Savannah River was fresh. The river itself was deep enough so that trading ships could dock right at the settlement. Upriver were vast forests that could be harvested and then floated down the river to both build houses for the colonists and to ship lumber back to London.

When the Revolution officially started in 1775, Georgia was still a young colony, but it went along with the idea of independence. For the first three years of the war, the British paid little attention to its southernmost rebellious colony. But as things continued to go badly in the northern colonies, the British changed their strategy and sent an invasion force toward Savannah.

The British landed at Tybee Island, near the mouth of the Savannah River, on December 23, 1778. No one opposed them. When the British finally marched on the city, only a small Continental force could be mustered, and they were no match for regular British troops. The Americans lost more than 100 dead while the British lost only 26. A major Southern city had fallen without a major battle.

Savannah was the first of two major Southern ports to fall to the British (it was followed by the capture of Charleston a year and a half later). Southern Tories in Savannah who had been careful to keep their opinions to themselves after the Declaration of Independence could now openly profess their continued loyalty to the Crown. However, in the farming communities to the north and west of Savannah, Tories still had to be very careful.

The British pressured the Creek and Cherokee Indians in Georgia to become their allies, but the Indians were confused about how to tell a Tory from a Patriot. All white men looked the same to them except that the British had instructed the Tories to wear pine sprigs in their hats. This blatant attempt to pit the Indians against Patriots resulted in most settlers supporting the Revolution.

In September 1779, the British discovered that the French fleet had ignored hurricane season and was sitting off the Georgia coast. On September 16, the French land forces commander, acting as spokesman for the newly allied French and American forces, demanded the surrender of Savannah. The British commander asked for 24 hours to think about it. He also continued building his earthworks. The French held off for the requested day, but discovered to their dismay that the British had built nine redoubts and mounted more than 100 cannons during the one-day truce.

The French waited another week before finally starting their own earthworks so they could shell the city from land positions. The bombardment began on October 3 and lasted four days. There were civilian casualties, but few British. On October 9, the combined French and American forces attacked the British redoubts and trenches.

The British had hoped that just such an attack—a formal assault on heavy defenses—would happen. The English soldiers were able to have almost complete cover in their trenches and redoubts while the French and Americans had to march across open ground toward those trenches.

The Allied attack across the open ground against the British forts was disastrous. The French and American allies suffered more than 800 casualties, at least a fifth of its army, while the British suffered only 18 killed and 39 wounded. Among those killed on the American side was General Casimir Pulaski, a Polish count who had trained Patriot cavalry. While still remembered in Savannah as a hero, not many others in the Patriot command system liked the count's arrogant demands to be made a general subordinate only to George Washington.

The successful British defense of Savannah had far-reaching effects. The French had been humiliated, and the Americans had been defeated again. Although the British in the North had not been successful in bagging Washington and his army, they had achieved total success here in the South. When the news reached Parliament about the taking of Savannah, those members who had been debating withdrawal from America fell silent. Perhaps this victory in the South was just the beginning and there was hope yet that the rebellion would be put down.

The British commanders in Savannah were more circumspect in their celebration. The truth was that the French fleet had landed a large number of troops without any opposition from what had been the greatest fleet in the world—the British. The woods outside Savannah were still filled with Patriots, so many that Tories still did not dare to try to organize their own armies. Yes, the city of Savannah had been taken, but not the colony of Georgia. Savannah would remain in British hands for the rest of the war.

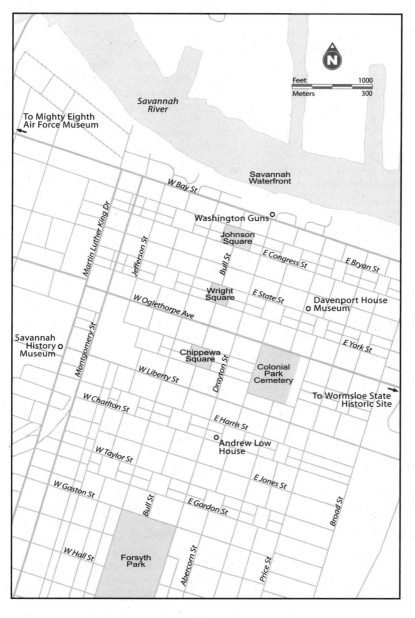

Savannah River

To Mighty Eighth
Air Force Museum

Savannah
Waterfront

W Bay St

Martin Luther King Dr

Jefferson St

Washington Guns

Johnson
Square

Bull St

E Congress St

E Bryan St

Wright
Square

E State St

W Oglethorpe Ave

Davenport House
Museum

Montgomery St

Savannah
History
Museum

E York St

Chippewa
Square

Drayton St

Colonial
Park
Cemetery

W Liberty St

To Wormsloe State
Historic Site

W Charlton St

E Harris St

Andrew Low
House

W Taylor St

E Jones St

W Gaston St

Bull St

E Gordon St

W Hall St

Forsyth
Park

Abercorn St

Price St

Broad St

Feet   1000
Meters   300

SAVANNAH TODAY

With a population hovering around 300,000, Savannah is one of Georgia's larger cities, but it retains a small-town feel because most visitors concentrate on visiting the historic area hugging the Savannah River. With the exception of Wormsloe Plantation, which requires a vehicle to be visited, all of the colonial sites are within walking distance of the historic downtown.

One aspect of Savannah that may surprise some first-time visitors is that just to the south of the contemporary street of businesses, Bryan Street, visitors will encounter the first of the tree-shaded squares complete with monuments, historic markers, and park benches. One word of warning— these squares also attract the occasional pan handler and scam artist who know that most of the people here are tourists. Keep your wits about you and use common sense.

Allow at least a full day to see the historic area, which is about one square mile. Add a night and another day if pursuing interests in civil rights and Civil War history. There is a civil rights museum near the historic area and Civil War–era Forts Jackson and Pulaski to the east, and Fort McAllister to the south.

POINTS OF INTEREST

Savannah History Museum ★★★★★
Savannah Visitor Center,
303 Martin Luther King Blvd., Savannah
T: 912-238-1779
chsgeorgia.org/shm/
Mon–Fri 8:30am–5pm,
Sat–Sun 9am–5pm
Admission: $4

This should be the first stop for anyone coming to Savannah. In the forward section of the building, formerly a train shed of the Central Georgia Railroad, a visitors' counter staffed with several employees is stocked with detailed street maps that direct visitors to historic houses and the squares for which the city is known. Below the visitor center and on the same level as the history museum is a nice gift shop.

The museum gives an excellent overview of the founding of the colony of Georgia on the banks of the Savannah River. Its development resembled that of no other colony. While other colonies were founded to get rid of religious dissidents, reward landless noblemen, develop cash crops, or find gold, Georgia was founded to give the poor of England a new start in life. Georgia's charter decreed that slaves and lawyers were both banned. (The slaves were banned because founder James Oglethorpe believed the colonists needed to work themselves and the lawyers were banned because of the filing of needless lawsuits.) Oglethorpe would later lose control of the colony he founded, and both slaves and lawyers would become a fact of life in Georgia.

Oglethorpe envisioned that Georgia's land would be able to support all types of crops. He experimented with a number of them, including raising silk worms, based on the idea that if high-grade silk could be delivered to England, the entire crop would be purchased to make clothes for the wealthy back in London.

Also explained in the museum is Oglethorpe's plan for building the city around public squares. Most of those squares still exist today. There is also a good display of the types of houses that the colonists built and the clothes they wore in everyday life.

Information about the September through October 1779 siege of Savannah and the resulting battle is prominently described in the museum. The museum's movie about the battle is well worth the time, as it gives an excellent description of what the battle meant to the Patriot cause.

Colonial Squares ★★★★★

Most of the public squares that Oglethorpe laid out in 1733 can still be seen today. Each one has its own character. There are parking meters found around the squares and on the side streets, but on-street parking is at a premium throughout this area. There is a parking garage near the intersection of Drayton and Liberty Streets, southwest of the Colonial Park Cemetery. This profile looks at three squares that have colonial ties. Maps showing the squares can be obtained from the visitor center. There are also tour books and a walking trail that give the complete history of each square.

Chippewa Square, at the corner of Bull and McDonough Streets, about four blocks directly east of the visitor center, has a magnificent statue of James Oglethorpe as its centerpiece. The statue was sculpted by Daniel Chester French, the same man who carved the seated Lincoln statue at the Lincoln Memorial in Washington. Oglethorpe symbolically rests his hand on his sheathed sword, suggesting that if negotiation does not work, he is ready to

draw his sword and engage in battle. Oglethorpe did just that when he twice attacked the Spanish colony at St. Augustine, Florida.

One block to the north is Wright Square, where the grave of Tomo-Chi-Chi, a Yamacraw chief, is located. Colonies to the north, including North Carolina and Virginia, often had to battle Indians for survival. By contrast, the Yamacraw welcomed the English and helped them grow crops. Some historians believe that if Tomo-Chi-Chi had not been so willing to help Oglethorpe, the colony may not have thrived as it did from the very beginning.

Another block to the north is Johnson Square. Here, under an obelisk erected in 1830, are the remains of Continental Army General Nathaniel Greene. Greene was one of the better strategic generals, though not a very good tactical general.

Greene's first service was as a quartermaster, but his talents in organizing soon pushed him to the top ranks. At age 32, he was the youngest general in the army. Greene was the most traveled general, fighting in New York and New Jersey before being given command of the army in the South, where he fought battles in North and South Carolina. Though he pushed the British out of both South and North Carolina, Greene never won a battle. That observation led Greene to comment, "We fight, get beat, rise and fight again." Greene believed that as long as his army could continue fighting, he could wear the British down, a strategy that eventually proved successful, ultimately resulting in independence for the colonies.

After the war, Greene, a Rhode Island native, was given land just north of Savannah. He died of sunstroke while riding on his land in 1786. He was 46 years old.

Four blocks to the south and two blocks east is the Colonial Park Cemetery. Used between 1750 and 1853, this cemetery is the last resting place for several prominent citizens of the city, including Button Gwinnett, a signer of the Declaration of Independence, who was killed in a duel over a question of honor in 1777. Two men who served in the Continental Congress are also buried here.

Still vital 270 years after they were created, Savannah's squares still serve their original purpose by providing the public with gathering places. Each is different from the next. Some are simple and unadorned. Some are planted with colorful flowers. Others are rich with historical significance that are explained by markers.

Davenport House Museum ★★★

324 East State St., Savannah (corner of State and Habersham)
T: 912-236-8097
davenporthousemuseum.org
Mon–Sat 10am–4pm, Sun 1–4pm
Admission: $7

The small, wooden colonial-era houses in Savannah have long ago been torn down to make room for more modern houses, but one of the older houses, built in 1820, is open for touring. Isaiah Davenport was a Rhode Island native who moved south to build houses for others. This house is a fine example of the Federal style that was popular in the early 19th century. It also was the house that launched the restoration of many other houses in the city. Once the house was saved from the wrecking ball in the 1960s, the Historic Savannah Foundation began to save other houses, creating the image of Savannah as a city today filled with historic houses.

Washington Guns ★★★★★

Along Bay St., Savannah

Located under a canopy on Bay Street along the sidewalk are two cannons that were captured from the British at Yorktown. Dubbed the Washington Guns after George Washington presented them to the Chatham Artillery in 1791 as trophies of war, they are two bronze six-pounders cast in 1756 and 1758. These were among the best mobile artillery pieces the British manufactured. Most cannons used by both the British and the Americans were three-pounders, dubbed "grasshoppers" for their tendency to jump off the ground in recoil when fired.

Waterfront ★★

No colonial-era structures survive along the Savannah River waterfront, but the cobblestone streets do. Watch your step if walking down from Bay Street down to the river to visit the numerous shops. There are several good restaurants along the river. At the eastern end of the waterfront is a statue of a young girl who used to wave at ships as they arrived from distant shores. Ship captains got so used to seeing her that they did not consider they had yet reached the port until they saw her waving her apron at them.

Andrew Low House ★★

329 Abercorn St.,
Lafayette Square, Savannah
T: 912-233-6854
andrewlowhouse.com
Mon–Wed and Fri–Sat 10am–4pm,
Sun noon–4:30pm
Admission: $7.50

This house belonged to Juliette Gordon Lowe, the founder of the Girl Scouts. It was built in 1849, but Mrs. Lowe did not inherit it until 1905 when her husband died. As might be expected, Girl Scouts and their leaders get special treatment.

Mighty Eighth Air Force Museum
★★★★★

175 Bourne Ave., Pooler
T: 912-748-8888
mightyeighth.org
Daily 9am–5pm
Admission: $10

Although this museum is not related to the colonial era or the American Revolution, it is valuable for any visitors who have an interest in aviation or World War II. It is filled with artifacts related to the men and bomber aircraft that won the air war over France and Germany. There are often veterans of the Eighth who have retired in the Savannah area who tell their personal stories. One interesting interactive exercise is manning a .50-caliber machine gun in a B-17 waist position while trying to shoot down German fighters coming in from all directions. Veterans of those gun positions point out that a gunner had only seconds to acquire a target that might be flashing by at more than 300 mph.

SITES NEAR SAVANNAH

Wormsloe State Historic Site ★
7601 Skidaway Rd. (10 miles east of Savannah's historic district)
T: 912-353-3023
Tue–Sat 9am–5pm, Sun 2–5:30pm
Admission: $4

Only the tabby (a colonial-era concrete-like material made from crushed sea shells) foundation ruins remain of the home of Noble Jones, one of the settlers who helped create Savannah in 1733. But those ruins are reached by driving down a spectacular avenue of oaks that makes the drive out of town worth the trouble. (The oaks, however, were not planted until the 1890s.) There is no evidence that the original plantation had such an avenue of trees, but the entrance to the site is attractive all the same. The dirt road under the oak canopy likely dates back to the period when the estate was built.

The home was not particularly attractive as it was designed to be fortified. (While the Indians were friendly, the Spanish to the south were not.)

Ask for driving directions to the site at the visitor center in Savannah.

GETTING TO AND AROUND SAVANNAH

Savannah/Hilton Head International Airport has more than 50 daily departures by eight different airlines. It is served by seven major car rental companies and three taxi companies.

Visitors will want to think about whether they intend to visit only the historic city, or venture out to the beaches on Tybee Island and Civil War forts, as that will determine whether or not renting a car would be helpful. If visitors plan to stay in a major hotel downtown and only want to see the city, there is no need for a car. There are plenty of restaurants and shops to visit in the historic area and along the waterfront where walking is by far the easiest way to get around. If there is no hotel shuttle from the airport but one is staying downtown, a cheap alternative is Chatham Area Transit (CAT), which charges a fare each way of only $1. The CAT Shuttle through the historic district is free and stops at 32 places.

Tourists who prefer a guided tour should look into Grayline Tours, which leaves from the visitor center every 30 minutes for a two-hour $25 tour of the historic area. The city's complete history is covered on the tour. Among the sites pointed out are those houses associated with the best-selling book *Midnight in the Garden of Good and Evil*.

There are two river boats, one seating 400 and another seating 600, that operate on the Savannah River and leave from the downtown waterfront. A sightseeing cruise runs $17; a dinner cruise is $44.

There are several horse carriage tours, all averaging about $20 for an hour-long tour. They leave from a variety of locations around the city.

There are too many specialty walking tours to list, but brochures for guides can be found at the visitor center. There are tours covering black history, Civil War, ghosts, architecture, even movie-setting tours and pub crawls.

SOURCES & OTHER READING

American Revolution in Georgia, 1763–1789, Kenneth Coleman, University of Georgia, 1958. *The Siege of Savannah*, Franklin, Hough, DeCapo Press, 1974

From Savannah to Yorktown: The American Revolution in the South, Henry Lumpkin, iUniverse, 2000

Savannah in the Time of Peter Tondee: The Road to Revolution in Colonial Georgia, Carl Weeks, Summerhouse Press, 1997

Savannah under Siege: The Bloodiest Hour of the Revolution, H. Ronald Freeman, Freeport Publishing, 2002

Storm over Savannah: The story of Count d'Estaing and the Siege of the Town in 1779, University of Georgia Press, 1951

ACCOMMODATIONS

Catherine Ward House Inn

118 East Waldburg St., Savannah
T: 800-327-4270 or 912-234-8564
catherinewardhouseinn.com
$159–$400

The Catherine Ward House, built in 1884, is an example of High Victorian Italianate architecture. It is listed on the National Register of Historic Places.

The Dresser Palmer House

211 East Gaston St., Savannah
T: 800-671-0716
gastongallery.com
$99–$275

This Italianate townhouse, built in 1876, provides a variety of spacious accommodations from king canopy beds with private bath and balcony, to rooms with twin beds. The inn most recently won a 2005 Best Breakfast Award.

The Marshall House

123 East Broughton St., Savannah
T: 800-589-6304 or 912-644-7896
marshallhouse.com
$139–$189

This B&B was voted best hotel in Savannah in 2004 and 2005. It was built in 1851, was the first building in Savannah constructed as a hotel, and is said to be haunted. The Marshall House is within walking distance of the city's historical landmarks. It is listed on the National Register of Historic Places and was restored and remodeled in 1999.

The Stephen Williams House

128 W. Liberty St., Savannah
T: 912-495-0032
thestephenwilliamshouse.com
$165–$375

The Stephen Williams House is a restored 1834 Federal mansion with accurate attention to historic detail and antique furnishings. It was honored with the 2003 Preservation Award by the Historic Savannah Foundation. It is listed on the National Register of Historic Places.

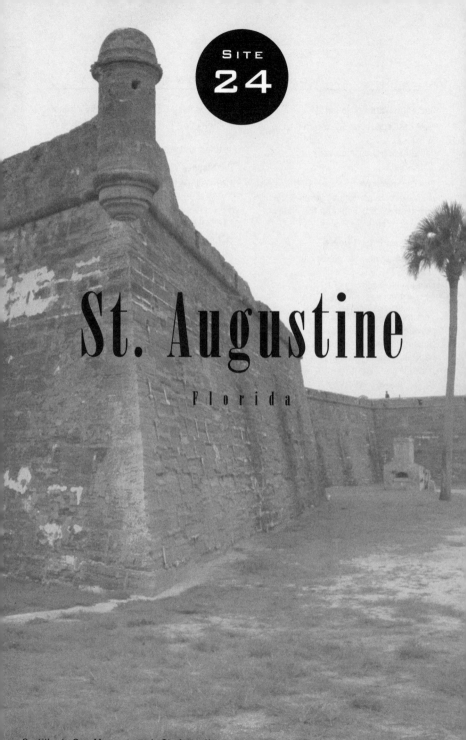

St. Augustine

Florida

Castillo de San Marcos guards St. Augustine

THE EARLY YEARS

St. Augustine, the nation's longest continually occupied city, was also one of Florida's first tourist destinations, long before Orlando took that title. In fact, tourists began arriving here in the 1500s looking for a fountain of youth. Though the fountain was never found, the city is nevertheless a great place to study early colonial history.

In 1513, Juan Ponce de Leon was an aging 56-year-old Spanish explorer, a veteran of Christopher Columbus's voyages to the New World. His reputation for cruelty was well established after years of trying to kill off the native populations on every island he had visited since he first landed in the Dominican Republic on Columbus's second voyage in 1493. When Ponce de Leon heard from a captured Indian that a "fountain of youth" could be found on a nearby island, de Leon listened closely to the man's tales that the spring would guarantee the drinker eternal life. It might even reverse the aging process.

The gullible Ponce de Leon bought into the story, and it was while on this quest that he sighted the coastline of what he would call "Florida" on Easter Sunday 1513. For the next seven years, Ponce de Leon searched the peninsula for that fountain. He never found it, and he died at age 61 after being wounded by Indians near present-day Sarasota.

Later Spanish explorers never believed Ponce de Leon's stories about the fountain of youth, but they did want to colonize Florida. They needed permanent colonies to protect the gold-laden Spanish fleets that were following the Gulf Stream up from Mexico and South America, and then crossing the Atlantic back to Spain. Five different Spanish colonies failed before the sixth one at St. Augustine finally was established in 1565. One of the first tasks of the Spanish soldiers assigned to the new town was to head north to the banks of the St. Johns River (near present-day Jacksonville) and drive out the new French colony. After executing the French and destroying almost all trace of their settlement, the Spanish had Florida all to themselves.

St. Augustine was often a military target. English privateer Sir Francis Drake raided it in 1586. In 1668, a pirate named John Davis rounded up the citizens and killed 60 of them, leaving their bodies in the streets. The Spanish rulers thought about abandoning the city for a more defensible site, but decided instead to build a powerful fort to protect it. That was the basis for the construction of Castillo de San Marcos, started in 1672 and finished in 1696.

The construction of the fort proved so sturdy that other homes in the colony began to be built of the same mined coquina rock and patched with tabby, a concoction of sand, crushed sea shells, limestone, and water. When it hardened in the sun, tabby was virtually indestructible.

In 1763, England made peace with Spain and Florida. In order to gain control of Havana, Cuba, which had been captured by the British the previous year, the Spanish traded Florida to England in exchange for Cuba. England never looked on Florida as one of the original 13 colonies, even though it was older than any of them. The Florida colonists, a mixture of Spanish and English, never considered themselves linked to the other 13 colonies.

Though originally a Spanish colony, Florida always attracted settlers from different parts of the Old World. In 1768, a number of Italians, Greeks, and Minorcans from the Mediterranean arrived in Florida to raise indigo, but the soil was not well suited to the plant from which a blue dye that was popular in Europe was made. When the indigo plantation failed, the colonists moved up the coast to St. Augustine, resulting in an even more complicated multicultural mix with the existing English and Spanish settlers.

During the American Revolution, colonial Florida remained loyal to King George III, and the Crown did not have to waste any resources putting down rebellions. When the United States was created at the end of the Revolution in 1783, some Florida residents assumed England would sell Florida to the new United States, but that did not happen. England kept its Florida colony.

Twenty years later, Florida changed hands again, but it still was not part of the United States. Instead, once again, it became a Spanish possession after Spain captured the British fort in Pensacola, 400 miles west of St. Augustine.

Times had changed. The gold had played out in South America, so there were no longer any Spanish gold fleets that needed protecting as they headed up the Florida coast. With no shipping lanes to protect, St. Augustine was of little use to the Spanish. The bigger problem was that the new United States kept encroaching on the colony. Using Indian raids into Alabama as an excuse, United States General Andrew Jackson made occasional forays into the western expanses of the Spanish colony.

Realizing that the United States was growing and would always be casting its eyes on Florida, Spain finally sold the colony to the United States in 1821 out of fear that Spain would eventually have to go to war to protect the colony.

The new US territory of Florida was problematic when it was first acquired because it was different from any of the earlier English colonies that had become states. Explored nearly 200 years earlier than the last English colony was founded, the territory's first settlement of St. Augustine had been a military outpost settled by soldiers to protect Spanish treasure fleets coming from South America. All of the other colonies had been founded either by religious dissidents, or as business ventures.

For two centuries the Spanish had given little thought to the idea that either the colony or the town could become a profitable outpost. While the English colonies were developing cash crops like tobacco, indigo, and rice to be shipped back to England, St. Augustine relied on food and goods imported from Spain to survive. If storms knocked off the timetable of those shipments, the colony suffered.

When the United States took over Florida, the settlers' culture of dependency continued for decades, which likely explains why Florida remained a small colony and state well into the early 20th century. It was not until the late 19th century when Henry Flagler started building his hotels in St. Augustine and his railroads through the city that Florida became the tourist destination it is today.

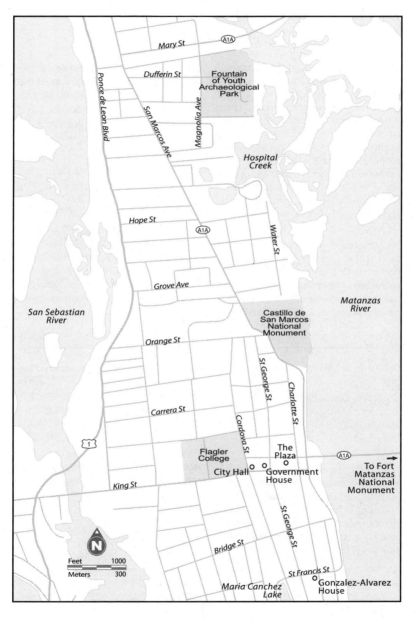

Mary St

A1A

Dufferin St

Ponce de Leon Blvd

San Marcos Ave

Magnolia Ave

Fountain of Youth Archaeological Park

Hospital Creek

Hope St

A1A

Water St

Grove Ave

San Sebastian River

Matanzas River

Orange St

Castillo de San Marcos National Monument

Carrera St

St George St

Charlotte St

Cordova St

1

Flagler College

The Plaza

City Hall

Government House

A1A

To Fort Matanzas National Monument

King St

St George St

N

Feet 1000

Meters 300

Bridge St

St Francis St

Maria Canchez Lake

Gonzalez-Alvarez House

ST. AUGUSTINE TODAY

Though it is the oldest city in the United States, founded in 1565, St. Augustine remains small, with a population of fewer than 12,000 permanent residents. Its economic lifeblood is visitors seeking historical stimulation rather than the pure entertainment found at the amusement parks in central Florida, so the town has worked hard to retain its architecture and colonial feel. That means there are plenty of downtown restaurants but no chains that would clash with the Old World look of the existing buildings.

St. Augustine is located less than 10 miles east of I-95, about one-and-a-half-hours from Orlando, meaning it is readily accessible to visitors who may have originally intended to spend all of their time at the amusement parks. Properly seeing the

city will take a day, but it will be a day well and inexpensively spent. Admission to the amusement parks in Orlando for a single day will run well over $500 for a family of four. The most expensive admission for any attraction in St. Augustine will be no more than $5.

There is a pleasant shopping district along St. George Street that begins at the Old City Gate near Castillo de San Marcos. Many restaurants are also scattered along this same walk. One suggestion for out-of-staters would be the Columbia House Cuban restaurant. Try Ropa Vieja, (literal translation, "old clothes"), a dish of shredded pork simmering in onions and peppers, followed with fried plantains, or small, sweet bananas.

POINTS OF INTEREST

Castillo de San Marcos National Monument
★★★★★

One South Castillo Dr., St. Augustine
T: 904-829-6506 ext 234
nps.gov/casa
Daily 8:45am–5:15pm
Admission: $6

Without Castillo de San Marcos, there would never have been the town of St. Augustine, or even a state called Florida. The construction of this fort and its successful resistance to regular attacks from several nations kept the Spanish in the New World for nearly 300 years.

It is worth visiting the fort for several reasons. It is an architectural gem, the only surviving example in the United States of

how Europeans of the 17th century constructed defensive works. And it is a marvel of construction thanks to its use of mined coquina, a native rock made of compressed shells and limestone. The walls facing the river are 19 feet thick, making the fort almost impregnable from shelling. The fort's long history makes it a good place to study how the various European nations established their colonies in the New World and then warred with each other by attacking outposts like St. Augustine.

While seeking the best routes to move treasure from Mexico and South America back to Europe in the late 16th century, the Spanish discovered the Gulf Stream, the natural ocean current that flows past Florida and up the eastern Atlantic coast. The Spaniards' opponents, the French, the British, and independent bands of pirates, also learned of the Gulf Stream. They recognized that Florida's bays and inlets would make good bases from which to prey on Spanish galleons. Spain would have to invest in defending its stake in the New World.

Spain reacted to the threat on its treasure fleets by starting work on a fort in 1672 to protect St. Augustine, which had been founded more than 100 years earlier. It took 23 years for the fort to be completed, but when it was, Castillo de San Marcos was a marvel of European engineering and design. It boasted four bastions thrusting out from the fort and numerous gun stations facing in all directions.

The fort came under attack in 1702 when British soldiers from Charleston, South Carolina, tried to remove the Spanish threat to the south of them. The fort was under siege for nearly two months, but the British could never mount an effective means of reducing the fort's thick, cannon ball–resistant walls. The British tried again in 1740 and again failed to take the fort.

The fort changed hands peacefully in 1763 at the end of the French and Indian War when the Spanish handed control of the colony over to the English. The fort changed hands again back to the Spanish, then to the Americans, and then in 1861 to the Confederates. The fort was even garrisoned during the Spanish-American War, giving it a 220-year history as a military installation before being formally handed over to the National Park Service in 1933.

Visitors today should set aside at least an hour and a half to see the fort. There is a display of cannons outside the walls along the river that is an interesting exhibit of military technology. Entrance to the fort is gained by a drawbridge over a dry moat.

Contrary to movie forts where the moats are filled with water, alligators, and sharks, the forward-thinking Spaniards kept the moat dry and used it as a storage pen for grazing animals. If a threat appeared on the horizon the animals were moved into the fort and the moat flooded. The fort's downstairs rooms feature a gift shop and museum displays explaining how forts were constructed. Walks on top take visitors to each of the fort's four bastions, which allowed defenders to create cross fires on any attacking enemies. Look carefully at the cannons and the mortars. Some of them were cast in the 1700s, making them some of the oldest cannons still on display in the United States.

Visitors interested in American Indian history will note that in 1837 more than 100 Seminoles, including Chief Osceola, were captured near St. Augustine, an event that led to the end of the Second Seminole Indian War. From 1875 to 1887, a number of Plains Indians were imprisoned at the fort in an attempt to educate them away from their traditional beliefs.

St. George Street ★★★

Enter St. George Street just across from the Castillo de San Marcos by walking through the city gate. At one time, the city was entirely walled. The only evidence left is this gate, reinforced in 1808.

St. George Street is lined with attractions, including the oldest wooden schoolhouse (dating back to the 1780s when Spain reacquired Florida), a number of tabby (a concretelike material made by mixing limestone, water, and crushed sea shells) houses and buildings, and wooden homes demonstrating Spanish architecture. The street also has some shops.

The Plaza ★★★★

St. George Street dead-ends into a central plaza laid out in 1598 at the order of King Phillip II of Spain who decreed that all colonial towns should have a central gathering area from which all streets would radiate in a spoke. Here is a statue of Ponce de Leon, the man who discovered Florida while looking for the elusive fountain of youth.

Government House ★★★★

48 King St., St. Augustine
T: 904-825-5033
Daily 9am–4:30pm
Admission: $2.50

At the west end of the plaza is the Government House, built in 1935 to replicate the 1764 British government building. There is a museum focusing on St. Augustine history on the main floor. Just west of Government House is the grave and monument to Confederate General W.W. Loring, a feisty, one-armed man who famously feuded with Stonewall Jackson.

Flagler College ★★★, 74 King St. and St. Augustine City Hall ★★★, 75 King St.

Admission: Free

Just west of Government House are a collection of buildings that anyone with an interest in architecture will enjoy seeing. A stroll through the grounds is sufficient.

Flagler College is housed in the former Hotel Ponce de Leon, built in 1888 by industrialist Henry Flagler. Flagler's hotels and the Florida East Coast Railroad that ran down to the Florida Keys played a big role in turning the state into a vacation destination early in the 20th century. Flagler was impressed with Moorish design, which is reflected in many of the buildings around the city.

St. Augustine City Hall, across from Flagler College, was originally the Alcazar Hotel, built in 1889 by Flagler. Today it houses both city offices and the Lightner Museum, a collection of art objects donated to the city. In front of city hall is an impressive statue of St. Augustine founder Pedro Menendez. Menendez was not a benevolent city father. He led the raid on Fort Caroline, near present-day Jacksonville, Florida. He executed every man, woman, and child in the settlement to send a clear message to the French that Florida was a Spanish settlement.

Gonzalez-Alvarez House/The Oldest House ★★★★★

Corner of Marine and St. Francis Sts.
T: 904-824-2872
staugustinehistoricalsociety.org
Daily 9am–4:30pm
Admission: $8

Parts of this house's coquina walls date back to 1702, giving it legitimate claim as the oldest house in the United States. It was continuously occupied by families until 1918 when it was acquired by the local historical society. The house's furnishings reflect the early colonial days.

Fountain of Youth ★

11 Magnolia Ave., St. Augustine
T: 904-829-3168
fountainofyouthflorida.com/
Daily 9am–5pm
Admission: $6

Was this tourist attraction, which really does have a fountain, the place Ponce de Leon was seeking? Maybe. The 15-acre site has some archaeological evidence that it was settled at the same time St. Augustine proper was settled. A cross made of coquina rock discovered in the 1800s is claimed to be the one de Leon fashioned once he landed on shore. Water drawn from the spring on the property is labeled and sold as originating from the Fountain of Youth.

Sites near St. Augustine

Fort Matanzas National Monument
★★★★★

8635 A1A South,
14 miles south of St. Augustine
T: 904-471-0116
nps.gov/foma
Daily 9am–5:30pm with ferry service starting at 9:30am
Admission: Free

Colonization of the New World was not only adventurous, it was murderous. Fort Matanzas literally means "slaughters."

In the mid-1500s both Spain and France were competing for land in Florida. Spain claimed all of the land dating back to 1513 when Ponce de Leon had first seen it, but that claim did not deter France from sending a colony to Fort Caroline on what is today the St. Johns River near Jacksonville, 40 miles to the north.

The Spanish considered the French to be interlopers on their land. Even worse than being unwanted colonists from another country, the French were Huguenots rather than Catholic. In May 1565, more than 600 settlers and soldiers sailed from France under the command of Jean Ribault to resupply the settlers already living at Fort Caroline. Sailing not long afterward from Spain was a convoy of 800 soldiers under the command of Pedro Menendez. He trailed the French ships, hoping to destroy the French colony.

The two warring parties clashed briefly near the mouth of the St. Johns before retiring. The French retreated to Fort Caroline and the Spanish sailed south until they came upon a harbor. It was there that Menendez started the outpost that would become the first permanent Spanish settlement, St. Augustine.

Both the French and Spanish were determined to destroy each other before more troops from the enemy country arrived. On September 10, Ribault and a force of French soldiers sailed south to attack St. Augustine. A storm blew them past the Spanish colony and shipwrecked them near present-day Daytona Beach.

While the French soldiers were sailing south, the Spanish soldiers under Menendez were marching north. They found Fort Caroline lightly defended with only a handful of soldiers, women, and children. All were executed. Not long after Menendez returned to St. Augustine, he heard from some Indians that white men had been seen on the beach south of the town. Menendez marched south and discovered 130 exhausted French soldiers, who had survived the hurricane. He executed all but a handful of Catholics and a few artisans he needed to help build the town of St. Augustine. A few days later, more French survivors from the shipwreck marched into the area. Menendez rushed south and killed them too. In two different expeditions, more than 250 Frenchmen were executed along the inlet that would forever be known as Matanzas Inlet.

After the British failed in their attack on St. Augustine in 1740, the Spanish realized that while Castillo de San Marcos protected the main harbor in front of the city, the river hugging the coastline was undefended. They began to build a fort at Matanzas Inlet, the same place where the Frenchmen had been killed more than 150 years earlier.

The fort was a smaller version of the Castillo with five cannons and a complement of 50 men. It proved its value in 1742, not long after it was finished, when the British tried to push past the fort to attack St. Augustine. The fort's cannons drove off the ships. This was the only time the fort ever came under fire. In 1763, when Florida was transferred to British rule, the fort was abandoned. It has been restored by the National Park Service.

The fort can only be visited up close by a ferry boat that spans the 100-yard-wide river. The short water trip is worth the time to examine the defensive architecture of the fort. But if traveling in the area before or after park hours, Fort Matanzas can be seen at a distance by pulling into a county roadside park just to the north of the national park gate. Look for the county park sign on the right of A1A. Take the wooden walkway into the marsh to view the fort to the south.

Some visitors might be tempted to skip seeing Fort Matanzas since it looks like a small version of Castillo, but this is the site where more than 250 Frenchmen were murdered and where that country lost its stake in colonizing the eastern coast of the United States. Had the French colony survived at Fort Caroline, the nation might have looked—and sounded—quite different from the way it does today.

GETTING TO AND AROUND ST. AUGUSTINE

Jacksonville Airport, 41 miles north of St. Augustine and served by 12 airlines and by seven rental car companies, is the most convenient airport. Daytona Airport, 58 miles to the south, is another option.

Once in St. Augustine, and if staying at one of the many bed-and-breakfasts in the historic area, there is no need for a car except when visiting the beaches several miles to the east. Virtually everything a visitor could want can be found within walking distance of the historic area.

There is the Old Town Trolley for visitors who do not want to walk. The Trolley makes more than 20 stops along the waterfront and in the historic area. A $16 pass is good for three days of riding and allows free on and off privileges.

Carriage tours can be found along the waterfront between Castillo de San Marcos and the Bridge of Lions heading east toward the beach. Rides through the historic area run about $15 to $20 for a two-and-a-half-mile ride as the driver gives details about the historic houses and buildings. Most carriages operate with a minimum of 10 people on board and the tour is subject to weather conditions.

There is a one-hour-and-15-minute river cruise boat operating out of the St. Augustine Marina for $15 per person. The same family has operated the river cruise for more than 100 years.

Seeing all that St. Augustine has to offer requires at least two days with an overnight stay.

SOURCES & OTHER READING

The Florida Bicentennial Trail: A Heritage Revisited, anonymous, Florida Bicentennial Commission, 1976

The New History of Florida, Michael Gannon, University of Florida Press, 1996

Religion, Power and Politics in Colonial St. Augustine, Robert Kapitzke, University Press of Florida, 2001

Seasons of Real Florida, Jeff Klinkenberg, University of Florida Press, 2004

The Settling of St. Augustine, Janet Riehecky, World Almanac Press, 2002

Accommodations

Casa de Solana Bed and Breakfast Inn

21 Aviles St., St. Augustine
T: 888-796-0980 or 904-824-3555
casadesolana.com
$119–$249

The original part of the house was constructed between 1803 and 1820 by Don Manuel Solana, the original owner. The main house of Casa de Solana is constructed of blocks cut from the native coquina stone, the same material used to build St. Augustine's fort, Castillo de San Marcos. The house features several other remnants of its original construction, including pegged beams, colonial window-panes, double-crossed doors, and hand-made bricks.

St. Francis Inn Bed & Breakfast

279 St. George St., St. Augustine
T: 800-824-6062 or 904-824-6068
stfrancisinn.com
$99–$239

Around the corner from St. Augustine's Oldest House is the city's oldest inn, the St. Francis Inn. It dates back to 1791. Gaspar Garcia, the first owner, was a sergeant in the Third Battalion of the Infantry Regiment of Cuba. In 1802, the property was purchased by Juan Ruggiers, a sea captain; and in 1838, Colonel Thomas Henry Dummett, a planter, purchased it. At the time of the Civil War, it was known as one of the best in St. Augustine.

Old City House Inn & Restaurant

115 Cordova St., St. Augustine
T: 904-826-0113
oldcityhouse.com
$89–$209

The Old City House, constructed in 1873, is in the style of Spanish Colonial Revival architecture. The coquina-stone facade on the inn was built from coquina found on the site. Legend has it that a ghost of a Spanish Soldier still guards the archway, unaware that he was killed by the misfire of his own musket.

Peace and Plenty Inn

87 Cedar St., St. Augustine
T: 877-468-365 or 904-829-8209
peaceandplentyinn.com
$89–$239

The Peace and Plenty Inn was built in the early 1890s by Walter Decker, who was employed by Henry Flagler, the multimillionaire railroad developer. Mr. Decker was instrumental in the building of the historic Bridge of Lions crossing the Matanzas River downtown. The inn was restored between 1996 and 2001 and is located one block from the historic center city.

Vincennes

Indiana

The statue of George Rogers Clark stands before murals inside the memorial.

THE WAR YEARS

T hough the town itself is far removed from what most people consider the heart of the American Revolution, it is historically significant because of what was won here. In addition, the national monument and the paintings housed within make this a worthwhile destination.

After the French and Indian War officially ended with the Treaty of Paris of 1763, England retained control of Canada and all of the land west of the Ohio River. The problem for the British was that while the colonies' governors recognized those boundaries, settlers, eager for their own land, did not. The British at Fort Detroit were unhappy with the Americans encroaching on their turf. The British had promised the Indian tribes who had helped fight the French that no settlers would push west of the Allegheny Mountains. But the Americans had not only crossed the mountains, they had ventured hundreds of miles beyond them.

With tensions heating up in 1775, the British in the western territories responded by building wooden stockades along the Wabash, White, and Mississippi Rivers. The British lieutenant governor of the territories, Henry Hamilton, arrived at Fort Detroit in future Michigan to step up the defense of British land. His plan was to encourage Indians to attack colonial settlers who had advanced as far as modern-day Louisville, Kentucky, known in those days as The Falls of the Ohio.

One of the pioneer leaders in Louisville was 26-year-old George Rogers Clark, who had a bold plan to fight back against the British. In the winter of 1777–78, Clark traveled to Williamsburg to get Virginia Governor Patrick Henry to approve a secret plan of raising 350 troops to suppress the British forts and eventually march on Detroit. It would be a bold invasion deep into the heart of British-held territory.

Only 150 men came to Clark's side, but he pressed on with his plan. In the spring of 1778, he captured two villages on the Mississippi River, Kankaskia and Cahokia, that were occupied by Frenchmen who were unaware that France had sided with the Americans in the Revolution. A group of Frenchmen from those villages traveled to Fort Sackville to convince those settlers to also switch sides from British to American.

Before Clark could arrive in Vincennes, Hamilton and a small force of British regulars and French militia who were still loyal to England arrived in Vincennes to force the townspeople to switch back their loyalties. Hamilton and his men then occupied Fort Sackville, a poorly constructed wooden stockade on the edge of the village. Hamilton intended to stay through the winter to check any further advances by Clark.

Back at Kankaskia, Clark launched one of the most amazing campaigns in American military history. Knowing he was in Indian territory, Clark boldly marched into an Indian village and told them of his plans to drive the British out of the region. Impressed with Clark's personal bravery, the Indians agreed that they would not harass the attacking force. They would wait to see if he was successful in defeating the British.

Clark and his men left Kankaskia and headed northeast toward Vincennes, 180 miles away. Under normal circumstances the march might have taken 10 days. It took 18 days because winter rains and melting snows had flooded the low-lying land until it was a virtual swamp. At times, Clark and his men were wading through water up to their shoulders as they tried to hold their rifles and powder horns above their heads. Because there was no dry land, there was no dry wood for building fires, and no game to hunt, as the deer had fled the flood waters.

When Clark and his men finally arrived under cover of darkness on the outskirts of Vincennes, they were cold, wet, hungry, and ready for a fight. Their powder, however, had been damp for three weeks. Clark had no confidence that he could attack now that they were outside the walls of Fort Sackville. The Frenchmen of Vincennes came to the rescue. When Hamilton and his men had occupied the town, they had confiscated the settlement's gunpowder except for a few barrels that some settlers had successfully hidden. When Clark arrived, that powder was distributed to his men.

Clark continued his aggressive plan by surrounding the fort and demanding that Hamilton and his 80 soldiers surrender to his supposed 500-man force. That was a bold request considering the fort was defended by two blockhouses, each armed with a three-pounder cannon. The British seemed to have the advantage, but Fort Sackville was not nearly as formidable as it looked. Both leaders recognized its weaknesses.

Clark began his attack at night. When an Indian party sent out by Hamilton was captured, Clark waited until daylight to parade them near the fort. He had the Indians sit in a circle and executed them by hatchet and sword in full view of the British soldiers. Hamilton asked Clark for a three-day truce. Clark, suspecting that Hamilton was hoping for reinforcements, refused. He demanded an immediate surrender, hinting that if he had to storm the fort, the defenders would face the same fate as the Indian patrol. He also told Hamilton that his artillery was on the way, and that he did not think Fort Sackville could stand a heavy cannonade. Reluctantly, Hamilton surrendered.

When Hamilton and his 80 men marched out of the fort on February 25, 1779, and faced Clark's 170-man force, only one of whom had been wounded in the battle, Hamilton asked where Clark's 500-man army was. Clark just swept his hands around him, wordlessly indicating that this was his army. Hamilton turned away in tears.

Clark was never able to complete his goal of capturing Fort Detroit, but its capture was never necessary. The British high command was concentrating its forces in the eastern colonies. Fort Sackville never again saw combat. The Indian tribes who witnessed the bravery of Clark walking directly into their camp eased their attacks on settlers in their new belief that the British would lose the war. Other tribes, now even more worried about encroaching settlers, continued attacking individual houses and small villages.

The Battle of Fort Sackville was small, but one of great consequence. By capturing the outpost and humiliating the British in the eyes of the western Indian tribes, the Americans had secured the frontier from any future alliances between the Crown and the Indians. Once the war was over, the presence of the Americans so deep in what had been British territory helped redraw frontier maps. The British, tired of warring with their former colonists, willingly gave up territory that would become the American Midwest.

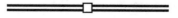

SITE
25

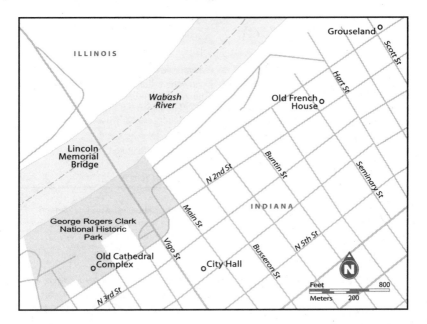

SOURCES & OTHER READING

Background to Glory—The Life of George Rogers Clark, John Bakeless, University of Nebraska Press, 1992

Conquest of the Country Northwest of the River Ohio 1778–1779 and Life of George Rogers Clark and the Winning of the Old Northwest, Robert Alberts, National Park Service, 1896

General George Rogers Clark, William Hayden English, Bowen-Merrill Company, 1896

George Rogers Clark and the War in the West, Lowell Harrison, University Press of Kentucky, 2001

Websites:

statelib.lib.in.us/www/ihb/resources/grcbio.html

statelib.lib.in.us/www/ihb/resources/grcexh1.html

VINCENNES TODAY

Vincennes is an unusual place in that it is a Midwestern city founded in colonial times (1732) as a French fur-trapping outpost. Founded 68 years before Indiana was even a territory, Vincennes is the oldest city in Indiana and one of the oldest in the Midwest, older than Chicago by 100 years. The city has remained small, with a population of about 18,000.

The Wabash River still flows past the town and still occasionally floods as it did when George Rogers Clark and his men marched overland to attack Fort Sackville.

POINTS OF INTEREST

George Rogers Clark National Historic Park
★★★★★

401 South Second St., Vincennes
T: 812-882-1776 ext 110
nps.gov/gero
Daily 9am–5pm
Admission: $3

There are two parts to George Rogers Clark National Historical Park. Visitors should start in the welcome center and museum and watch the 30-minute movie on Clark and his attack on Fort Sackville. The well-acted movie is essential to understanding the monumental accomplishments of Clark and his men. The small museum has life-like displays of what the British, the Americans, and the Indians looked like in 1779. Particularly striking is the Indian.

Once a small number of visitors has accumulated, a National Park Service ranger will lead the group to the memorial, explaining along the way where the fort was located (in front of the memorial with the west wall located 35 feet from the Wabash River). The fort itself was crudely built with no side measuring the same as its opposite side. The longest section was about 205 feet long and the shortest around 165 feet long. In two corners were wooden blockhouses, with five cannon ports each from which the fort's two three-pounder cannons could be aimed.

One of the first points the ranger will make during the presentation inside the memorial is that George Rogers Clark was not the famous explorer who took part in the Lewis and Clark expedition to explore the Louisiana Purchase. That was George's younger brother, William, who was only nine years old when George was capturing Fort Sackville in 1779. Because there was an 18 year in age difference between the two brothers, they had little contact with each other until they were adults.

The ranger will likely make two other points. One was that Clark's mission was twofold: to capture British outposts, and more important, to discourage the Indians from further supporting the British by raiding settlers on the Kentucky frontier. (Ironically, on July 4, 1776, the same day the colonies issued their Declaration of Independence, six Indian tribes had agreed on a common alliance to side with the British.)

The ranger will also put Clark's mission into perspective with regard to how the Revolution was going in the east. At the time, the war was going poorly for the Americans. Only a year earlier, Washington's army had barely survived the winter at Valley Forge, Pennsylvania. In June 1778, the Battle of Monmouth, New Jersey, had proved to be a standoff. Though the French had come into the war on the side of the Americans, their fleet had been unable to win any major battles against the British. On December 29, 1778, the British had captured Savannah, Georgia. Indians had killed settlers all along the frontier from New York southward over the last year. It was clear early in 1779 that the outcome of the Revolution was still far from decided.

Clark's mission on the frontier was a secret between him and Patrick Henry, the governor of Virginia. It was so secret that few other Patriot leaders were likely even aware that there was going to be any fighting at all on the western frontier.

The Clark Memorial itself was started in 1931, finished in 1933, and dedicated by President Franklin Roosevelt in 1936. Despite being finished in the midst of the Depression, rangers are careful to explain that the Memorial is not a Works Progress Administration or Civilian Conservation Corps project (two bureaucracies set up in the 1930s to make work for civilians). It had been authorized in 1928 to honor Clark, and the Roosevelt administration kept the contract in force as the Depression widened. The memorial is reminiscent of the Thomas Jefferson Memorial in Washington, D.C. at 180 feet across and 80 feet tall. The memorial is surrounded by 16 Doric columns under a huge inscription circling the memorial, "The Conquest of The West—George Rogers Clark and the Frontiersmen of the American Revolution."

Once inside the memorial, visitors will likely stop and look around with awe.

Those who have visited the United States Capitol Rotunda will be reminded of it by the huge paintings and the echoes made by people talking. The Clark Memorial has seven murals, each one 16 feet wide by 28 feet tall. It took artist Ezra Winter two and a half years to paint them. The murals trace the highlights of Clark's mission, ending with the surrender of Fort Sackville by the British. The statue of Clark, in the center of the memorial, is seven and a half feet tall on a base of five feet. A set of headphones and written explanations in front of each mural explain Clark's mission in detail.

It was not until the British and the Americans sat down in Paris in September 1783 to hash out the Treaty of Paris officially ending the American Revolution that the full impact of the capture of Fort Sackville became clear. American negotiator Benjamin Franklin pointed out to the British that they had lost the outpost in 1779 and Americans had spent the last four years advancing into the territories that had once been legally held by the British. In fact, Fort Sackville was fully 80 miles north of the Ohio River, the previous border that had once separated England's lands from those claimed by the colonies.

Franklin likely surprised himself with the deal he negotiated that was finalized by signing the treaty. Without much arguing that the Americans had occupied land to which they were not entitled, the British gave up the Northwest territories, more than 270,000 square miles. The treaty also gave the Americans full control of Lake Michigan, rights to use the other Great Lakes, and rights to much of the land along the Mississippi River. What the British called the Northwest Territories would one day be carved into the states of Ohio, Indiana, Illinois, Michigan, Wisconsin, and eastern Minnesota.

Clark and his 170 soldiers had accomplished much more than capturing one woe-begotten, poorly constructed wooden fort when they forced the surrender of Fort Sackville. They had literally added the land that the United States would come to know as the Midwest.

It became apparent after the war that the bureaucrats and politicians back east did not understand Clark's western mission and what its accomplishment meant to the future of the nation. When Clark mailed his detailed receipts for the money he had personally spent on outfitting the mission, they disappeared. When Clark continued to press for reimbursement over the years, he was repeatedly turned down because he could not produce copies of the receipts he had mailed. Decades after

Clark's death as a debtor, a clerk stumbled upon the receipts sitting in a box in Richmond, Virginia. Clark's accounts totaled to the penny what he had been claiming he was owed by the government.

George Rogers Clark lived until 1818, dying at age 66 in the house of his sister in Louisville, Kentucky. If the people in the eastern colonies still had not recognized what Clark had done for the nation, his friends in Kentucky did. Part of the oration given at his funeral was, "The mighty oak of the forest has fallen, and now the scrub oaks sprout all around."

The Old Cathedral Complex ★, beside the memorial, dates back to 1749 and is the oldest parish church in Indiana. The current building has been there since 1826.

SITES NEAR VINCENNES

Old French House ★★

Near the corner of North First and Seminary Sts., Vincennes
T: 812-882-7886

Built in 1806 by a fur trader, this is a rare example of a vertical log home. It can be viewed from the street.

Grouseland ★

3 West Scott St., Vincennes
T: 812-882-2096

Spring, summer, and fall Mon–Sat 9am–5pm, Sun 11am–5pm; winter Sat–Sun 11am–4pm
Admission: $5

Grouseland was the home of Indiana Governor William Henry Harrison in 1804. Harrison became nationally famous when he defeated the Indian Prophet at the Battle of Tippecanoe, Indiana, about 185 miles to the northeast, in 1811. Governor Harrison parlayed this victory into seats in the US House and Senate and later into his run for the presidency in 1840 with the slogan "Tippecanoe and Tyler Too!" (John Tyler was the vice presidential candidate.) In 1840, Harrison was elected ninth president of the United States, but he died within a few weeks of taking office.

The house, featuring furniture from the early 19th century, is open for touring.

Getting to and around Vincennes

Vincennes is off the beaten path for most travelers looking for colonial or Revolutionary War sites, at least 50 miles from the nearest interstate highway. The town has to be reached by car. Once at the Clark Monument, however, it is easy to see both the monument and museum.

Evansville Regional Airport is 50 miles south of Vincennes and is served by three airlines and five rental car companies.

Terre Haute International Airport/Hulman Field is 52 miles north of Vincennes and is served by four rental car companies.

There is no obvious way to duplicate the grueling march of Clark and his men from Fort Kaskaskia to Fort Sackville, though the locations of the beginning and ending points of the march are known. Though the two forts were major population centers in their day, there is no direct road between the two, nor is there a historic walking trail.

Travelers wanting to try, however, can get a good road map and drive southwest about 120 miles to find Fort Kaskaskia State Historic Site on the Mississippi River just north of Chester, Illinois. There are remnants of the fort there and the Kaskaskia bell that was rung in celebration by the townspeople when they learned that Clark's men were not going to harm the town. Do not expect to find the same swampy conditions Clark and his men found unless the Wabash is in flood stage.

Accommodations

Motels:

Best Western Inn of Old Vincennes

1800 South Old Decker Rd., Vincennes
T: 812-882-2100
$65–$75

Quality Inn Vincennes

600 Old Wheatland Rd., Vincennes
T: 812-886-9900
$58–$70

Bed-and-Breakfasts:

Cool Breeze Bed and Breakfast

1240 S.E. Second St., Evansville
T: 812-422-9635
coolbreezebb.net
$80–$95

The house was built in 1906. The second owner was Joseph Graham, who, with his two brothers, was owner of the old Madison Square Garden in New York City.

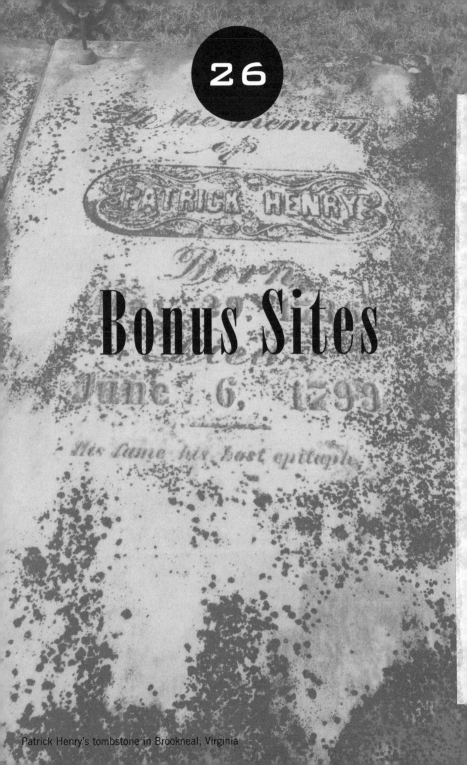

26

Bonus Sites

Patrick Henry's tombstone in Brookneal, Virginia

BONUS SITES

There are many houses that have ties to the American Revolution still standing, but only a few can be tied to specific men who played roles in winning the nation's independence. There is only one preserved battlefield where legendary Daniel Boone fought. There is only one place that Benedict Arnold betrayed to the British. There is only one town in the nation better known for witch trials than for an incident which almost sparked the war. All of these sites are found in the following bonus sites.

Adams National Historical Park

Quincy, Massachusetts
T: 617-770-1175
nps.gov/adam
Closed from November-March

More than 200 years of Adams family history is contained here at the home of the second and sixth presidents. John was one of the moving forces of the independence movement, but he found the office of vice president of the United States to be "the most insignificant office that ever the invention of man contrived or his imagination conceived." His last words on July 4, 1826 were, "Thomas Jefferson survives" but his friend had died a few hours earlier. As a young boy, John Quincy Adams was a witness to his father's involvement in founding the nation, but his own, single term as president from 1826–1829 was chaotic with opposition to him coming from the allies of Andrew Jackson, who would go on to win in 1830. Both of their houses, their church and their graves may be seen at this park.

Blue Licks Battlefield State Park

Mount Olivet, Kentucky
T: 800-443-7008
parks.ky.gov/resortparks/bl

This is a small park, mostly dedicated to recreation, but it was also the site of a major battle of the Revolution 10 months after Cornwallis had surrendered at Yorktown, Virginia. It is considered the last real battle of the war. One of its notable participants was Daniel Boone, the famed explorer and settler of Kentucky whose name appears on a monument on the battlefield. More than 70 Kentuckians died in an ambush at the river staged by British redcoats and their Indian allies. The site itself is just outside the park near the old bridge over the river. A monument with Boone's name listed is on site.

Federal Hall and Trinity Church

26 Wall St., and Wall and Broadway Sts., New York
T: 212-825-6888
nps.gov/feha

This building was built in 1842, but is on the site where George Washington was inaugurated president of the United States in 1789, and where the Bill of Rights was adopted by Congress. Inside is the Bible on which Washington placed his hand during his swearing-in ceremony. This is where John Peter Zinger was tried and acquitted of libel, one of the landmark cases defending freedom of the press. Nearby is Trinity Church at

Broadway and Wall Street. In the church's cemetery is the grave of Alexander Hamilton. Hamilton was an artillerymen during the war before making his name helping write the Constitution and as the first treasury secretary.

Fraunces Tavern Museum

54 Pearl St. (at Broad St.), New York
T: 212-968-1776
fraruncestavernmuseum.org

Built in 1715 as a private residence and turned into a tavern in 1765, this was one of the meeting places for the New York members of the Sons of Liberty, the same group that organized the Boston Tea Party. After the war, it became famous for its "long room," where General Washington read his farewell address to his officers. That room is preserved with period furnishings, as are a number of period oil paintings.

Monticello

Charlottesville, Virginia
T: 434-984-9800
monticello.org

The home of Thomas Jefferson, the nation's third president, is somewhat removed from most other colonial and American Revolution sites, but visiting is well worth the trip. Jefferson designed the home and many of his inventions are still on display and still in use. There is an excellent museum explaining Jefferson's life at the foot of the mountain on which Monticello rests. Many tourists skip the museum and take in just the house. This is a mistake. Just a few miles beyond Monticello is Ash Lawn, the home of James Monroe, the country's fifth president. The house will likely surprise visitors due to its modest appearance.

Montpelier

Montpelier Station, Virginia
T: 540-672-2728
montpelier.org

Montpelier is the home and gravesite of James Madison, the nation's fourth president and the main writer of the Constitution. His wife, Dolley, was considered a driving force in the nation's early history. The house is undergoing restoration through 2007 to remove wings that were not part of the original house. The home will remain open through the restoration process, making it a unique opportunity to watch restorative rebuilding of a historic property taking place. The house is filled with period furniture.

National Archives

700 Pennsylvania Ave., N.W., Washington, D.C.
T: 866-272-6272
archives.gov

Arrive early on any day because this is a popular destination for both tourists and school children. This is the repository for the original copies of the Declaration of Independence, United States Constitution, and the Bill of Rights. The documents are displayed in dim light under thick glass.

Red Hill—The Patrick Henry National Memorial

Brookneal, Virginia
T: 800-514-7463
redhill.org

If Monticello is out of the way, the home and grave of famed Virginia orator Patrick Henry is even farther out of the way, just to the northeast of Danville, Virginia. In protesting the Stamp Act, Henry growled, "If this be treason, then make the most of it." At a church he shouted, "Give me liberty or give me death!" While serving as governor of Virginia, he authorized the secret mission of George Rogers Clark to capture the British-held fort in what is now Vincennes, Indiana. He is also known for refusing to ratify the Constitution until the Bill of Rights was adopted. Henry's reconstructed house and his original law office are open for touring.

Salem

Massachusetts
T: 877-725-3662
salem.org

Salem tourism focuses on two subjects: maritime, including the role of privateering during the Revolution, and the Salem Witch Trials of 1692. Those trials, brought about by local hysteria and superstition, resulted in the trials and hangings of several women and teenaged girls suspected of being witches.

United States Military Academy (West Point)

Highland Falls, New York
T: 845- 938-4011
usma.edu

No battles were fought here, but Benedict Arnold was caught smuggling plans of West Point's fortifications to the British. The military academy was not founded until 1802, but this narrow section of the Hudson was vital to protecting the lower part of the river. A huge iron chain that once stretched across the river to catch British ships is on display at Trophy Point, as are other captured war trophies. The West Point Cemetery outside the Old Cadet Chapel is filled with famous graves from the Civil War period and later, as well as Revolutionary War soldiers. Outside the main gates to West Point (entering requires photo ID) is a fine museum. Bus tours of West Point are also boarded at the museum.

INDEX

INDEX

INDEX

INDEX

INDEX

INDEX

INDEX

INDEX

ABOUT THE AUTHOR

Clint Johnson is a full-time writer who lives in the mountains of North Carolina near one of the gathering sites for the Overmountain Men who defeated the Tories at Kings Mountain. One of his ancestors serving in the South Carolina militia lost a leg at that battle in 1780.

Johnson has written six other touring books, which all cover the American Civil War, including: *The 25 Best Civil War Sites,* also published by Greenline Publications, *Touring the Carolinas' Civil War Sites* (17 point-to-point driving tours in the two states), *Touring Civil War Sites in Virginia and West Virginia* (17 point-to-point driving tours), *In the Footsteps of Robert E. Lee, In the Footsteps of Stonewall Jackson,* and *In the Footsteps of J.E.B. Stuart.* He has also written *Civil War Blunders* and *Bulls-Eyes and Misfires: 50 People Whose Obscure Efforts Shaped the American Civil War.* To order personalized copies, visit his website at clintjohnsonbooks.com.

ACKNOWLEDGMENTS

Some people who deserve special thanks in this book are my wife, Barb, who helped research each site's accommodations and how to get around, and who also took the first whack at editing the text. She also accompanied me to navigate through New York, New Jersey, Pennsylvania, and Massachusetts. She has been along on many a field trip to distant Civil War and Revolutionary War sites.

I also want to thank my Civil War reenacting buddy Martin D'Autrechy of the 26th Regiment of North Carolina Troops and his wife, Claudia, of Burlington, New Jersey, for helping gather research materials and photos of the Trenton, Valley Forge, Morristown, and Valley Forge sites.

Thanks to Lisa Simpson of Fort Ticonderoga, New York, for a personal tour of this splendid historic site, and thanks to the entire staff of the Old Barracks at Trenton, New Jersey, for a before-hours tour and suggestions of other places to visit in New Jersey.